ALSO BY BOB SULLIVAN

Gotcha Capitalism

Your Evil Twin

STOP

GETTING

RIPPED

OFF

BALLANTINE BOOKS | Trade Paperbacks | New York

STOP

GETTING

RIPPED

OFF

Why Consumers Get Screwed,
and How You Can Always
Get a Fair Deal

BOB SULLIVAN

For Grampa Sullivan
Who taught us to avoid getting railroaded,

and Grandma McFadden
who taught us to be nice about it.

A Ballantine Books Trade Paperback Original

Published in the United States by Ballantine Books, an imprint of The Random House Publishing Group, a division of Random House, Inc., New York.

BALLANTINE and colophon are registered trademarks of Random House, Inc.

ISBN 978-0-345-51159-1

Printed in the United States of America

www.ballantinebooks.com

9 8 7 6 5 4 3 2 1

Book design by Jo Anne Metsch

When you believe in things you don't
understand, you suffer

—Stevie Wonder,
"Superstition"

CONTENTS

PART I

WHY CONSUMERS GET SCREWED

"Life was easier" in a war zone, she said. "You had
your camaraderie. You don't have that here.
It's a dog-eat-dog world here."

Staff Sergeant Sandra Rolon grabbed for her piece of the American dream at precisely the wrong moment. The forty-nine-year-old, who had served in the Middle East during the Iraq War, bet everything on a $468,000 Bronx home in mid-2007. With only limited resources for a down payment and her military salary, she had no choice but to sign up for a subprime loan with a 9.8 percent interest rate. The initial monthly payments during the interest-only period would be $4,152. They would escalate later. At the time, the U.S. Army Reserve administrator's salary was $56,000 a year, or less than $5,000 per month. Her mortgage bill—before taxes and insurance—would be more than 80 percent of her real income.

Rolon had plans, however. She would supplement her income by remodeling part of the house and taking on tenants. She was also assured by a mortgage broker that if the payments overwhelmed her, she could refinance as soon as three months after closing. Housing values, after all, moved in only one direction. There was always more equity to tap. So she took the leap of faith.

But Rolon was scammed by construction workers, who took $8,000 from her and left her basement in unrentable condition. At the same time, the housing market in the Bronx hit the skids. With no equity in her home, the refinancing parachute disappeared.

Rolon never made it past the first two mortgage payments.

The desperate situation led her to a startling observation: "Life was easier" in the Middle East, she said to The New York Times. "You had your camaraderie. You don't have that here. It's a dog-eat-dog world here."

Soon after, Rolon had her wish. She was back in the Middle East, this time serving in Camp Bucca, Iraq—a U.S. prison camp. Her deployment offered a temporary reprieve, thanks to the Civil Relief Act, but within a few months she received a new default notice from her loan servicer. She no longer lived in the Bronx home as her primary residence, it said, so the bank was going to begin foreclosure proceedings.

IT'S A CHILLING notion that a woman who had devoted her entire adult life to the service of our country would conclude that it's easier to serve in a war theater overseas than fight a bank at home.

The picture is cracked in so many ways. Who sold Rolon a mortgage with a monthly payment that nearly equaled her income? What bank underwriter approved a loan that was dependant on rental income without evidence of a signed lease from a tenant? How can a member of the U.S. military be abandoned to the wolves of high finance with such heartlessness?

As author of msnbc.com's Red Tape Chronicles for the past several years, I have been asking these kinds of questions throughout the boom and bust of the housing market. I consider my role that of a consumer advocate. After all, banks, cell-phone companies, cable-TV providers, and other conglomerates have enormous marketing budgets that are used to trick people, and armies of lawyers they deploy to protect their interests against the whims of small print. Consumers usually fight these battles alone. As I pore over such tales, I am always inclined to give consumers the benefit of the doubt, and I usually stand ready to criticize greedy companies who take advantage of vulnerable people. The companies should, and usually do, know better.

Often, critics of my work will send me loud and obnoxious emails that boil down to this: "Why do you defend people who are stupid?" I usually dismiss them as mean-spirited. But sometimes, a more thoughtful message arrives offering a similar, but tempered, observation. It might say, "You can't protect people from themselves," or, "Aren't adults responsible for their own actions?"

They have a point. Who could read Rolon's story and not ask,

"Isn't someone who takes out a mortgage with payments that are almost equal to her monthly income just asking for trouble?"

And, in fact, aren't the millions of consumers who bought houses they couldn't afford the real problem, and the real cause of the 2008 economic meltdown?

In a word, yes.

In my line of work, I usually challenge this kind of seemingly obvious statement with explanations that dig a little bit deeper. Consumers can't control the price of homes near good schools; to be good parents, they simply must pay those high prices. Consumers shouldn't be expected to become lawyers just to buy a home. Or my favorite: We won't let people buy a toaster that might catch on fire, why do we allow people to buy mortgages that set the whole world's economy on fire?

While all that's true, I must confess it grants too much leniency to the people who sign on the dotted line. And it raises this irresistible question: If consumers were smarter, would we have avoided the housing meltdown and economic collapse?

HAVE A LOOK at this question, and see how quickly you can answer it.

Look at the menu below. If you order a Lancaster Special sandwich and onion soup, how much should you leave for a 10 percent tip?

Soups—Made by Our Chef Daily	
Onion soup	.60
Soup of the day	.60
Vichyssoise in summer	

Burgers	
Beef burgers, broiled to order:	1.85
1/4 lb. of the finest beef available, seasoned to perfection and served on a buttered bun	1.95

Wine cheddar-cheese burger	1.95
Blue-cheese burger	1.95
Pineapple burger	1.95
Bacon burger	2.10
Wine cheddar-cheese & bacon burger	2.25

Sandwiches

Sliced Turkey—garnished	1.30
Turkey Salad—garnished	.95
Chicken Salad—garnished	.95
Tuna Fish Salad—garnished	.95
Sliced Beef Tongue—garnished	1.50
Grilled Wine Cheddar-Cheese	.75
The Lancaster Special	1.95
Corned Beef, Melted Swiss Cheese, Sauerkraut	
on Seeded Rye . . . Need we say more?	

Minimum Check at Lunch 1.00

The question isn't hard. The Special costs $1.95 and the soup 60 cents, for a total of $2.55. Ten percent of that is 25.5 cents. Let's say either 25 or 26 cents is an acceptable answer.

If you answered this question correctly, consider yourself part of an elite group, because when the U.S. Department of Education asked U.S. adults to answer it as part of a nationwide study, only 42 percent answered correctly. Less than half of American adults were able to pick two numbers from a list, add them, then perform the most basic of all percentage calculations—simply moving the decimal point one column to the left to calculate 10 percent.

You might be surprised by this abysmal performance. But then, if you think about your last dinner with a group of friends, perhaps you won't be. Remember that dreaded moment when the bill came, and the splitting began? Cell phones and calculators were whipped out. Shrugs swept around the table. Finally, most of you gave up and threw down $20 bills or credit cards.

College-educated, successful professionals are regularly brought to their knees by vexing math problems like this: Add up a burger, half a plate of nachos, an iced tea, and tax, then divide by two. Heck, you've probably seen people melt merely at the prospect of calculating a 20 percent tip. (Here's how: Move the decimal point one to the left and double the result. If the bill is $45.13, take 4.51 and double it. A $9 tip will do the trick. Now you don't have to pay for that iPhone Tipulator app.)

What's going on here? Can't Americans *add and subtract*?

In a word, no.

That lunch-tip question might have reminded you of a pesky word problem from high school math. Perhaps some folks who could easily calculate 10 percent of $2.55 suffer a bit of brain lock when asked a question like that in paragraph form. Still, it's a very real-life query. And so is the question below. Have a look, then guess how many Americans guessed wrong when they were asked:

You need to buy peanut butter and are deciding between two brands.

Estimate the cost per ounce of the creamy peanut butter. Write your estimate on the line provided:_____

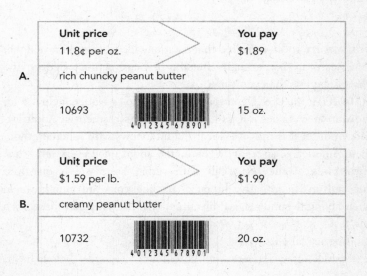

Unit price		You pay
11.8¢ per oz.		$1.89
A.	rich chuncky peanut butter	
10693	‖‖‖‖‖‖ 4 012345 678901	15 oz.

Unit price		You pay
$1.59 per lb.		$1.99
B.	creamy peanut butter	
10732	‖‖‖‖‖‖ 4 012345 678901	20 oz.

Again, not a difficult problem. If this were a math class in high school, I would immediately recognize what is sometimes called "freshman logic." The numbers were designed to work out fairly evenly, to avoid leaving behind students who have trouble with decimals. If peanut butter costs $1.59 per pound—and there are 16 ounces in a pound—the price is close to 10 cents per ounce. Or, you could take another, just-as-easy route. If 20 ounces costs $1.99, then simple division tells you that one ounce must cost about 10 cents.

Division, however, is a bridge too far for most Americans. When this question was asked by the Department of Education, six out of ten adults gave the wrong answer.

Perhaps you are sympathetic to the plight of students who identify themselves as "verbal" rather than mathematical, and division is often where many of the math un-inclined trip up. But look at it this way: This isn't a division problem. It's a basic life problem. A consumer who missed this question isn't really qualified to shop at a grocery store. That means six in ten adults probably get cheated every time they buy bread and milk. What do you suppose happens to them when they are sitting with the financing manager in the back room of a car dealership?

YOU MIGHT HAVE expected that a nationwide test would reveal that Americans are bad at math. But the problem is much deeper, and more sobering, than you think.

In 2003, the U.S. Department of Education's National Center for Education Statistics ran its third National Assessment of Adult Literacy. The test is massive, involving interviews with nineteen thousand Americans, so it's only conducted about once every ten years. Two-thirds of the test dealt with verbal literacy, but one-third focused on "quantitative literacy." Its questions are impressive in their ability to simulate real-life situations. It's not a math test, it's a life test.

America failed.

Overall "grades" were split into four categories: below basic,

basic, intermediate, and proficient. Originally, the top rating was to be "expert," but researchers changed their minds, noting that basic check-balancing skills shouldn't be labeled as expert. Here's the final tally:

- Below basic: 22%
- Basic: 33%
- Intermediate: 33%
- Proficient: 13%

Let's break these numbers down a little more for you. More than half of U.S. consumers were categorized as having basic or below basic quantitative skills. But what does that mean? It means they could not:

- Determine whether a car has enough gasoline to get to the next gas station, based on a graphic of the car's fuel gauge, a sign stating the miles to the next gas station, and information given in the question about the car's fuel use.
- Calculate the cost of raising a child for a year in a family with a specified income, based on a newspaper article that provides the percentage of a typical family's budget that goes toward raising children.
- Calculate the total cost of ordering office supplies, using a page from an office-supplies catalog and an order form.
- Determine what time a person can take a prescription medication, based on information on the prescription-drug label that relates timing of medication to eating.

Naturally, as the required math proficiency increased, fewer consumers were able to complete the tasks. Only one in seven Americans qualified as "proficient." That means that only one in seven Americans can reliably perform tasks such as these:

- Calculate the yearly cost of a specified amount of life insurance, using a table that gives cost by month for each $1,000 of coverage.

- Calculate an employee's share of health insurance costs for a year, using a table that shows how the employee's monthly cost varies with income and family size.

If you're wondering why Americans pay too much for health insurance, the fact that most people have no idea how much they pay for health insurance might be one hint.

Of course, no one starves to death because they can't find a number on a piece of paper. But what if they can't even calculate their own salaries? The literacy assessment found that 22 percent of Americans were incapable of:

- Calculating the weekly salary for a job, based on hourly wages listed in a job advertisement.
- Calculating the cost of three baseball tickets using a form that provides the price of one ticket, and postage and handling charges.
- Calculating the cost of a sandwich and salad, using prices from a menu.

It bears repeating: Nearly one in four Americans can't figure how much their lunch costs! If we are giving high school degrees to people who are not capable of calculating when they will run out of gas, what their weekly salary is, or the cost of a sandwich and soup, we are doing a grave disservice. Something has gone horribly wrong.

IF YOU'D LIKE to, try your hand at another question from the survey, this one requiring a little bit more narrative understanding. Then guess how many test-takers are at high risk of running out of gas someday.

On March 9 you filled your car with gas. Calculate how many miles per gallon your car got since you filled it up with gas on March 2.

- The mileage was 43,083.
- You bought 12.5 gallons.
- You paid $18.25.

AUTOMOBILE MAINTENANCE RECORD

Month of __March_____ 19 _92_____

Date	Mileage	Gasoline No. Gals	Amount	Repairs	Oil and Grease
1					
2	42775	13.1	$19.10		
3					
4					
5					
6					
7					
8					
9					
10					
11					
12					
13					
14					
15					
16					
17					
18					
19					
20					
21					
22					
23					
24					
25					
26					
27					
28					
29					
30					
31					
Total					

This problem involves slightly more advanced skills than the earlier questions. In the end, however, it's a simple matter of subtracting two numbers (43,083 − 42,775) to get mileage driven, then dividing the result by the number of gallons used: 12.5. Yet the results were dismal. Only 29 percent answered correctly.

Not surprisingly, quantitative abilities are an excellent predictor of life success and household income. Adults who earn $100,000 per year or more had an average test score right on the edge of "proficient." Adults who scored in the "basic" range had an average income ranging from $20,000 to $60,000. And those who couldn't get out of the "below basic" rating were stuck with an average salary of less than $20,000 per year.

Breaking down the numbers by gender or race is even more disturbing. Only one in ten U.S. women registered as proficient in 2003. Worse yet, only one in twenty-five Hispanics, and one in fifty African-Americans, scored proficient.

Education level mattered, but not as much as it should. Those with a college degree were six times more likely to be proficient than those who stopped their education after finishing high school. On the other hand, even the majority of those who hold a college degree weren't rated as proficient—69 percent, in fact, were not.

That means most college graduates (and most adults who held advanced degrees, too), were unable to answer a "proficient" question asked by the Department of Education involving home loans. Only one in five test-takers of any stripe were able to correctly tell questioners how interest on a home equity loan is calculated. In other words, more than 80 percent of Americans were unable to complete the most basic task a home-buyer faces when trying to select a mortgage.

One vital key to running a con on someone is what economists sometimes call "asymmetric information"—one side simply knows much more than the other in a transaction. With most Americans incapable of even describing the cost of a home loan in 2003, you can assume that the vast majority of mortgages sold during the 2000s decade were classic asymmetric transactions. The stage was set for the biggest con in human history.

How did we arrive at a place where Americans had so much money and so little understanding? There are many answers, but here are seven.

1. INNUMERACY

The problem of adult illiteracy in America is widespread and alarming—an estimated 14 percent of Americans, or one in seven, can't read. Terrible, but perhaps not surprising, as you've no doubt heard a statistic like that before. There are seemingly incessant studies of the problem, with multiple institutes devoted to dealing with it and public-service radio campaigns drawing awareness to it.

The problem of mathematical illiteracy is much less well-known. In fact, it is downright obscure—so obscure that we lack a ready-made term to describe the group of people who can't calculate restaurant tips or balance their checkbook. Saying someone "can't count" is in no way the equivalent of saying someone "can't read."

John Allen Paulos tried to change that in 1988 when he published the book *Innumeracy*. In it, he describes the genesis of the wide-spread epidemic that has led to a gap between the "numerate" and the "innumerate." Innumerates hate math and are sometimes proud of it. They can easily be identified when they say things like "I'm a word person." Numerates, on the other hand, can easily win a bar bet from innumerates by asserting that in a tavern full of fifty people, there almost certainly are two people who share the same birthday. In fact, they'll win the bet most of the time even if there are as few as twenty-five people in the bar. (Don't believe me? Read on.)

Innumerates almost never realize their precarious situation. Often, they are the kind of people who are quite sanctimonious about being right and precise. In describing this phenomenon, Paulos tells this story of a rather annoying character at a dinner party.

The same people who cringe when words such as *imply* and *infer* are confused react without a trace of embarrassment to even the most egregious of numerical solecisms. I remember once listening to someone at a party drone on about the difference between *continually* and *continuously*. Later that evening we were watching the news and the TV weathercaster announced that there was a 50 percent chance for rain on Saturday and a 50 percent chance for Sunday, and concluded that there was therefore a 100 percent chance of rain that weekend. The remark went right by the self-styled grammarian, and even after I explained the mistake to him, he wasn't nearly as indignant as he would have been had the weathercaster left a dangling participle. In fact, unlike other failings which are often hidden, mathematical illiteracy is often flaunted. [People say] "I can't even balance my checkbook. I'm a people person, not a numbers person," or "I've always hated math."

In this passage, Paulos puts his finger on one of the root causes of the economic meltdown. Think back to high school for a moment: Rare is the institution where the captain of the math club wanders the hallways proudly sporting a C on a leather jacket. In fact, the usual wearer of the C, the high school quarterback—or for that matter, any student, really—is much more likely to curry favor by joking about failed algebra tests. There is, Paulos asserts, "a perverse pride in mathematical ignorance." Until recently, you may even have heard a perverse pride from people who didn't understand their investments or their home loans. "Oh, I let my broker handle all that."

It may be cute that the quarterback can't add, but unless he eventually lands a multimillion-dollar contract and an agent to count money for him, he will quickly become a burden on society. For example, he'll be much more afraid of getting killed by a shark (odds: 1 in 300 million) than by a car accident (1 in 18,000) or by heart disease (1 in 7). He'll happily drive after two or three beers at 3 a.m. and eat endless bags of potato chips, but he'll cancel a seaside vacation after an isolated news report involving a shark attack. People who don't understand numbers are prone to making terrible risk assessments. This puts them, and us, at grave risk.

AREN'T THERE 365 days in a typical year? Then wouldn't you need at least 366 people in a jam-packed bar to be certain two patrons will share the same birthday?

The answer is yes . . . and no. In high school, you were probably told that math problems have only one answer. But in the real world, that's quite far from true. You see, numbers aren't quite so black-and-white.

Despite what you may have heard, numbers do lie, and they make an excellent tool for deception. People naïvely grant numbers, just like photographs, far too much credibility. Those who do are easy targets.

In another great tome on the problem of mathematical foibles called *The Two-Headed Quarter*, Loyola University Maryland professor Joseph Ganem shows how often numbers are used to trick consumers. If a little bit of context is withheld, seemingly unbiased numbers can quickly make a fair transaction unfair. A coin flip might seem like an even fifty-fifty bet, for example, unless one party knows that the coin being flipped has heads on both sides—the classic asymmetric transaction. Ganem sees many house, car, credit-card, and insurance transactions through the lens of a two-headed quarter.

"Numbers are a perfect vehicle for making true but misleading statements," he writes. "Deception works by not revealing the whole story. A two-headed quarter works in a magic trick by presenting a false choice."

In the world of personal finance, he sees many two-headed quarters. Here are a few:

- A credit-card convenience check that promises, in large print, to let people transfer balances for the low interest rate of 2.9 percent—then tacks on a 3 percent transfer fee.

- Tax-refund anticipation loans. The Jackson Hewitt tax-preparation company says it charges a small 3 percent fee for consumers to receive their tax refunds instantly. Sounds small. But the annual percentage rate for such a loan is more than 100 percent. As Ganem points out, consumers would be better taking a cash advance from a credit card at 29.99 percent to cover the seven days of waiting for the refund to arrive.
- A rent-to-own store he surveyed charged a low price of $17.99 per week to rent a bedroom set. Best of all, consumers who rented it would own the set after two years! Here's the problem: The value of the set was $935, but after two years, the consumer would have paid $1,870.96. Clearly, $17.99 was a lie—the rental store was instead providing a loan with an APR of nearly 80 percent.

In each case, the key to making the number lie was in the "framing." Simply changing the furniture rental price terms from weekly ($17.99) to monthly ($77.96) can dramatically change the perception of the transaction. Revealing the APR unravels the lie altogether. But rental furniture is often marketed to down-on-their-luck buyers who are literally living week-to-week, paycheck-to-paycheck, so the framing as a weekly payment works as a perfect trap.

There are many ways to construct a two-headed quarter. One is an outright cheat, so that the "house" knows more than the gambler—say, that the coin is fixed. But another, more subtle two-headed coin is to keep one party in the dark about the subtleties of the transaction.

What if a bettor became convinced, through poor education or belief in myth, that a coin flip is really a 75–25 proposition? Obviously, the house would win a lot of money. This suggestion might sound absurd until you consider our country's fixation with casino gambling. Einstein once remarked, "No one can possibly win at roulette unless he steals money from the table while the croupier isn't looking." He was right. Every single casino game is rigged so the house has slightly better odds than the bettors. A roulette ball lands on red 47.37 percent of the time. The payout is two to one, but the risk is slightly greater—about 5 percent greater. Remember this rule in all gambling, and in most financial transactions: The house always wins.

Why all this talk about gambling? To make the point that numbers often lie. Simple math would expose the lie of the $17.99 furniture rental, but we've already learned that much of America is blissfully ignorant of simple math. Step the complexity up just a small amount—say, imagine a "pay option ARM" (adjustable rate mortgage) with a teaser rate of 1.9 percent and an initial rate of 7.9 percent that adjusts to 8.9 percent after two years—and you can swindle a lot of home-buyers by saying, "Look at this low monthly payment."

AS FOR THAT bar bet, math students will readily recognize the "birthday problem." Believe it or not, with just twenty-three people in a room, the odds are better than 50 percent that two have the same birthday. This is not immediately obvious to most people—wouldn't you need at least 183 people, or half a year's worth, to get those kinds of odds?

The problem lies in the oft-misunderstood world of probability. The question is not whether one person's birthday matches the other twenty-two in the room, but rather whether *any two* of the twenty-three match each other. Person A has twenty-two potential matches, but person B has an additional twenty-one potential matches, and person C has an additional twenty matches, and so on. There's about a 6 percent chance that Person A will have a match (22/365), but there's also a nearly equal chance that Person B will have a match (21/365), and person C, and person D, and . . . so on.

Adding up all these possibilities quickly tilts the odds in your favor. In fact, among twenty-three people there are 253 pairs of possible matches, making the odds better than 50 percent that you have a match. With fifty people in a room, the odds jump to 97 percent.

Numbers can do the funniest things! Sometimes they can even provide a happy ending, particularly if you are on the right side of the "asymmetry."

In a wonderful children's book, *One Grain of Rice,* the heroine, an Indian girl named Rani, outwits an oppressive king who is starving all his subjects. She does him a favor, then asks for a simple wish to be granted: She just wants a single grain of rice the next day. And she asks that the reward be doubled each day for a mere thirty days: two grains on day two, four on day three, and so on. The king laughs at her seemingly trivial request and grants it without a second thought.

Of course, Rani's people never starved again. She had fooled the raja into forking over half a billion grains of rice by day thirty (to be precise, 536,870,912 grains of rice).

Unfortunately, consumers are usually the victims of such compounded (or in this case, logarithmic) calculations, lured by what sound like small investments into what quickly become impossible obligations. Clever framing of these kinds of math problems lies at the core of the bad mortgage or the double-priced bedroom set. Numbers really can lie. No wonder people are afraid of them.

Just how afraid of mathematics are the American people? Every year, roughly 50 million Americans file their taxes using one-page, simple forms such as the 1040EZ. That form rarely requires entries on more than ten lines, and it can be boiled down to these three questions: What was your income? Which personal deduction are you entitled to (a multiple-choice question)? And how much in taxes have you already paid? Yet fully one-third of EZ filers—around 20 million Americans—pay someone else to fill out this tiny form.

That statistic says something about fear of the IRS, of course. But on a deeper level I think it describes an utter lack of confidence in performing mathematical calculations when something important is really on the line.

While this general apprehension about math might be the first condition necessary to create an environment that allows massive scams to be perpetrated on millions of consumers, a secondary element has recently emerged that has turned this scamming into a science. It has a name: behavioral economics.

2. BEHAVIORAL ECONOMICS

For decades, economists constructed models of industry built on the presumption that consumers generally behaved rationally—that they always seek out better prices and better products, for example. Now, a new branch of economics challenges the fundamental error of these old models. Consumers, it turns out, do the strangest things, too. For example:

You might think of your friends as either risk-averse or risk-tolerant. One friend might readily drop a few thousand into a new stock at the drop of a hat, while another wouldn't do so without spending months on painstaking research. Risk tendencies are much more complex than that, however.

Surprisingly, people's tendency to take risks depends on circumstances. Study after study has shown that average consumers are more risk-averse (conservative) when they stand to gain, but much more risk-tolerant when they stand to lose.

In one classic example, subjects are told to choose between a sure $3,000, or an 80 percent chance at $4,000 but a 20 percent chance at ending up with nothing. Nearly four out of five take the sure bet—take the money and run. But when the question is framed differently, the results are reversed: When subjects are told they face either a sure loss of $3,000, or an 80 percent chance at a $4,000 loss but a 20 percent chance of losing nothing, a stunning 92 percent, this time, take the bet.

This test has important implications for personal finance. People take riskier bets on the way down, and many debtors who take desperate chances only dig their holes even deeper. A person drowning in debt will often borrow more money, even as loan terms become steadly more onerous, out of faith that one more shot in the arm will turn the tide. It rarely does.

This phenomenon also explains why people seem to sell stocks at the wrong time—when a stock is performing well—but hold on (or even double down) when a stock is falling. Or, put more simply, people hate risk when it threatens gains, but seem to take on more risk when they are losing hope.

Here's another behavioral puzzler: *copycatting*. You've witnessed this every time you yawn just because someone else in the room has yawned. Scientists are discovering that consumers are hardwired to imitate each other's behavior. Specific parts of the brain called mirror neurons are designed to help us be copycats. Imitation is a good thing; it helps people learn and organize into societies. But it's also a secret weapon for marketing companies. By simply creating the impression that "everyone is doing it"—buying a home, driving a convertible, living the good life with credit cards—companies dip deep into our brains and trick us into doing something that's not really good for us.

And another: *anchoring*. Where you start a discussion about numbers impacts where the discussion ends. If someone offers you a salary of $45,000, then eventually raises the offer to $50,000, you'll feel much better about your pay rate than if the offer of $50,000 came first. Here's one study that shows the dramatic impact of anchoring. Real estate agents were asked to appraise a home based on a twenty-page packet of information where the only variance was the list price. When the list price in the packet was $119,000, the average appraisal was $114,000. When the list price was $149,900, the average appraisal that came back was $128,700. By varying the "opening bid," the professional assessment differed by a full 10 percent.

Salespeople have known this for years, of course. The first offer in any negotiation, however ridiculous, is designed to shift the entire discussion up or down by an entire price range. Most people fall for it every time.

Here's one you can probably relate to: *endowment effect*. People value things they have greater than things they want; or put another way, they exaggerate the value of goods they own. You might insist that the old, beat-up Mustang convertible you have in the backyard is worth at least $1,000 if you sell it. But if you wanted to buy said convertible, you'd only be willing to pay $700 for it. This endowment impulse has great implications for the housing market. Consumers selling homes are notoriously attached to their place, believing this garden or that wallpaper makes it oh-so-more attractive, and insist on a premium price. They forget not everyone likes wallpaper. Or flowers. Then they wonder why the house is taking so long to sell.

One more: *confirmation bias*. Decisions are hard, but once we make them, we like to believe we've made the right one. So people tend to like their real estate brokers, their financial planners, and often hold on to the belief that they got a fantastic deal on a home purchase long after friends know otherwise. That's why car salesmen have an easy time convincing buyers they "got a steal" as they walk out the door after overpaying. Everyone craves affirmation, and confirmation.

Confirmation bias might explain some other well-known mistakes people make about their own skills, sometimes called a *superiority bias,* or better yet, the *Lake Wobegon effect:* 72 percent of online daters say they have above average looks (at least 23 percent must be wrong); 42 percent of workers think their performance places them in the top 5 percent; 93 percent of drivers say they are above average; 94 percent of college professors think they are at the top of their "class"; and nearly everyone believes he or she has superior intelligence. Perhaps more on point for our discussion, 32 percent of adult Americans overestimate their credit scores, while only 4 percent underestimate them.

Understanding all these peculiar choices has made the jobs of marketing companies and public relations professionals easier than taking candy from a baby. Just convince people they are making a smart choice, getting a great deal on a mortgage, or getting themselves out of debt with a secret program that credit-card companies don't want them to know about—and you've won.

Endless research has chronicled the downfall of our society driven by marketing companies and hyperconsumerism. It's hard to argue that marketing isn't making us dumber. During the 1990s, the public relations industry grew 250 percent. The industry has enjoyed double-digit growth through most of the current decade. At the same time, revenues in television news have slowly sunk, and newspaper revenues have been entirely torpedoed, leading to the closure of several large-city papers. The market for paid—spun—information is exploding at a time when the market for unbiased information is disappearing.

Meanwhile, the main purveyor of the world's information today, Google, treats all information sources as completely equal, even if one provides bald-faced lies aimed at stealing your money. It makes no distinction between a PR firm, an advertisement, an outright scam, and a news site. A search for *home loan* or *adjustable rate mortgage* on Google at the height of the housing bubble was just as likely to return a series of advertisements for "1 percent interest" mortgages; a *BusinessWeek* story about the perils of exotic loans; or a press release from the National Association of Homebuilders saying, essentially, "party on."

With all these forces bearing down hard—consumers, already afraid of numbers, pelted from all sides by advertising, poked and prodded endlessly to exploit their most unconscious weaknesses, with unbiased sources all but disappearing—it would seem regular folks don't stand much of a chance against this massive engine of economics.

Yet another, equally nefarious device is often exploited by the world of business: distraction. Consumers often don't pay attention to what they're doing. In his book *The Undercover Economist,* author Tim Harford describes the elegantly simple way that Starbucks gets the absolute maximum amount of money from their coffee drinkers. When a company sets a price for an item, it faces two risks—underpricing, thereby leaving some cash on the table that it could have grabbed from shoppers; and overpricing, which would drive consumers away. So how does Starbucks deal with this eternal commerce conundrum? It does both. By including a sliding scale of prices—Short, Tall, Grande, Venti—Starbucks offers a range of prices to satisfy even the most distracted, least price-conscious consumers. The incremental cost of sizing-up a Starbucks drink is negligible—a bit more milk, a tiny bit more paper. But by tricking shoppers into jumping from a Tall to a Venti, Starbucks gets consumers to pay $3.95 rather than $3.10. Heck, some drinkers even pay 25 percent more just for a larger cup of hot water for tea! Think of it this way. Starbucks is saying, "If you don't want that money, we'll be happy to take it from you."

Want to feel really silly? Economists sometimes call this "Goldilocks" pricing, as in "This amount is too small. This is too large. But this is just right." Makes you want to jump out the window and just run away, doesn't it?

Now, are consumers really *that* gullible? Or is something even deeper happening here?

3. EDUCATION

About three in four U.S. fifteen-year-olds told international researchers in 2003 that they got good grades in math classes. It's a good thing they weren't going to school in Finland, Canada, the Czech Republic, or even Iceland.

Every three years, the Organization for Economic Cooperation and Development (OECD) runs an international test of fifteen-year-olds around the world, so nations can compare their educational systems. All the world's industrialized nations participate, along with several non-OECD members—more than forty nations in all. In 2003, the focus was on math achievement.

The U.S. teens scored highest for grade inflation—more U.S. teens said they got good grades than the teens of any other nation. But when it came to actual math skills, the United States landed near the bottom of the countries tested. In addition to the countries listed above, the Netherlands, Latvia, Poland, and even Hungary outperformed the United States, which found itself nestled among a group that included Italy, Serbia, and Uruguay—and twenty-fifth among the thirty developed nations studied.

The study also noted that the Czech Republic, which landed thirteen spots above the United States, spent only one-third as much to educate its students. The United States was said to have the poorest outcome per dollar spent on education. Perhaps most disturbing and what gave pause to many U.S. educators was the trend line:

"The gap between the best and worst performing countries has widened," said Andreas Schleicher, who ran the study and wrote the report.

Any number of international studies unearth much the same results: The nation that first landed a man on the moon is being left in the dust by developing countries in math and science studies. The news was so disturbing that President George W. Bush appointed a panel in 2006 to investigate the problem and propose some answers. The National Mathematics Advisory Panel published its findings a year later.

Its complaints run the gamut: Textbook publishers seem to confuse heft with utility, as children's math textbooks can be seven hundred to a thousand pages long, far longer than those from nations with better test scores; teachers are ill-prepared for mathematics instruction. It all added up to a disturbing result:

"Close to half of all seventeen year olds cannot read or do math at the level needed to get a job at a modern automobile plant," the panel's report concluded. "Barring some other special knowledge or talent that would allow them to earn a living as, say, a plumber or artist, they lack the skills to earn a middle-class paycheck in today's economy."

The researchers zeroed in on one specific, and perhaps fatal, flaw in math education. U.S. students seem to fall off a cliff when the subject is fractions. The report said that about half of U.S. eighth-grade students could not solve a word problem that involved fractions. Absent the ability to work with fractions, U.S. math students hit their ceiling in math studies at a very young age.

"The sharp falloff in mathematics achievement in the U.S. begins as students reach late middle school," the report said. "Difficulty with fractions [including decimals and percents] is pervasive and is a major obstacle to further progress in mathematics, including algebra." And, it should now be clear, in settling restaurant tabs and buying cars and homes.

IT'S DARN NEAR impossible to learn something if your teacher doesn't know it. Johnny will never be able to work with fractions if Johnny's teachers can't.

As the presidential report was swatting away at U.S. students for not understanding fractions, other researchers were poking away at teacher-education programs, with disappointing results. The National Council on Teacher Quality surveyed seventy-seven top teachers colleges to find out how well they were preparing future educators to teach math in 2003. Its findings: Teachers weren't required to know math to enter the colleges' programs, and even worse, they weren't required to know it when they graduated, either.

Standardized tests are required for entry into these schools. One such test is called Praxis, sort of like the LSAT for law schools. Praxis does include math questions: elementary-school-level math questions. In other words, aspiring fifth-grade teachers need only prove that they could pass a fifth-grade math test! Only one of the seventy-seven schools studied required proof of proficiency in high school math.

"Almost anyone can get in [to teachers schools]," the report said. "Compared to the admissions standards found in other countries, American education schools set exceedingly low expectations for the mathematics knowledge that aspiring teachers must demonstrate."

Education certification is controlled at the state level. The report found that eighteen states had no requirement that elementary teachers attend even a single math course.

But the standards for graduation are even worse. The Praxis II, administered at the end of coursework, to make sure the teacher is ready to enter a classroom, has no separate mathematics quiz in any state. Because the questions are all scored together, it's possible for teachers to answer every single math question wrong and still receive a passing grade!

It's not enough for teachers to successfully add and subtract, the report found. Nor is it sufficient for teachers to be "one chapter ahead of the students" and know just enough to teach the material from a book. To inspire youngsters to memorize times tables and follow the disciplined rules of division, teachers must have a deeper understanding of why multiplication tables work, or why algebra matters. Without the skills and conceptual understanding, they are unlikely to effectively teach math lessons—in the same way that reading teachers must know more than how to read and must understand phonics, word attack strategies, and numerous other literacy skills to teach reading.

It shouldn't be surprising that math skills are rare among elementary school teachers. People attracted to teaching young kids skew toward verbal and communication skills and often end up attracted to coursework that augments those skills. Society often permits excellent communicators to neglect so-called right-brain, analytic studies. It does so at great peril to our society's math skills, and to nearly every consumer's pocketbook.

Massachusetts officials decided to take on the math-teacher training after hearing some of these distressing results and started sending an educator named Michael Klugerman around the state to bring teachers up to grade. Before he delivers his seminars, he administers a short pretest. Of two hundred teachers he tested in a recent year, less than half could answer such questions as "30 is what percent of 75?" and "What is 14 divided by 1/2?"

"Elementary teachers are phobic about math," Klugerman told *The Boston Globe*. "I've seen that very much in my classes. There's a lot of anxiety about math."

Parents have picked up on this deficiency, of course. At school board meetings parents have revolted and demanded better math instruction. "Math wars" have pitted fans of old-fashioned memorization against fans of "reform math," which stresses conceptual understanding over drills. In California, parents can send their kids away to summer camp—Money Camp—which teaches them practical mathematics such as how to compute compounded interest for loans. But so far, these efforts have amounted to little more than sound and fury.

THE HARD THING about fractions is that you can't really calculate them by "feel." Simple addition and subtraction are fairly observable in the regular course of life: You've invited eight friends to your house, but three guests don't like beer. One six-pack and a four-pack of Smirnoff Ice should cover at least the first round of drinks. Even simple multiplication seems to be second nature. If you plan to make two sandwiches for lunch every day this week, a loaf of bread with at least twenty slices will do the trick. These kinds of problems don't require much brainpower. The answer comes almost instinctively. But let's twist things, just a little.

Back to those eight friends (nine, including you). You have three-quarters of a container of half-and-half in the fridge. You know everybody will want coffee. Do you have enough creamer? The answer won't come quickly, but let's give it a shot.

How much cream goes in a cup, an ounce? A tablespoon? Maybe two. But how many tablespoons are in a pint? Only bakers keep facts like that at hand (it's thirty-two).

You might then remember that the break room at work offers Land O Lakes Mini Moo's, and people generally seem to use two of them. A quick glance at Google tells you that a Mini Moo's is three-eighths of an ounce. And so it begins. How much is two Mini Moo's? And then how many two—Mini Moo's servings are in three-quarters of a pint of half-and-half?

At this point, most people would grab their coat and car keys, head to the grocery store, and just buy more creamer. Let's just hope they check the sugar bowl before leaving.

If fractions are the Waterloo for the majority of elementary-school students today (and perhaps for you, too), we should back up the equation just a little further in school. Pupils learn arithmetic in this order: addition, subtraction, multiplication, then division. Fractions are just an advanced way of expressing division (three-eighths is really three divided by eight). Working with fractions ultimately requires division, and that's where a lot of the trouble begins.

I think the reason is obvious: The answer *isn't* obvious. It might be obvious how many beers or slices of bread you need in the examples above, but it's not obvious how much creamer. There's only one way to get the answer to this creamer dilemma: You must work it out. You must sit down with pencil and paper (lucky people can do this in their heads) and calculate the answer. It requires discipline. It requires applying a multistep prescription. It's not trivial. And it can't really be done with a cell-phone calculator.

Long division is hard. For example, to divide 3 by 8, you must add a place and a decimal point, multiply 3 times 8, subtract 24 from 30, write the answer of 3 and carry over the result of 6, then multiply 7 times 8, enter the result of 56, write in the answer of 7 and carry over the 4 (when will this end?), then multiply 8 times 5, write in the result of 40 and the answer of 5, and there you have it (0.375). Don't worry if you didn't stay with me. That's the point. Fractions aren't obvious.

I'll leave it to the endnotes to express the calculation for how many two–Mini Moo's servings are in twelve ounces. Let's just say you didn't need to waste the gas, unless the sugar bowl was empty.

In fractions, as in long division, there really is no shorthand way to get the right answer. You must take the long road. Americans aren't too pleased when there isn't a shortcut. We are the land of shortcuts. That's why you can buy anything now and pay for it later. That's why we play Guitar Hero over learning how to play guitar. And why college graduates believe their business degrees give them the right to a six-figure salary (by the way, why do we let nineteen-year-olds take classes in "management" anyway?).

This trouble with fractions and with division in general has a profound impact on our nation's financial savvy. Fractions are the gateway to many other mathematical concepts. Chief among them, percentage. A population that has trouble calculating percents—and doesn't even really understand how to work out percentages—can't possibly shop intelligently. All those "15 percent off" sales are crippling us.

4. STUART SMALLEY

That's all right, you think. Really, how bad is it that our party host ends up with an extra container of cream at the end of the night? It's just another $2.69 down the drain. What really matters, you think, is that she's a gracious host with a warm heart who makes her friends feel at home.

That's true. In the end, we should all be judged by what's in our hearts, and not in our bank accounts. And it's true that we care about her heart when she adds a back deck, signs on to pay $20 per square foot for construction of the 375-square-foot project, and pays $11,000. Her friends all tell her how beautiful the deck is. When she buys a car and doesn't realize the payments are $40 more every month than they should be because the loan was packed with a useless warranty extension, her friends say she was brave for going to the car dealership by herself. When she signs up for a pay-option adjustable-rate mortgage so she can buy a house way beyond her means, everyone will say the home is a great investment—even if they chuckle behind her back.

A close friend will readily tell her she has a piece of lettuce between her teeth after a meal on a double date. But when it comes to financial matters and other big life decisions, affirmation is everywhere. We are a nation of Stuart Smalley mirrors. You remember Smalley, a faux TV therapist played by then comedian Al Franken on the NBC comedy *Saturday Night Live*. Smalley sat in front of his full-length mirror every week and proclaimed repeatedly, "I'm good enough, I'm smart enough, and doggone it, people like me!" Well, we no longer need mirrors for such unconditional affirmation. Positive reinforcement rules the day now in so many corners of America, whether discussing dog training, child rearing, or friends' life choices.

Confrontation is frowned upon, as are uncomfortable conversations that reveal the truth. Who dares tell a friend that he's wasted money on financial advice?

As the nation's housing market overheated, how many friends do you recall saying, "You know, I'm not sure this is a good idea."

Positive reinforcement is discipline's antithesis, and right now Stuart Smalley is in and long division is out. Can't do math in school? That's all right, you're a verbal person! Don't understand your retirement fund? That's okay. It's even cute. At least you are a good hugger.

This overly permissive cultural leaning can easily be observed in the way people spend their money every day. For those who argue that consumers' bad choices were the real culprits in the meltdown of our economy, no evidence is more powerful than the uninterrupted march to accumulate things that was so easily observable in the last decade.

5. GREED

Perhaps you've noticed that many of your friends can rave about the superior handling and stability of their four-wheel-drive vehicles, and maybe even the car's "maximum approach angle." Yet most of them never even engage that second axle. The problem is so severe that some SUV dealers actually have to remind customers that they must slip the car into 4WD at least once a year to ensure the mechanism keeps working properly.

Welcome to the world of Bobos, so elegantly described in David Brooks's book *Bobos in Paradise: The New Upper Class and How They Got There*. Brooks ushered in the new millennium by describing this new breed of well-to-do, a combination of BOhemian rebels and BOurgeois aspirants. They don't flaunt their riches by spending money on expensive artwork or extravagant jewelry. Instead, they throw thousands of dollars at "utilitarian" objects they purchase at stores such as REI or Restoration Hardware. Only the best hiking boots or pizza cutters will do for Bobos. They flaunt their money and success more subtly and, they believe, more honorably, by spending cash only on smart, functional purchases. They wouldn't think of making coffee without grinding the beans to insure freshness and wouldn't fail to use a conical burr grinder such as the one Solis Maestro sells for around $100. Of course, nothing smaller than a 2,200-square-foot house that's prewired with Ethernet cable and has a garden sprinkler system would do.

Brooks's tome is actually sympathetic to Bobo culture, which he sees as a natural marriage of sixties idealism to eighties conspicuous consumption. Excess by any other name is still excess, however. A $500 hammer, whether bought by NASA or by a yuppie, is a waste either way.

Before the decade was out, all those down winter coats had begun to jam-pack even the twelve closets spread conveniently throughout the largest suburban McMansions. Eric Abrahamson and David H. Freedman, in a delightful book called *A Perfect Mess,* described the natural response to overconsumption—the swiftly growing "organization" business. While Container Store employees push closet counseling or vacuum packs for sweaters, Public Storage and its competitors sell an even more comprehensive solution—rent extra space off-site for all that extra stuff. In 1980, the average square footage of a new home was 1,740 feet. By 2004, the average was 2,349. Yet no one seemed to think it odd that even more space was needed to store the winter clothes.

A backlash was inevitable.

George Will wrote in *Newsweek* at the height of the economic collapse in February 2009 that the government should not interfere with falling housing prices—and he forcefully made the point that many Bobo haters have longed to hear. There is no need to buy $500 boots when $100 boots will probably do the job:

The price difference between "the best" and the adequate often is much larger than the quality difference. All over America, local magazines identify, for the benefit of food snobs and other poseurs, their cities' "five best breads" and "five best lattes," as though settling for the sixth best would be a hardship. Come the recovery, Americans will be better off, and perhaps also better.

It is hard to have sympathy for consumers who are dragged out of their homes by banks while clinging to their granite countertops and Wolf kitchen ovens. And it is undeniable that greed has played a major role in the screwing of America. I've written hundreds of stories about con artists. In nearly every case, the victim's own greed helped the criminal. People do fall for those Nigerian scams. Should we ever feel sorry for someone who is lured with the promise that they'll receive 10 percent of a $20 million windfall? Like a clever wrestler, con artists always turn the eagerness of their opponents against them. Bobos and Bobos-to-be clearly exhibited a sense of entitlement as the housing boom carried on, one after the other deciding they deserved a three-car garage with room for a boat. Mortgage brokers often had an easy time taking candy from these financial babies and handing out subprime mortgages in return. You might even think they deserved each other and deserved to go down in flames. If this crowd got screwed out of $30 a month by their cellphone providers and $100 a month by cable TV, so be it.

But there is a problem with this picture. It's fundamentally flawed. It's a myth. Despite the $500 hammers and $200 sneakers you've heard so much about, American consumers are actually getting by with less—much less—and spending a lot *less* than their parents.

I know you don't believe me, so I'll prove it to you. Average consumers spend less, far less, on such items as food, clothing, and even entertainment than they did in 1970. For example, a generation ago, families spent 20 percent of their monthly budget on food. Today, it's only 10 percent. This holds true even when ever-growing restaurant bills are included. Despite the emergence of designer brands in everyone's closets, the average family of four spends 20 percent less on clothes than their counterparts a generation ago.

On the other hand, basic housing costs eat up more than twice as much of a family's budget as they did in the 1970s.

It all boils down to this: Families today spend about 75 percent of their income on the basics. In 1970, that figure was 50 percent. Put another way, today's parents have about half the discretionary spending power that their parents did.

The phenomenon is described in Elizabeth Warren's book *The Two-Income Trap*. Her main point: Most U.S. households now survive only because husband and wife both work. Higher incomes have simply created a dog-chasing-its-tail effect of raising housing costs without providing the expected income relief. In fact, families have far less left over after paying the essentials every month. Following is a chart that shows the dramatic differences in some of these fixed expenses. Notice that income has nearly doubled because both partners work, but basic expenses have nearly tripled.

How is it, then, that families afford all those pairs of $200 sneakers and all those $4 lattes?

One phenomenon we did not explore in the behavioral section of this chapter is called personalization. People tend to overgeneralize events that happen to them, leading them to incorrect generalizations about overall trends. Everyone in a seaside village where a shark attack occurs believes that shark attacks are on the rise. Similarly, every time someone hears a story about $200 sneakers, they assume everyone is buying $200 sneakers. In fact, average consumers are spending far less on items like these.

Let's take that grand symbol of Bobos lives, the stainless-steel refrigerator. It may seem extravagant, but is actually dramatically cheaper than the fridge that their parents purchased. A look at a 1971 Sears catalog reveals that a midrange fridge cost $399. That would be two weeks' work for an average laborer in 1971. In 2009, a midlevel Sears fridge cost $500, less than two days' work. The story is the same for other household items. A midlevel TV in that 1971 catalog cost $429—$2,150 in today's money. A dishwasher cost $249 ($1,250 in 2008 dollars).

GENERATIONAL SHIFT

Comparing budgets for two typical, four-member families

	"Tom and Susan," single-income family, mid-1970s [adjusted to 2004 dollars]	"Kimberly and Justin," dual-income family, 2004	Percentage change
Husband's income	$42,450	$41,670	−2
Wife's income	$0	$32,100	+1,000
Total family income	$42,450	$73,770	+74
Tax rate (% of income; local, state & federal)	24 percent	30 percent	+25
Taxes	$10,300	$22,280	+116
After-tax income	$32,150	$51,490	+60
MAJOR FIXED EXPENSE			
Home mortgage	$5,820	$10,250	+76
Day care (7-year-old)	$0	$5,660	+1,000
Preschool (3-year-old)	$0	$6,920	+1,000
Health insurance	$1,130	$1,970	+74
Automobile #1 (purchase, upkeep, insurance)	$5,640	$4,275	−24
Automobile #2	$0	$4,275	+1,000
Total fixed expenses	$12,590	$33,350	+165

Source: Elizabeth Warren, co-author with Amelia Warren Tyagi of *The Two-Income Trap: Why Middle-Class Mothers and Fathers Are Going Broke.*

The story holds true for annual clothing expenditures, too. While $400 Jimmy Choo shoes are held up as an ideal, clothing prices have in truth plummeted thanks to the arrival (okay, market saturation) of cheap imports. Anyone who's purchased a complete Friday-night outfit at Target for $40 can attest to that.

The U.S. Department of Labor completes an extensive survey of consumer spending every year. It found that from 1984 to 2005, the percent of household income spent on clothes plummeted by 50 percent.

Sure, people have more gadgets and more clothes, but these purchases have little to do with rising personal bankruptcies.

"Yes, people are spending more on home electronics, but the dollars just aren't that big," says Amelia Warren Tyagi, co-author of *The Two-Income Trap*. "Maybe they spend a couple of hundred dollars more on stereo equipment. But they are spending less on tobacco. This is not to say that there's no frivolous spending going on, but as you add it all up, there's no more frivolous spending than there was a generation ago."

WHERE THE MONEY GOES

Average annual expenditures per household

	1984	%	1995	%	2005	%
TOTAL	$22,546		$33,597		$46,409	
Food	$3,376	14.97	$4,691	13.96	$5,931	12.78
Housing	$6,728	29.84	$10,571	31.46	$15,167	32.68
Transportation	$4,393	19.48	$6,121	18.22	$8,344	17.98
Health care	$1,061	4.71	$1,747	5.20	$2,664	5.74
Clothing	$1,376	6.10	$1,771	5.27	$1,886	4.06
Entertainment	$1,089	4.83	$1,687	5.02	$2,338	5.15
Pension/life insurance	$2,062	9.15	$3,517	10.47	$5,304	11.43

U.S. Department of Labor, Bureau of Labor Statistics.

So where does all that extra money go? Why are families struggling so much? There is only one answer.

Housing.

During the six years from 2000 to 2006, the average family's housing costs soared 32 percent. Even more striking is the amount of income most families are paying to stay in their homes. Banks used to hold to a standard that mortgages should not be approved unless the monthly payment was 25 percent or less of the buyer's gross income. That limitation, which had slowly eroded for years, disappeared during the boom—right along with the near extinction of the "conforming" loan market. The government entities you've now heard so much about—Fannie Mae and Freddie Mac—helped prop up the mortgage market for decades by agreeing to buy up so-called conforming loans: what was once imagined as mortgages for average homeowners with average incomes. Only loans of less than $417,000, where the buyer could keep payments near or under 25 percent of their income, were considered conforming loans. But as the housing market exploded, the number of loans under those two thresholds declined dramatically, sending most lenders into the nonconforming loan market—sometimes also called the Wild West of the housing market. In nonconforming-loan land, the Fannie Mae and Freddie Mac income rules didn't apply, so banks began approving mortgages for buyers who spent 40, 50, or even 60 percent of their income on housing expenses.

The U.S. Census Bureau defines *house poor* as spending more than 30 percent of income on housing expenses. In 1999, 26.7 percent of U.S. households were considered house poor. By 2006, the number had jumped to 34.5 percent. And a full 15 percent of consumers—or one in seven households—spent 50 percent of their money on housing.

Compare that to 1975, when only 9 percent of U.S. consumers spent more than 35 percent of their income on all housing-related costs, including insurance.

Mortgages, more than lattes, are the cause of middle-class anxiety.

I'm not trying to say that consumers bear no responsibility for their financial situation. I've already conceded that consumers make bad choices, don't pay attention in math class, and overindulge on extras. But that's not the whole story; in fact, it's a sideshow.

I make this case because underneath every tale I tell about consumers getting screwed, I hear this response: They had it coming. They were lazy, they were dumb, they were selfish. Screw them! I see this with every single Red Tape Chronicles column I write. It is, I believe, the moral underpinning—rationalization, really—of those who make their living by cheating others.

This line of thinking, however, is bankrupt. Like all rationalizations, it cannot stand the light of day. Consumers who want their kids to attend good schools aren't lazy and selfish, and they certainly don't deserve to be nickeled-and-dimed at every turn. Only so many homes qualify the kids for good elementary schools, and their scarcity has sent prices skyrocketing. The dream to buy a home near a good school does not make someone a fair target for financial deception. As well, senior citizens who've worked for forty-five years don't deserve to be tricked into reverse mortgages that rape them of their equity.

These people deserve to be protected, and on this count, our country has failed them miserably. The real reason Americans get screwed so often is because our government permits it and, in many ways, encourages it.

6. NO REGULATION

In 1999, Harry Markopolos began pelting the Securities and Exchange Commission with overwhelming evidence that Bernie Madoff was a billion-dollar con man. In a now famous memo he wrote a few years later, he didn't mince words: "Madoff Securities is the world's largest Ponzi scheme." He then included hundreds of pages of nearly incontrovertible evidence. He concluded, "In this case there is no SEC reward payment due the whistle-blower so basically I'm turning the case in because it's the right thing to do. Far better that the SEC is proactive in shutting down a Ponzi scheme of this size rather than reactive."

We all know how that turned out. Madoff stole billions from baseball legend Sandy Koufax, talk-show host Larry King, New York Mets owner Fred Wilpon, a who's who of Jewish charities, and hundreds of other helpless people and organizations. Madoff was simply taking in money from new investors and using it to pay off other investors, a rudimentary Ponzi scam writ large. When the time came to pay everyone, there was nothing. The SEC, which is charged with keeping Wall Street neat and clean, did neither. Apparently, it didn't even read its own mail.

If the SEC isn't hunting down folks such as Madoff, do you really think it's protecting you?

Of course, an alphabet soup of government agencies is charged with making sure the American marketplace is fair and honest. Sadly, their track record isn't much better. Cell-phone companies fraudulently extending consumers' contacts without their knowledge? That's the Federal Communications Commission's area. What did the agency do about it? Forward complaints to the companies. Toys tainted with lead sent to U.S. kids by Chinese companies? The Consumer Product Safety Commission told its single toy tester to step it up a notch. Poisoned food seeping in through the nation's ports? The Food and Drug Administration reduced its ranks of inspectors. Mortgage advertisements luring home-buyers with promises of 1 or 2 percent mortgages? The Federal Trade Commission issued a press release asking for them to stop advertising these misleading "teaser" rates—in 2007, six years after the practice began, and after the housing bubble had already burst.

All of these federal agencies are staffed by hundreds of employees who care deeply about their work and want consumers to be treated well. Many win individual, small battles on behalf of victims. But collectively, their ranks have been decimated for decades. The Federal Trade Commission, for example, had nearly two thousand employees in 1979. By 2006, the staff had been cut almost in half. Meanwhile, its workload was massively expanded to include new subjects such as Internet security, identity theft, spam, and the Do Not Call list. Like all other consumer-protection agencies, the FTC couldn't keep up.

This, you see, was by design.

During the throes of the housing collapse, *Mother Jones* magazine wrote an exposé titled "This Was No Accident." At its core was Phil Gramm, the former U.S. senator who got himself kicked off the John McCain campaign when he was caught on tape calling the economic downturn a "psychological recession" in early 2008. Gramm, who was a longtime chair of the Senate Banking Committee, made a habit of thwarting SEC requests for more staffing. He also presided over the 1999 Financial Services Modernization Act (aka Gramm-Leech-Bliley Act), which did away with most Depression-era controls on banks. But nothing set the stage for the boom-and-bust cycle of the housing market more than Gramm's other brainchild, the Commodity Futures Modernization Act. The law paved the way for the Trojan-horse financial instrument that was at the core of the mortgage-industry meltdown—the credit default swap. Swaps were a form of insurance that let mortgage lenders pretend they had no risk on their books from loans they'd granted, so they could sell even more loans (theoretically, if a homeowner did fail to pay, such insurance would cover the losses). Ultimately, that gave banks the moxie to lend out nearly $100 for every $1 they took in, a crazy formula that should sound quite a bit like Bernie Madoff's Ponzi scheme to you. Gramm's law ensured that swaps could be bought and sold outside the prying eyes of government regulators such as the Commodity Futures Trading Commission. No one seemed to wonder what would happen if lots of people stopped paying their mortgages all at once.

Before the decade was over, credit default swaps were bought and sold and resold so much that their total value was estimated at $62 trillion: four times the value of the entire housing market. Within a decade, they would first take down insurance behemoth AIG, then lead to the domino effect we now know as the recession of 2008–9.

While corporate America was looting the country, the cop on the beat was asleep at the wheel.

The age-old response to unfair behavior by those who defend hands-off governing is simple: Consumers have the ultimate power. They can leave. If they hate the way their bank treats them, they can withdraw their money and go elsewhere. If enough leave, the bank will go out of business. That's how capitalism works.

Anyone who believes that is even more naïve than overly optimistic home-buyers who can't pay their mortgages. Changing companies is always easier said than done. There are early-termination fees, a lack of competitors, cleverly designed paperwork headaches—what economists call switching costs. Then, there is the biggest hurdle of all: false advertising. If consumers can't compare prices and punishments *before* purchasing a service, they'll never get a good deal. I'd take a pure form of a market economy with little or no government involvement any day. But we have nothing of the sort. Generally, we have industries where corporations enjoy powerful monopolies and legal immunity from misbehavior, all the while requiring shoppers to act as if they should abide by the rules of a free market. False advertising is so rampant in the banking industry, for example, that the Federal Reserve did a study of bank account switching costs in 2008 and described the current system by this bitter phrase: banks employ a "bargain-then-rip-off" strategy to reel in customers and then exploit them. (The less sarcastic name for it is "two-period models." Period one is free gifts to college students for opening credit-card accounts. Period two is oppressive interest rates soon after graduation.

Of course, the Fed hasn't done anything about bargain-then-rip-off pricing. That's not a bad label for most marketing plans today. In many parts of the country, it's illegal to sell a home that's not earthquake proof. That might sound like government intrusion to you, until you think about the buildings that collapse when tremors hit third-world cities. It's illegal in most places to sell food without submitting to health inspections. I can't imagine anyone would choose a restaurant that bragged it was evading inspections. When you buy gas, you probably notice a sticker which indicates that a government agency has regularly checked the station's pumps to make sure a gallon of gas really is a gallon of gas when you buy it. These are normal government functions. Without them, everyone would have to be an expert on everything—carrying around measurement tools for the gas station, for example—and commerce would come to a screeching halt. People have come to expect that if they buy a new car, the brakes will work, and thank God for that. Why in heaven's name would we allow creation of mortgage products that would send the world into recession and call that a free market?

No, simple comparison shopping can't get us out of the mess we're in. Take another rarely understood phenomenon, inflation by degradation. Sometimes, the costs of things goes up even though the prices haven't changed. That's easy to see in the grocery store. When a quart of mayonnaise is suddenly a thirty-ounce jar . . . a twenty-nine-ounce jar . . . a twenty-eight-ounce jar—you see a new kind of inflation in action. Perhaps, you think, the tiny print on the bottle should be enough to tell consumers what they're getting, but consider this example. Assume an airplane ticket between New York and Washington, D.C., cost $200 five years ago, and the airline's on-time rating was 90 percent. Say the flights cost the same amount of money today, but now the on-time rating is 40 percent. Isn't the first ticket far more valuable since it comes with a near assurance that it won't ruin your entire day? Without federally mandated on-time reports, we couldn't possibly compare the true costs of flying. Now, think about all the other ways companies you deal with have cut back on product or service without lowering price (just about any customer-service phone call should come to mind), and you'll see what I mean by inflation by degradation. Without basic minimum standards, it's impossible to comparison shop—and it's impossible to know ahead of time if you're getting screwed, no matter how enterprising a shopper you might be.

The chief reason that Americans get screwed so often is that they are willing participants in a marketplace that requires trust, then someone pulls the rug out from under them. Be thankful consumers are still willing to trust anyone. Faith in the future is a fundamental

American value that sets our nation apart and has enabled us to cross the ocean of space, perform real miracles of science, and defeat Hitler. Taking advantage of that unbridled—perhaps sometimes naïve—American optimism, and in fact destroying it, tears at the very heart of what makes our country great. We shouldn't focus our energies on turning people into bitter skeptics; we would be better served making our world safe for dreamers.

7. MAGIC

A young Israeli named Uri Geller became a household name in the United States during the early 1970s, enrapturing audiences with his seeming powers of telepathy and psychokinesis. His face landed on all the major magazine covers, and eventually he became perhaps the world's most famous magician. Schoolchildren around the country began trying to imitate his signature trick—bending spoons with his mind. In many households, broken soupspoons became a subject of familial strife.

In one famous video clip, after Geller bends a spoon on live television, he exhorts his fans to believe that they, too, can have this amazing power. All they have to do is want it.

"If there is a radio that is broken? Want it to start working. Television broken—just want it to start working," he urged his fans. If Geller were in the prime of his career today, he would write a book and try to get it adopted by Oprah's Book Club with that kind of positive talk.

But the Oprah of 1970s was Johnny Carson, the original king of late-night television. Carson was himself a magician, and he had concerns that Geller was going a little too far with his gags. Claiming trickery is one thing; claiming paranormal powers, and getting paid for them, is still another. So Carson invited Geller on the show, but he also called in his own magician-in-residence for help: the Amazing Randi.

By 1973, the Amazing Randi had sat on Johnny Carson's couch

many times. James Randi spent the first half of his career pulling harmless gags on TV, himself one of the world's most famous magicians.

But he has spent the second half of his life as the world's leading skeptic, exposing fraudulent magicians and psychics who've stolen from vulnerable consumers. Geller's appearance on Johnny Carson marked a turning point for both men. Randi convinced Carson to sit Geller down in front of a table full of spoons and other props that had been quarantined before the show to prevent any chicanery. Randi, himself a proficient spoon-bender, knew that the spoon trick required only a few minutes of preparation—prebending—to loosen the metal enough so that a magician could appear to move the metal with only the lightest touch and deep concentration.

Geller, of course, was powerless on the *Tonight* show that night. The video of the episode is nearly painful to watch, as Geller flaccidly moves his hands over objects, can't nudge the spoons, in his thick accent teases Carson for being skeptical, and eventually concedes, "I don't feel strong . . . I'm feeling being pressed."

The incident launched Randi's career as the world's most famous skeptic. He opened the James Randi Educational Foundation for the study of the paranormal and pseudoscience. He even established a $1 million prize for anyone who could demonstrate psychic power. The award was established in 1996 and has not yet been claimed.

And he continued to run investigations—some airing on Carson's *Tonight* show—exposing charlatans who tricked consumers out of their money by claiming they had superpowers.

In the early 1980s, televangelist Peter Popoff was pulling in millions of dollars during massive faith-healing ceremonies. Using a technique that's familiar to anyone who's ever turned on a television late at night, Popoff would call up sick and frail audience members, lay his hands on them, then scream out that they were "healed." The audience member, overwhelmed by the gesture, would faint on cue. Then, Popoff would implore viewers to send more money.

One day, Randi attended a Popoff gathering—with a small radio frequency receiving device in tow. Here's what Randi's radio picked up from a scratchy broadcast on a secret frequency in the auditorium:

"Hello, Peetie, can you hear me? If you can't, you're in trouble."

It wasn't the voice of God that Popoff heard. It was his wife, whispering in his ear through a small radio device.

"Johnson," she would say in his ear, and describe the woman so Popoff could find her in the audience. "She wants to get rid of the walker." Popoff would then approach Miss Johnson, call her by name, then seem to magically know everything about her through divine providence.

"You live at 1627 Tenth Street? Is that right?" he asks in one video.

"That's right," she says, and beams. He lays his hands on her, a spotlight glows, and after a healing moment Popoff grabs her hand and says, "Take a few steps just to make the devil mad. She's not gonna need that walker anymore." The amazed audience roars.

Randi unmasked Popoff's magic trick in grand fashion. The incriminating audio recording was paired up with video of a Popoff event and shown on an episode of the *Tonight* show. Before each event, Randi explained, Popoff's wife worked the crowd, making what appeared to be idle small talk, but she was really casing marks for Popoff's "healings." She also had the audience fill out prayer cards. Then, during the event, she secretly told her husband everything he needed to know to maintain the illusion of supernatural powers.

Carson called it "very disturbing." Today's audience might readily recognize a wireless trick, but in 1980s the technology still looked like magic. Popoff eventually admitted to using a hidden radio and declared bankruptcy soon after.

Randi has collected all this debunking and written several books of skepticism, including one that should be required reading before high school graduation: *The Encyclopedia of Claims, Frauds, and Hoaxes of the Occult and Supernatural.* He hosts an annual skeptic's conference. At eighty years old, Randi can still easily convince a crowd that he can pull playing cards out of people's ears—or even bend spoons.

"Magical thinking, you know, is a slippery slope. Sometimes it's harmless enough, but other times it's quite dangerous," he says.

His white beard now seems impossibly long for a man of such modest height, and his face shows a rich topography that's the result of many furrowed brows. Still, when he makes appearances, he usually ends up sitting next to the prettiest girl at the table.

Ask Randi the most obvious question after a trick—how did you do that?—and he manages to pull off some magic.

"Many times," he confessed to me, "magicians don't really know why their tricks work. They just work." Pushed to explain a little bit more, he put it this way: Charlatans don't bother creating detailed schemes for deception. They just have a good feel for what fools people. And they have a good feel for people who are fools.

A huckster's most important tool, he said, is the blind faith of the victim.

"In the end, people really want to believe," Randi said. "Everyone wants to believe in magic. Since you were a kid, you were taught to believe in magic."

Those who pay for visits to psychics are often desperate for someone to tell them what to do. Those who see financial advisers usually feel the same way. Everyone wants to believe someone can win them a little more money, get them a little better deal on a car, or give them exclusive access to a time-share property. Magicians, hucksters, con artists, and salesmen all tap into the same force, Randi said to me.

"Everyone wants magic to be real."

To prove the power and lure of magic, one need only catch up with Geller and Popoff several decades after their encounter with Randi. In the past few years, Popoff has reemerged on late-night TV selling "miracle water" that promises to heal the sick, so long as the sick donate large sums of money to Popoff. Geller now straddles a fine line between claiming he's psychic or a magician. He has a hit TV series that airs in a dozen countries around the world, he's produced documentaries and TV specials, and he even has a line of watches and jewelry that's sold on QVC. On his website, he makes clear who he thinks got the last laugh:

The people who are uploading these videos on YouTube, imagining that they are exposing me, are really giving me priceless exposure. They're creating the most brilliant free publicity I could ever have, and certainly manufacturing more controversy . . . thus enhancing the mystery and mystique around Uri Geller.

The skeptics have been doing this for over 35 years! Wow! That's a long publicity and PR campaign—and it's all free! To calculate that in financial terms: if I had to pay for all this, I believe a Madison Avenue public relations agency would have charged me many millions of dollars over the decades. That's what the "Get Geller" bunch have supplied me with on a silver tray: FREE PUBLICITY. There is NO such thing as bad publicity (unless you are John Edwards and you're running for president). . . . Whether you think I'm a fake or you believe I'm a miracle worker, I can assure you of one thing: I must be among the best PR gurus in the world. I've shown that I know how to reinvent myself over and over. . . .

I don't mean to brag, but you skeptics, especially the ones obsessed with Uri Geller . . . eat your hearts out.

IT'S OKAY TO LIKE MAGIC . . . SOMETIMES

We tend to talk about naïveté as if it's a bad thing. I can't think of anyone I know who'd like to be called naïve. Yet, being called skeptical isn't exactly a compliment, either. If someone accused you of being incapable of believing in magic, he or she probably wouldn't invite you to a child's birthday party in the next breath. Childlike enthusiasm is delightful in adults, and yet it is childlike enthusiasm that lands consumers in terrible car loans.

On the other hand, the most skeptical (and paranoid) people I know are often the biggest scam victims. Those kinds of folks tend to see the world as very black-and-white, so all a con man has to do is get on their good side. Then, they are likely to fall for the trap hook, line, and sinker, all the while congratulating themselves for their skepticism.

So is being naïve good or bad?

Like many questions that face adults, the split between naïve and skeptical is not so black-and-white. Sometimes, it's good to believe in magic. Sometimes, it's even good to believe you're getting a good deal. As we mentioned above, for a market to function at all, there must be some naïveté, some trust. For investors to bet on a small business, they must believe in a dream. In almost every purchase, there is always a moment when one person holds both the money and the thing being purchased. Someone has to trust the transaction will be completed in good faith, or there is no transaction. In every element of commerce, there is a leap of faith, a moment of trust. From our earliest days, we are conditioned to make this leap of faith. Driving down a road and trusting that cars won't hit you is such a leap, one we take thoughtlessly every day. That a website such as eBay functions at all—actually functions well millions of times a day—shows that this trust is well-placed most of the time. Yet, this trust is exactly what Randi and his enemy hucksters exploit.

You've heard this endlessly: If it sounds too good to be true, it probably is. But if it just sounds pretty good, well, what then? How can consumers find the right spot on the dial, the right place on the spectrum between skepticism and faith while navigating our increasingly complex financial world? Particularly when you can't count on those who design our markets to protect you? How can you learn the difference between the leap of faith required to buy your first house, or the leap of entrepreneurial spirit required to start a small business, and the leap of a too trusting fool about to get screwed on a car deal? By sprinkling a little knowledge on top of your instincts. By developing those instincts through personal experience. And most of all, by learning the art of good judgment.

This is the subject of *Stop Getting Ripped Off*. In this book, we will go through your monthly bills one by one and see where every pitfall and booby trap may be. We'll talk about how to fight back when a company has taken you for a ride, and how to sense such shenanigans even before they start. Then we'll show you how to put it all in practice through the Pitfall-Proof Pyramid, where you'll learn how to get, keep, and grow your money the right way. When we're done, businesses will be afraid to try to screw with you. But before we get started on the specifics, I want to share a few general principles.

TAKE ME OUT TO THE BALLPARK

Teenaged boys who play football have another game they love to play in the hallways of high school: push-and-shove. The game is simple and can really be played anywhere. To those who aren't endowed with spare muscles and spare adrenaline, the game is a perpetual mystery. But it has real purpose, helping to teach balance, engagement, aggression, and restraint in a much less tense environment than football practice. The boys also think it impresses the girls. In other words, it's fun.

Math nerds play a similar game, but one that perhaps you haven't heard of. It's called the Fermi problem, named after Italian physicist Enrico Fermi. They use it to stretch mental muscles. If you've never seen it in action, you might be impressed. It's also a bit less dangerous than watching push-and-shove at close range.

The game works like this: Someone throws out seemingly impossible mathematical problems, like these:

How many taxicabs are there in Chicago?

How many piano tuners are there in New York?

How many grains of rice would it take to build a line from New York to Seattle? To Tokyo? To the moon?

How many square inches of pizza are consumed on a college campus during a single semester?

Of course, these are questions without answers. There simply is not enough information to precisely calculate how many square inches of pizza are consumed (Whose pizza? What semester? How many lactose-intolerant students are there?).

Those details don't bother our mathematical football players, however. They're just having fun. Much to your surprise, they aren't troubled by imprecision the way you might be. A defendable ballpark figure is all they're looking for. And in fact, thousands of Fermi players long ago determined that New York has somewhere around five hundred piano tuners. Here's one way the game is played, courtesy of MathForum.org:

Approximately how many people are in New York City?
10 million.

Does every individual own a piano?
No.

Would it be reasonable to assert that individuals don't tend to own pianos; families do?
Yes.

About how many families are there in a city of 10 million people?
Perhaps 2 million.

Does every family own a piano?
No. Perhaps one out of every five does. That would mean about four hundred thousand pianos in NYC.

How many piano tuners are needed for four hundred thousand pianos?
Some people never get around to tuning their piano; some people tune their piano every month. If we assume that on average every piano gets tuned once a year, then there are four hundred thousand piano tunings every year.

How many piano tunings can one piano tuner do?
Let's assume that the average piano tuner can tune four pianos a day. Also assume two hundred working days per year. That means that every tuner can tune about eight hundred pianos per year.

How many piano tuners are needed in NYC?
The number of tuners is approximately 400,000/800, or five hundred piano tuners.

You probably don't care how many piano tuners there are in New York, particularly if you don't live in New York or don't have an ear for music. But perhaps you should. For starters, the first guy to solve the Fermi problem always gets the girl. I've seen it. And he probably has a much better shot at keeping a roof over his future family than the quarterback.

Just like push-and-shove, Fermi problem-solving has practical implications in the real world of competitive math. Scientists regularly engage in gross estimations before they dive into a problem with more precise measuring tools. This saves them from many embarrassing errors. A rough estimate that predicts results helps in early detection of a major error—if a result is far outside an esti- mated answer, something must be wrong and the experiment must be stopped.

Employing that very same skill—the rough estimate, the ballpark answer—is one of the best ways to make sure you aren't getting screwed during a business transaction.

Let's change our Fermi problem ever so slightly.

You're buying a $13,000 car and you plan to put down $3,500. Quick: What should your monthly payments be?

Faced with this problem, the vast majority of consumers would either (a) run to an Internet calculator, or (b) trust whatever the friendly salesman says. Sadly, if A is not available, B is often the only choice, and it's fraught with peril.

So how could we attack our consumer Fermi problem? Here's one way.

Round the loan amount up to $10,000. Figure on a four-year loan. That's $2,500 a year. Divide that by twelve months and you know that principal alone would cost you something a little north of $200 a month. That's already a pretty decent starting guess. You already know that a salesman who says $279 a month is trying to pull a fast one on you. But we can get much more precise without much more effort.

How much do interest charges add to the payment? That's a harder question, but it can be estimated fairly quickly with the right approach.

Start here: Assume an interest rate of 5 percent. You know that 5 percent of $10,000 is $500, a good guess at annual interest costs. You're borrowing the money for four years, so make the total interest $2,000. Fortunately, you aren't borrowing all $10,000 for all four years, you are paying it back a little every month, and the balance slowly shrinks toward zero. So let's say the average loan balance is halfway between $10,000 and zero, or $5,000. So let's cut that interest charge in half—$1,000. Now, divide that by four years, for $250, and by twelve months to get a little more than $20. And now we have monthly payments of $220–$230.

Notice I've ignored the $500 difference in car price—the loan amount is really $9,500, not $10,000. That's okay. I've rigged this math problem so the numbers would be easy to work with, and you should, too, every chance you get. If you like, at this point you could notice that your original working number was 5 percent less, and you could rachet down your estimate 5 percent, so now you have $210–$220 a month.

Here's the right answer: Monthly payments would be $218.78. Total interest paid on the loan at 5 percent is $1001.36. Not only was our final estimate pretty darn close, but notice how close our original estimate of a little north of $200 was.

Score one for Fermi.

This little game is much more than intellectual gymnastics, however. It's typical for a car salesman to (a) arrive at the sales desk with a monthly payment number than bears no resemblance to your estimate and (b) claim to be bad at math. In the above situation, he might show up and say, "Have we got a deal for you! My manager says we'll give you the loan for 279 dollars a month!"

At this point, with your blood boiling, you are unlikely to download an auto-loan-amortization calculator onto your cell phone and plug in the numbers. You're better off saying something like "It can't be more than 230 dollars a month. Something's wrong. And I'm leaving."

At that point, your salesman will probably say you forgot to add sales tax to your math. Here's another chance to panic, but there's no need. Say sales tax is 7 percent in your state. So add 7 percent to your estimate (that's $7 for every $100 . . . or $14 for every $200 . . . so let's add $15–$20 a month), and you have an updated payment of $225–$240 a month. You are very much in the right ballpark, and nowhere near $279 a month.

This is when he says something like "But you forgot about the loan-origination fee/undercoating/extended warranty protection." Or my favorite: "Oops, we forgot to calculate in the rebate." (Yes, that's happened to me. Dealership, you know who you are.) That's when you really do get up and walk out.

Don't misunderstand me. Precision, as we learned earlier in this chapter, is a lost art and should be employed before any financial transaction is consummated. In my example, I hope you bring a laptop computer with a prebuilt spreadsheet to the dealership and fight them and their math down to the penny. But you won't always have your spreadsheet nearby. During intense negotiating, things can quickly change. Roughing out numbers gives you parameters to work with and provides a fantastic check on sales staff. Think of it as a safety net for a high-wire finance act.

A related principle is something I call the guidepost. You might already have begun to formulate one in your head from the last example. It costs roughly $200 per month for every $10,000 you borrow to buy a car, before interest charges. So a $20,000 four-year loan starts at $400 a month, a $25,000 loan at $500 a month, and so on. Obviously, the interest rate matters—but a range from 1 percent to 7 percent gives you a payment range of $210 to $240 for $10,000. So this gives you a good guidepost when deciding how much car you can afford, and what kind of malarkey the car salesman is giving you.

Another handy guidepost can be used for home purchases. A mortgage has far more variables than a car loan, so this guidepost really requires gentle handling. Still, it's quite useful. A $400,000 home purchased with a traditional thirty-year mortgage, with 20 percent down, will lead to mortgage payments of about $2,000 a month. In other words, every $100,000 you add to the loan costs you roughly $500 in monthly payments. So a $100,000 home purchased with

$20,000 down costs $500 a month. An $800,000 home bought with $160,000 down costs $4,000. And a million-dollar property bought with $200,000 down costs $5,000 a month.

With mortgages, small differences in interest can make a big difference in payments because the money is borrowed over much longer spans. My rough estimation counts on a 6.5 percent interest-rate loan (for a $200,000 home the payment is actually $1,011). If that rate shrinks to 5.5 percent, my calculations are off a bit—now the payment is $908. Similarly, with a 7.5 percent mortgage, the payments are $1,119. Massaging my Fermi mortgage requires a bit more work. Still, it's a good starting point when roughing out what you can afford. If you are considering an adjustable-rate mortgage, the Fermi mortgage is a good guidepost for you to compare to and find out how much pain you are postponing. If your payment *should* be around $2,000 a month, but you're starting off with $1,600 payments, you should know you are borrowing trouble in the future.

Speaking of borrowing in the future, here's another rule of thumb. For every $1,000 in credit card balance you carry on a high-interest card, you'll pay roughly $1 every day. So a $1,000 balance will cost you about $30 in interest every month, and a $5,000 balance costs $150 monthly. That doesn't sound too bad . . . but remember, every dollar in interest you are charged lands in your balance column. Carry that $5,000 balance for a year and it's now a $6,800 balance. Please note, this is a very blunt tool, as credit card interest rates can vary by 25 percent or more. But it does serve the purpose I intend: to help you get a grip on your finances.

Roughing it . . . estimating . . . has gotten a bad name in recent years. Parents of elementary-school math students have correctly lamented the awkward substitution of estimation for old-fashioned pencil and memorization. But estimation isn't all bad. Not only was it good enough for Enrico Fermi, it's actually a sign of quantitative intelligence. Researchers at Johns Hopkins University have conducted experiments showing that people who seem to have good "gut instincts" for math often end up near the top of their calculus class, too. In one test, students were shown a series of yellow and blue dots for just an instant. Some students are good at quickly counting how many of each has appeared, or at least estimating whether there were more yellow or more blue. Students with excellent standardized math scores could spot differences as subtle as ten yellow dots versus nine blue dots. Poor students couldn't even distinguish between five yellow and three blue.

Such raw math instinct is an important survival skill in the animal kingdom—that's how two baboons might instantly assess the wisdom of fighting a gang of six, suggested *The New York Times*. But why would it be connected to a student's ability to calculate derivatives?

No one seems to know. But clearly, it's good to know when an enemy is bigger than you are. And clearly, many consumers seem bad at that basic, instinctual judgment. One of your first tasks to become a survivor in the animal kingdom of consumers is to get good at rough judgments.

THE SOCIOPATH BEHIND THE NEXT SALES DESK

Another critical economic survival tool is the ability to negotiate. Negotiation, of course, can be a rough-and-tumble game. It also lies at the heart of a market economy. Not everyone likes to do it, but then, not everyone likes eating vegetables either. But if you won't participate in a little rough-and-tumble negotiation, then you're not participating in a capitalist society. Much of this book will fall under the broad category of negotiating tactics, but before I send you out into action, you must be armed with this knowledge:

Negotiation is one thing. Lying is quite another. You never want to try to bargain with a flat-out liar. You'll lose.

How likely is such a troubling encounter? If you believe author and psychiatrist Martha Stout, very likely. She says one in twenty adults is a born liar—a sociopath. The sooner you figure out who those folks are, the less often you'll end up screwed.

What makes born liars special? They have no conscience. They won't sweat, stammer, or even fail a lie detector test while repeating utter falsehoods. They won't feel bad about cheating on tests or taking a little old lady's money. You and I might stretch the truth once in a while; few people haven't made a large mistake and tried to cover their tracks impulsively with fibs. But a normal adult still feels bad about such lies. Sociopaths, rather chillingly, feel nothing. That's a critical difference. And it's something you will face nearly every day of your consumer life.

In her groundbreaking book, *The Sociopath Next Door,* Stout argues that this condition is far more prevalent than most people imagine. One in twenty sounds like a lot, doesn't it? But think of every car salesman you've ever met; every coworker who said one thing and did another; every lover or friend who has betrayed you. The numbers start to add up. There's no way to determine an exact number of sociopaths, of course. They are elusive. Few are ever diagnosed, and they certainly don't answer surveys truthfully. All you have is your hunch.

How do you recognize a sociopath? Many people will report a physical, or visceral, reaction. You might feel queasy or dizzy, or even disoriented, talking to a person who's a sociopath. Sociopaths often have the additional traits of charisma and persuasiveness; if you find yourself changing your mind about something quickly with seemingly little new information, you might be under the spell of a sociopath. Perhaps you went to a dealership looking to buy a compact car and ended up with an SUV, for example. Or you were dead set against taking out a second loan on your new home, but a mortgage broker convinced you otherwise. Such a quick change of heart might be information about you—perhaps you are too easily influenced—but you could also be in the presence of a sociopath. Any salesman will try to push you toward spending more money, and that's fine. You say no. If someone tries to talk you into something you've already said you don't want, that should be a warning signal. If you have to say no twice, you should consider yourself in a danger zone. Three times and you should probably vacate the situation.

Sociopaths, however, are rarely so obvious. Instead, they will have an uncanny ability to charm, and to nudge. A mind that is uncluttered by conscience is capable of incredible manipulation. If you take the mind-set of a scientist, it can be impressive to watch. As I write this, I am in a coffee shop sitting five feet from a couple who seem to be buying their first home, discussing finance options with their real estate agent. As I eavesdrop, I hear the agent steer the couple toward a mortgage broker she knows. She is far too skilled to say something direct, however. Her tactics are far more subtle. When the husband says he likes the credit union he belongs to, the agent takes a carefully orchestrated approach to reel him in.

"Well, credit unions are good, but a lot of them are closed on weekends and nights," she says. "You want someone who's going to be available anytime because these things happen very fast. Someone who will be with you all the way."

She then urges them to get a Good Faith Estimate from her friend first, which they can take back to their credit union if they like. The agent probably knows half of consumers won't bother to get that second estimate when the rubber hits the road and a house purchase is really on the line.

Then, she says something that the couple miss, but any trained observer would hear loud and clear.

"I don't get any kickbacks from him or anything like that," she says, unprompted. Doing so would be illegal, so why would she say that? It's possible her agency gets the kickback instead and funnels part to her through a bonus. It's certainly a curious choice of words.

Why is it important to recognize you are dealing with a sociopath, and not just a talented salesperson? Because no normal adult can avoid disaster in a standard negotiation with a sociopath. Just as you can't win a poker game when you are the only one not cheating, you cannot negotiate fairly with a sociopath and win. So what should you do?

Lie.

Let's say for a moment there are two kinds of buyers in the world: hagglers and nonhagglers. The biggest mistake nonhagglers make during intense negotiations is to show their cards far too soon. Now there's a surefire way to lose a poker game. Nonhagglers impulsively tell the truth, like this: "Well, I have three thousand dollars for a down payment and can pay four hundred dollars a month," when those things are actually true.

Before you buy your next car, I want you to prepare a few standard lies before you even walk into the dealership. Here are a few:

"I only have XXX dollars in my bank account." (Make it the amount you want to pay as a down payment.)

"I love the car I'm driving now."

Or the most useful of all:

"I'm expecting an important call from work" or "My aunt is in the hospital and I may have to leave quickly."

Note that these aren't really lies. A real lie would be fabricating your income on a loan application to inflate the amount of money you can borrow. Instead, think of these negotiating fibs as efficient "dealer-speak." For example, "I only have XXX dollars" means "I don't feel like bickering for an hour over down payment. That's all I'm spending." When the dealer tries, as all dealers will, to kidnap you and lock you up in the back room of the dealership, fake a cell phone call and get up to walk out. Don't be honest. Don't say, "I'm tired of sitting here," or, "Why is this taking so long?" That tells the dealer he or she is winning. Simply say, "Got to go to work," and head toward the door. You'll get where you want to go much faster.

Of course, the best thing to do when you find yourself negotiating with a sociopath is to quit and find a normal person to buy from. But that's not always possible. At car dealerships, frequently the finance guy in the back room is the real sociopath, and you won't get to him until you are eighteen steps down the road to buying a car. You won't always be able to back out at this point. Sometimes, you'll have to fight fire with fire.

I am using the strong language of lying because many people just don't believe salesmen or financial brokers lie to them. Their brain's trusty limbic system, which offers constant feedback on the emotional level, is telling them this nice man in the white shirt really does want to help. That's exactly the part of your brain that sociopaths tap into. I want to help break that spell for you. I don't want you to lie to get something. I just want you to lie to get out of something, to avoid buying something you don't want or spending money you don't have. A salesperson will always try to "frame" a price negotiation by aiming high. You must respond by aiming low. And you must believe what you are saying. You must believe your own lies, and you shouldn't feel bad about them. If you do, you'll be the only one at the table who does.

HOW TO STAY IN THE GAME

The inability to negotiate. Lack of finance education. Poor math skills. Development of advanced marketing techniques. Lack of government regulation. Whatever reason you believe people are apt to get screwed as they move through their financial life, I can tell you one thing victims all have in common: They don't have a grasp on their finances. Losing that grasp is easy in a world of revolving credit-card debt, adjustable-rate mortgages, and volatile 401(k) balances. Often the advice you get is not to worry about those things on a daily basis. Many people don't even want to look at their 401(k) balances these days. That's exactly wrong. Every consumer should be engaged with their financial picture at all times. I don't believe in obsessively checking your brokerage-account balance daily, but I know far more people who got in trouble by paying too little attention than too much.

Investing can be a little like baseball: a lot of standing around waiting for something to happen with frantic action mixed in occasionally. Naturally, baseball gets boring when you're not playing. So baseball managers have devised a way to make sure that bench players keep their "head in the game." They'll go up to a benchwarmer in the middle of an inning and quiz him, "What's the count?" As in, how many balls and strikes has the current hitter faced? If the player's not paying close attention, he'll fail the test and stay on the bench.

I'm going to play baseball manager now and ask you a series of "What's the count?" questions. Can you answer them?

1. How much cash do you have in your primary checking account right now?
2. What's your retirement-account balance?
3. What are the interest rates on your credit cards? Which has the lowest rate?
4. How much money did you spend last month?
5. How much would you need to survive for three months if you lost your job?

In a recent study, more than one-third of participants failed the credit card question, and that should be the softball, given that it's a fairly static number.

If you can't answer some of these questions, you have dangerously checked out of your financial picture. You have, for example, lost track of your monthly budget, and your long-term financial plans. You're detached. Blame Visa and MasterCard if you like. Robert Manning, author of *Credit Card Nation,* talks about the cognitive disconnect that was fomented by the credit card associations beginning all the way back in the late 1960s. Before then, most Americans lived by a relatively simple principle: Earn money, spend money. But credit cards reversed that order of things, which brought with it an astonishing cultural change. When people spend money before they earn it, a cognitive disconnect soon develops between how much you spend and how much you earn. Now, half of Americans spend more each month on credit cards than they pay. It's easy to forget to watch your pennies if no pennies are to be seen. Study after study shows people who fork over actual cash (and feel the immediate pain of money leaving their hands) spend less than people who pay with plastic or some other automated means. They have literally and figuratively lost their grip on money.

Losing your grip, of course, is another way of saying you're suffering from anxiety, and nothing is more anxiety-producing than having no idea what's going on. Think of the last time you went to the doctor with a mysterious pain. No matter how bad the diagnosis was, you felt better knowing what was wrong. The less you know about your financial picture, the more you are likely to feel a low-level, background anxiety (or just plain guilt) every time you spend money or make dinner plans. People tend to think of strict budgeting as restrictive and oppressive, but in reality it's liberating. Nothing is more liberating than spending $50 that you *know you have* and in fact have planned for on a nice dinner.

However, once consumers are in the full-blown stage of credit card revolving, they no longer even think about their total debt. They simply focus on their minimum monthly payment. Similarly, they focus on monthly car payments, monthly mortgage payments, etc., detaching entirely from their larger financial picture.

Losing your grip on your finances has another important effect. In his groundbreaking relationship research, John Gottman describes the impact that emotional "flooding" has on partners during fights. When emotions run too high, such as during a conflict, physiological changes take place that prevent the brain from functioning properly. In other words, sometimes people don't think during a fight—their brains can't even process. This you know from experience: Sometimes you say things you don't mean, or at least things you wouldn't have said if you were thinking. Similar flooding occurs when people feel insecure around numbers and they've lost their grasp of their debt, income, and savings. Then, when the moment of truth comes, and they are standing before that shiny new pair of shoes or the flat-screen TV, they just buy it. Why not just add it to the pile? And when the car salesman says your payment should be $279, who are you to argue?

This is not a book about turning debt into wealth; there are plenty of those. I don't espouse any particular debt-reduction philosophy, no more than I support any kind of diet or self-help book. I believe that most of them work just fine, as long as you pick one and stick to it. If you have bad eating habits, anything you do to observe what you eat and limit it will make you healthier. Any personal-improvement program you undertake—say, speaking up more at work—will make a difference, as long as you stick to it. And any work you do to pay off debt will reduce your debt. Every one of these approaches will take a long time.

Instead, I'm here to help you make immediate improvements to your financial situation by helping you to stop getting screwed. I want you to keep more of the money you make, and to stop giving it away to amoral companies that have spent years studying ways to trick you. I want to give you a back-to-basics approach to buying cars, homes, insurance, and everything else you need. I want you to be treated fairly. Then, I'm going to show you how to apply all these rules in a simple formula—your Personal Pitfall-Prevention Pyramid— so you will have a strong financial foundation and a future that can't be shaken by charlatans and evil math wizards.

Some of this material may be familiar to you. Great, skip ahead. But all the research I've shared so far in this book—and everything I learned from the thousands of emails, letters, and calls I received after the publication of *Gotcha Capitalism*—tells me that America could really use a how-to guide for wrestling with transactions in the twenty-first century. That's what I aim to provide here.

Music fans will recognize the quote at the beginning of this book as the work of Stevie Wonder in his timeless hit "Superstition." As the Amazing Randi would tell you, people frequently believe in things they don't understand . . . and suffer. But you don't have to. It's time you stopped getting screwed, by starting to understand all the elements of your financial life.

I'M ON A mission. I want to fix capitalism before it's too late.

Thomas Jefferson once said, "An enlightened citizenry is indispensable for the proper functioning of a republic." In case you haven't been paying attention, the previous decade has proven that something else is indispensable to the proper functioning of our republic: a functioning economy. When the world of business breaks down, all our lofty goals disappear quicker than an auto salesman who just grabbed your down-payment check. If there's no money, no one worries about parks or roads or feeding the poor or poor health care. Therefore, in order to form a more perfect union, we need a healthy economy.

Yet something funny happened during the Great Depression. We selected an alternate form of government for our economy: dictatorship. Back then, we let a cabal of mysterious, rich bankers push all the levers and knobs in an effort to restore financial order. Their success or failure remains a hotly contested issue for historians.

This governing body for our economy is rarely contested. Wall Street sets the rules, whether we're talking about mortgage interest rates for million-dollar properties or $35 overdraft fees on checking accounts. Everything is done to satisfy the titans of New York.

This was never more evident than in fall 2008, when Secretary of the Treasury Henry Paulson, a former Wall Street executive, asked for $700 billion—that's six months' worth of federal tax revenues!—in a three-page memo. Sure, there was token discussion and opposition for a few days. The memo got a little longer, but basically Hank got what he wanted. Ultimately, he used the money however he wanted.

"Trust me," he told us. "I'll take care of you." And with that, Hank Paulson reached into your bank account, took an extra six months' worth of taxes from you, and gave it to America's banks. We spent more on the bailout in one day than we spent on the entire Iraq War. Try this, for fun. Look at your most recent two-week pay stub, find the box that indicates how much you paid in federal taxes, and multiply that by twelve. Then picture yourself walking into your bank and dropping that pile of cash off at the front desk. That's what happened during the bailout.

Yet, we all did it with hardly a peep. In fact, a few weeks later, we elected hundreds of congressmen and congresswomen who voted to take this money from us. A small gathering of Ralph Nader supporters outside the New York Stock Exchange, and some feisty complainers outside the AIG insurance company building in Manhattan, were the only true whispers of opposition. Why did we all line up like lambs to the slaughter for the bailout?

Because all the experts told us to. A steady stream of columns by America's most respected economists told us it was the bailout or else. One commentator on CNBC said that the American economy was five hundred trades away from complete meltdown, as if he were watching a fuse burn down toward a detonator, and the bailout was a last-second bucket of water. It all felt like a movie, with economists riding in at the last minute to save us. Fed chairman Ben Bernanke got his Ph.D. studying the Great Depression and the flawed government reaction to it. It's easy to imagine him feeling like Professor Indiana Jones, propelled suddenly from a bookish office to the dangers of a real-world crisis—his chance to go back in time and save us from the Great Depression.

We all know how things turned out. The bailout bucket they brought was more like a water pistol. The market devoured that $700 billion and asked for more, more, more, the way giving people-food to a dog always makes him beg for more. Soon after, everyone's 401(k) was cut in half anyway.

I know, I know, without the bailout things would have been much worse (worse? I'll owe money for fifty years and half my retirement money disappeared and you tell me things could be worse?). My point here is not to debate the tactics of the economic rescue plan. My point is this: Do you recall any great national debate about the merits of the bailout, the stimulus plan, bailout #2, stimulus #2, or the foreclosure rescue plan? Do you recall illuminating discussions on your local television station about what would happen to the money, how the bailout would work, how the purchase of toxic securities would kick-start home sales? Of course not! Such conversation wasn't even considered polite at the time. We were to leave those details to the kings and queens of high finance.

Should we really have expected things to turn out any differently? This was the same group who had engineered the crisis through the deluded notion that low interest rates and the elimination of all mortgage regulation would be good for the country. The group then steadfastly maintained this view as $15-an-hour laborers purchased $550,000 homes. Even as things began to turn sour, in 2007, when any fourth-grader with a calculator could see that America was overdrawn and headed for disaster, the deluded dictators of the economy maintained that we were only hitting a speed bump.

If a skyscraper collapsed because of poor design, would you hire that architect to rebuild it?

Why did we let these fools design the bailout? There's a simple answer: We don't have an enlightened citizenry. Or more specifically, enlightened consumers.

Try this question on for size: How many personal-finance classes did you take in school? You spent 2 million minutes sitting in a hard chair in high school. If you spent even one thousand of those minutes on life-essential tasks such as how to balance a checkbook, how to calculate credit card interest, or how to buy a home, you are in the minority. Only three states in the United States require a personal-finance course. You probably spent hundreds of hours learning how to calculate the value of x, or memorizing the vice presidents during the 1800s. You almost certainly spent time learning how to put on a condom in light of the AIDS epidemic. But nothing on credit scores.

Well, if the housing meltdown and the resulting worldwide economic disaster isn't an epidemic worth attention, I don't know what is. America needs to act with HIV-crisis-like haste to teach its people financial safety. No one should walk into an auto dealership or a mortgage broker's office without the proper protection, lest you leave with a problem that could drag you down for years or even decades.

Getting a bad mortgage is not as bad as contracting a disease. But it's close. We need to find a cure before the next financial outbreak takes down half the planet's economies.

This book, I hope, will be part of that cure. It picks up where school, family, and mortgage brokers have let you down. I will provide a primer on how to conduct business in the most important facets of your financial life. I will not be telling you how to make a quick killing in the stock market. Instead, I will tell you how to avoid getting killed. We'll go inside car dealerships and real estate agent offices and insurance companies and we'll unmask all the ways these industries are designed to cheat you, and all the ways employees are trained to deceive you. Then, I'll give you the antidote you need to get fair treatment, all the time. You will not get rich quickly. But you won't feel like a sucker, and that's even more valuable.

Two years ago, when *Gotcha Capitalism* was published, many of my readers already knew, deep down, what was going on. They knew they were getting screwed. Every month, their cable and cell-phone bills were jam-packed with extra surcharges. Their credit cards were layered with hundreds of dollars in fees. Their mortgages were designed to be unintelligible. "Confusion marketing" was designed to manipulate them and make it impossible to determine the real price of things. In that book, I laid out the case that this was no mere irritation: It was an attack on our way of life, and our economic system. With prices invisible, competition skewed, and fairness on vacation, capitalism was in peril. Only companies that cheated best, with profits and business models built on straw, could win in that toxic atmosphere. At the time, many of Wall Street's most celebrated companies were rotting from the inside, but only a few people knew.

Within a year, the disaster struck. Brand-name companies were betrayed by their own lies and unsustainable business models. The subsequent unwinding of America's unfair housing market led to a calamity even bigger than I had predicted.

We can't let this happen again.

By learning the antidote to Gotcha Capitalism, you'll begin putting hundreds or thousands of dollars right back where they belong: in your pocket. And you'll be doing something even more valuable: You'll be part of a movement to save American capitalism. You'll be "voting" on how our country's economy should work. Every time you fight a bank overdraft, keep home-purchase closing costs low, or outsmart your cell-phone company, you will be doing your part to restore the proper functioning of our free-market system. By turning your back on thieving corporations and their scheming ways, you will rid our economy of those leeches that drain it of life: bad companies with hollow profits that are destined to fail spectacularly someday.

And I promise, you'll feel good doing it.

Now, let's get started.

PART II

STOP GETTING
RIPPED OFF—
ONE DEAL AT A TIME

1

The Twenty-First-Century Checking Account

I recently overdrew my checking account at Chase Bank by 60 cents, and my unemployment check was set to be electronically deposited later the same night. The overdraft would only exist for a few hours. The bank charged me $35 for a 60-cent overdraft. If this were interest, it would be 6000%, but since it is a fee, it is okay.

—KATE HANK,
a Red Tape Chronicles reader

Once upon a time, a checking account was simply for depositing paychecks and writing checks. As long as you noted the checks in a register, you were safe. If you bounced a check, it probably was your fault.

Those days are long gone.

Now, check writing is probably the least of your checking-account worries. Today, your checking account can be accessed at least six ways—ATM withdrawals, signature debit purchases, PIN debit purchases, online bill pay, and other electronic transactions such as wire transfers. And, of course, checks. In industry terms, your checking account has far more velocity now, making it far more vulnerable to hackers, and, more important, far more difficult to keep track of your balance.

The result? In 2007, Americans spent $17.5 billion making banks richer through overdraft charges, probably the most lucrative hidden fee in America. The notion of a free checking account is largely a charade. Banks created the overdraft phenomenon and stoke it by quietly adding features such as "courtesy overdraft protection," all the while tightening the screws more and more with each passing year. Overdraft fees now cost nearly $40 per transgression, and because the fees are often "stacked"—one overdraft leads to another, then another, and so on—one single lapse can easily cause a $5 hamburger purchase to ultimately cost $200. That means it's more important than ever to protect yourself, and your checking account, from heading south of zero.

It's not easy. There are other bank-designed booby traps, such as "Check 21." This new electronic processing system for checks means banks get your money instantly when someone cashes a check you write (no more "float"), but can still hold on to checks you deposit for long stretches of time (up to eleven days). In short, the money comes out much faster than it goes in. That's a recipe for overdrafts. Banks even vary *by deposit type* how quickly they credit your account when you deposit money. (Hint: At one major bank, online transactions are credited at 10:45 a.m. every day, in-person teller transactions aren't credited until 2 p.m., and deposits at newer ATMs don't make it until 8 p.m.!) Not knowing these rules can be costly.

But how would you know them? In 2007, 20 percent of banks were in violation of the Truth in Savings Act, a federal law requiring clear and conspicuous disclosure of their fee schedules. Quick: What does your bank charge for an overdraft?

In total, Americans donate $36 billion in fees to U.S. banks every year, or about $400 for every adult American. Virtually all of that spending is unnecessary. Anyone using the right tricks can have checking and savings accounts for free. This chapter will show you how.

BALANCING YOUR CHECKBOOK MONTHLY?
NO, DAILY

You'll hear plenty of old-fashioned advice about balancing your checkbook to prevent accidental overdrafts. If you're the type to do that every month, God bless. Software can help, too. But balancing a checkbook today is so much harder than it used to be; and even a monthly balancing won't really protect you from the $39 overdraft fees I'm talking about. Anybody can make a string of unexpected debit purchases during a month of bad luck (but not if you follow my advice and don't make debit purchases). Anyone can misunderstand checking-account deposit-credit policies. Anyone can accidentally click twice while using online bill pay and suddenly find their accounts unfunded.

Checking accounts are misnamed at this point—their real name should be something like "electronic transaction accounts" or "e-accounts." And for these accounts, we need a whole new branch of personal accounting.

In a moment, I'll tell you that you don't really have to balance your checking account to the penny every month. I want you to set up your finances so they run on automatic for you, without any fear of overdraft fees, and I'll show you how. But first, I want you to consider the simple proposition that change is good.

Here's the fundamental flaw introduced into your life by the debit card: There are too many transactions yanking money out of your primary wealth-holding account. For the vast majority of consumers, the modern checking account is the staging ground for most of their money. Paychecks are automatically deposited into it; money sits there earning paltry interest while you wait to pay bills, then you spend it. Think about it; if your after-tax paycheck is $1,500 twice each month, then $36,000 flows into your checking account every year. What do you get for that? If you have to claim more than $20 in interest earning on your federal taxes each year, then consider yourself lucky. My point is this: Whatever bank you use for direct deposit of your paycheck, you are giving that bank a hell of a deal. Why be loyal? If you suffer an overdraft fee and your bank isn't playing ball with you, break off the relationship. Join a credit union or a smaller bank. These almost always have lower fees, less brutal policies, and higher interest rates. Save yourself two overdraft fees and earn yourself an extra 0.5 percent interest, and you've just pocketed more than $200 annually. Then buy your spouse something nice for Christmas. That's sure worth the trouble.

But even if you don't switch, the knowledge that you *can* switch is really valuable. When you're having a protracted conversation with a bank manager about excessive fees, the most convincing argument you have is the front door, because if you announce you are walking out the front door, you'll often find your foe will come around to your point of view.

One special note about switching banks. Many of the suggestions I make rely on effective use of online banking tools. These are still evolving, particularly at small banks. Most are now free, but they are not all created equal. Before you sign up with a new bank, ask to see a demonstration of its website and its online bill-paying tools. Ask friends who use the site. If a bank's online tools are hard to use or come with any fees attached, you should probably keep shopping around.

Now, back to the concept of the everything-but-the-kitchen-sink checking account, the place where you "stage" all your money. This is a bad setup and I want you to change it immediately. You should never make ticky-tacky purchases or weekly cash withdrawals from the main staging place for your money. That's a recipe for disaster. Eventually, you're going to trip up, screw up, and be hit with a fee. You're also going to lose track of your balance and the normal ebb and flow of money into and out of your account. Using one account for all these things is a big mistake.

What you need is an allowance debit card.

Here's what I mean. I want you to set up a second bank account, either at your primary institution or, even better, at a second bank.

Then each month, I want you to automatically send yourself spending money. That's the only account I want you to use for debit purchases or ATM withdrawals. In fact, you can go to your primary checking-account bank and ask them for an old-fashioned "ATM card" rather than a debit card to help you avoid accidental purchases out of your number one account.

When you divorce all those workaday transactions away from your "staging" account, a funny thing happens: You will be stunned at how easy it is to balance your checking account. One or two deposits each month, then five or ten checks/payments each month, and that's the end of it. No more hunting through your purse for ATM receipts. No more hours spent wondering where that other $2.23 went.

Here's how it would work in the checking account we've already described. Each month, there are two deposits totaling $3,000. On the first of the month, move $500 from your holding account to your spending account. During each month, make your payments as they come up. Here's what your primary checking account would look like:

HOLDING ACCOUNT		Deposit	Payment	Balance
Nov. 1	paycheck	1,500		1,500.00
Nov. 2	spending money		500	1,000.00
Nov. 5	cell phone		92	908.00
Nov. 5	auto loan		492.93	415.07
Nov. 5	electric		54.22	360.85
Nov. 5	auto insurance		89	271.85
Nov. 15	paycheck	1,500		1,771.85
Nov. 28	student loan		322.09	1,449.76
Nov. 28	cable		38.98	1,410.78
Nov. 28	rent		1,000	410.78
Nov. 30	rainy day savings		300	110.78

When was the last time your checking-account monthly statement looked that neat and clean?

Obviously, your own monthly recurring payments will vary, but I want to call your attention to a few other things about this monthly payment sheet. For starters, notice how the payments are lumped together. That's no accident; nor is it due to some convenience initiative by the electric company and the cell-phone company. Some of your bills are due at around the same time of the month. By batching them together, you can keep your grasp on how much you are paying all at once. And by lumping them into two sets, you can essentially assign certain bills to check A and others to check B each month. This makes it easier to make sure you are running from ahead instead of running from behind.

Notice the savings payment comes at the happy end of the month, when you have something left over, which leaves you a little breathing room for unexpected emergencies. Many personal-finance columnists urge consumers to "pay themselves first," which is nice if you can do it. But ten months of extra interest earned by paying yourself first can be ruined by one bout with overdraft fees, so I wouldn't go that route unless I had a nice cushion to work with every month.

The big message here is that you have a rough idea of your cash flow all month long. If it's the beginning of the month, you know you have $1,500 minus $500 in living expenses and about another $700 in bills; if it's the end of the month, you know you have $1,500 to work with and $1,400 in bills.

The key to all of this, of course, is that you never dip below the equator and turn that balance red. You always know what you have, and you don't muck it up with long lists of $20 withdrawals and $1.98 bagel purchases.

All those daily activities are going on in your allowance account, which looks like this:

ALLOWANCE ACCOUNT		Deposit	Payment	Balance
Nov. 2	spending money	500		500.00
Nov. 2	ATM		50	450.00
Nov. 4	dinner		92	358.00
Nov. 5	Tony's Pizza		7.34	350.00
Nov. 9	ATM		100	250.66
Nov. 12	movie		27.23	223.43
Nov. 15	ATM		100	123.43
Nov. 20	gum		1.12	122.31
Nov. 28	fast food		5.33	116.98
Nov. 28	fast food		6.20	110.78

The beauty of the two-account system is that you don't really have to keep eagle-eyed watch over your spending account. Here's a little-known secret benefit to keeping close tabs on your budget. It's not oppressive or depressing, or even anal retentive. It's liberating. On the other hand, nothing creates more anxiety than spending-spending-spending and never knowing how much you've spent or what you have.

To make this work, an absolutely critical element is to be sure that no overdraft protection is connected to your allowance account, and that no minimum balance is required. This card is intended to be used until its empty, then no more. It will provide its own very specific, very brutal corrections if you try to spend more than you have. Your transaction will be denied.

Important note: This entire system breaks down if your bank attaches automatic "courtesy" overdraft protection to this account. When this account is empty, you simply want it to stop working. Because you'll never write checks against it, this account will be bounce-proof. And so will you.

One more note on your allowance card. Obviously you'll be using this card for lots of ATM withdrawals. So it's critical that you find a bank that doesn't impose ATM fees, and that refunds other banks' fees. The average consumer pays almost $100 each year in withdrawal fees. (Many withdrawals now cost $2 at your bank + $3 at Bank of America = $5. Do that twice a month and you reach $120 by the end of the year. Boy, would that eat into your allowance.)

This is why shopping around for your allowance card is critical. Credit unions and small banks tend to have the most generous terms, but no one offers infinite largesse. Most banks limit their fee refunds to $10 or $15 each month, so it's better to take out larger sums less frequently. Still, even if you do pay a fee here or there, you're getting a 50 percent discount because you're only paying the "foreign" bank where you make the withdrawal, not your own bank.

A special note to couples: Married couples and others sharing joint accounts know keeping track of spending and finances can be among the most vexing topics in a relationship. For them, the allowance-account strategy can be a godsend. Most couples never think they'll have the kind of miscommunication that sees them both withdrawing $300 from the ATM on the same day to make sure they have cash for that big weekend trip. But it happens. All the time. The best way to stop it from happening is to make it impossible. Opening a joint allowance account is one option—as long as that account is bounce-proof, as I've described. But a more practical solution is to open a holding account that's used for all paychecks and common bills, then giving each partner an allowance card.

Whatever system you use, I want you to adhere to one simple premise—stop using one checking account for everything.

Of course, I know some of you out there want to keep better track of exactly what you're spending and when you spend it. You know the truism that if you really want to get control of anything in your life—how much you eat, how much you spend, how much you exercise—you've got to write down everything that happens. Nothing is more sobering to a dieter than a diary of food intake; ditto for big spenders.

Good news: Keeping all your spending in a separate account makes this infinitely easier.

A growing list of online software companies such as Mint.com and Buxfer.com will even help you convert your spending account into useful pie charts and balance sheets. These sites also offer fee-busting tools that are indispensable. When your balance gets near some critical amount—either near a zero balance or near a minimum-balance requirement—Mint and Buxfer can send you a warning email, or even an instant text message to your phone (or your spouse's phone). That will let you deal with the problem immediately and perhaps even make some simple, profitable choices like post-poning a sweater purchase for a week until you're sure you have the money to cover it.

Some consumers might not like the idea of giving a single com-pany so much information about their financial life. Such privacy concerns are valid. Still, you can choose how much you tell each site—you can limit the data shared to certain accounts, such as the allowance account I'm describing. That will protect your privacy and still provide automatic warnings.

Now, if you really want to nickel-and-dime a bank, sweep money into a high-interest-bearing account such as an Internet-based ING Direct savings account as soon as you get it. Then, transfer the funds into your staging/bill-paying account at the last minute to pay bills. A note of caution, however: You're now playing on the bank's home turf, moving money around to cover checks and hoping everything clears at just the right time. You might lose, and one bout with over-drafts can ruin a year's worth of extra interest. Proceed with care.

DON'T TRUST THE BALANCE

A final note about ATMs, bank websites, and even tellers. They will lie to you about your balance. Not intentionally, of course. But you simply cannot trust what you're told when you ask the simple bal-ance question. Why? Bank laws vary by state, but for the most part banks have the right to hold deposited funds for five days before allowing you to draw on them. Worse yet, they have the right to undeposit funds for thirty days or more if a check you deposit turns out to be fraudulent or is returned for insufficient funds. Banks may tell you that your account has been credited. They may say the funds are available. An ATM may include the funds in your balance. But that does not mean you cannot bounce a check or incur an overdraft. If you want to move money back and forth to maximize interest, you've got to know your bank well and follow a rigid strategy. Remember, one slipup and you can easily pay $150 in fees, wiping out much of your hard-earned gains.

That's why I don't recommend these advanced money-management skills for most people. These are games that can be won by the most diligent of the detail-oriented among us. But they open the door to costly errors. I'm trying to make your life simpler.

Don't Get Screwed by Banks

- Stop using your checking account for everything.
- Never buy things with a debit card unless you are sure there is no "courtesy" overdraft protection. If you're not sure, pay with a credit card and be sure to pay the bill on time.
- Use online tools to monitor your balance frequently, even daily.
- Sign up for text message warnings of low balances.
- Group monthly bills around paychecks so you always have a grasp of your cash flow.

2

Credit Card Math

I recently received an email from American Express Blue that my credit limit was being reduced to $5,600 from $22,300. My balance at the time was $5,440, leaving me with an available credit of $160. I have been a "cardholder" since 1996, have excellent credit, and have never, never been late. What ticks me off is that this is going to adversely impact my credit score. I am sure these credit card issuing companies can do whatever they want, but it's not fair that they can affect my credit score for no fault of mine.

—SAJI THOMAS,
a Red Tape Chronicles reader

Chew on this: A credit card with an $8,000 balance will suck more money out of your wallet every month than $45,000 in student-loan debt. Don't believe me? That's credit card math for you. I'll prove it later in this book. For now, I want you to keep in mind how devastating credit cards can be to anyone's financial life. What's in your wallet? A financial Trojan horse. Credit cards are wrapped up like gifts from banks, but when their full army of hidden fees and finance charges are unleashed, the attack can be hard to withstand.

This is a very exciting time for credit card users, however. The industry that never met a fee it didn't love finally killed its golden goose, and during the 2008–9 recession credit cards became a light-ning rod for antibank sentiment. Much of the populist anger over the bailout was aimed right at card-issuer misbehavior. First the Federal Reserve, then later Congress, passed rules that banned many of the most egregious behaviors. Starting in 2010, these blatantly unfair tactics are now verboten:

- Universal default—raising a customer's interest rate because an unrelated bill was paid late.
- Two-cycle billing—a math trick that often doubled the appropriate finance charge.
- Retroactive interest hikes—the practice of applying new rate hikes to past balances. There are some exceptions, however.
- Automatic overlimit fees—customers must now agree in advance to overlimit fees.

Don't feel bad for Capital One, American Express, MBNA, and all the other card issuers, however (I know you don't). Even before the ink had dried on President Barack Obama's signature on the Credit Card Accountability Responsibility and Disclosure Act, card company mathematicians were hard at work inventing new tricks and traps. Here's one of my favorites: It's now possible to be charged a foreign-transaction fee without even leaving the United States. You online shoppers, listen up.

Foreign travelers have known for years that they are subject to a 3 percent fee for every transaction that's performed in a foreign country. Starting in the middle of 2009, banks began charging foreign fees to U.S. consumers who shopped stateside but purchased from companies based elsewhere—say, on the Web. The most obvious example is airline tickets purchased online from firms such as Ryanair or Air Malta. Here's one you might not forsee: routine GPS map updates purchased from Dutch-based TomTom.

The Web is worldwide, you know. And it's easy for shoppers to click around and not realize they're buying from an overseas firm. No matter: Bank of America can take 2 percent of each purchase, and Visa an additional 1 percent.

As card issuers continue to digest the new rules, expect such new fees to pop up everywhere. When trying to regulate the industry, Congress is playing a game of Whac-A-Mole. Beating back one unfair fee does nothing to stop a new one.

That's why this chapter will say much more about how credit cards and credit card math can be used to your advantage. There will always be creative financing by banks. Credit cards are designed to confuse you and make you pay extra for everything you do. But it doesn't have to be that way. Once you've mastered the plastic, you can start mastering your financial future. But first, you must understand the rules of the game as they've been set against you.

WHEN IT COMES to credit cards, there are three kinds of users: those who pay their bills in full on time every month; those who occasionally run a balance and pay interest; and those who never pay their balance in full and are playing Russian roulette as "revolvers." The advice each group needs is very different, so at the end of this chapter, you'll finds tips by type of card user.

There are some important tricks you need to know about, no matter what kind of cardholder you are. Even if you pay your bills on time almost every month, these tricks could be costing you hundreds of dollars each year. Everyone needs to understand credit card math. Even if you are the ultimate responsible card user, someday your number will come up. When it does, you'll slip down the rabbit hole into credit card Wonderland, and you'll need to act fast to minimize the damages.

How crazy is this Wonderland? You responsible cardholders out there likely hold *too few* credit cards. While the proper number of cards remains an industry secret guarded more carefully than the Colonel's fried-chicken recipe, you need to know that your practice of keeping most of your charges on a single card with a single bank is a bad habit—at least in our twisted world of credit scores. The higher a balance you keep, the more money you borrow from credit card companies, the bigger the mistake.

As the years pass, we are learning more and more about the secret sauce that is used to generate the three-digit number that dictates your financial prospects in America. We still don't know everything. But thanks to the fine work of people such as John Ulzheimer, who once worked at Fair Isaac, the keepers of the credit-score secret formula, we know quite a bit. Ulzheimer wrote a book called *You're Nothing but a Number* and also runs a site called Credit.com. He often preaches that "credit utilization" is an incredibly important factor in your score. Let's say you have only one credit card, and that card has a $3,000 limit. Now, let's say you spend a lot on your card each month, maybe $2,000 in personal and work expenses, perhaps in a quest to earn "valuable" rewards points. You carefully pay it off in full each month by the due date to avoid any finance charges. That's bad. Very bad. It means you often use almost all the credit you have, and the credit-score people think that means you are likely to begin defaulting on your loans. In fact, *you could be killing your credit score.* Depending on what time of the month your score gets pulled, near-the-limit utilization could knock thirty, forty, or even fifty points off your score.

To counter this effect, Ulzheimer recommends—get this—never using more than 10 percent of your credit limit. That means never running a balance higher than $300 on that $3,000-limit card. That's something you won't find even if you read every last sentence of your cardholder agreement. You remember, that's the leaflet with eight-point "mouseprint" that's tucked into your monthly bill once a year enumerating all your rights.

From the perspective of your credit score, you are better off spreading your charges among multiple cards. That, of course, is how many people end up in serious credit card trouble, and one of the many ways that the credit industry pushes consumers in impossible and contradictory directions. I don't recommend you use five or six cards, because even the most responsible consumers will eventually screw up and miss a payment when their finances are spread so thin and wide. But I do recommend you always have at least one card that is spotless, which can be used during those emergency months when you might run a balance that approaches half of your available limit. And I recommend paying special attention to credit utilization during the two or three months before you make a major purchase that will involve a loan, such as a car or a house. If need be, spread your charges among two or three cards to keep your utilization low.

ON AVERAGE, AMERICANS DON'T OVERUSE CREDIT CARDS

Now, before I get to credit card math and other crappy things banks do, I want to speak a bit more to the credit puritans. I know there are plenty of holier-than-thou card users who never run a balance, and they think the rest of the population is stupid and greedy. They snicker when they hear data points like this: The average American family has $8,000 in credit card debt.

We should snicker at those numbers, which are included in every story that lampoons credit card consumers, because they represent that journalists are bad at math. And as we learned in the introduction, so is the self-satisfied crowd.

When financial reporters insult indebted cardholders, they are indulging in the classic mean/median/average mistake. Let me illustrate. Take ten cardholders. Nine have $1,000 in debt, and the tenth has $11,000 in debt. What's their average debt? It's $2,000 ($20,000/10). What is their median debt? It's $1,000. Which is the more "accurate" indication of typical debt?

Now, to exaggerate my point. Take ten cardholders. Nine have $100 in debt, and one has $99,100 in debt. What's the average debt? It's $10,000. Write that in a story, however, and you are unfairly besmirching the nine centurions. But that's what you normally get in stories about credit card debt.

Here's a much more accurate picture of America's addiction to credit. Nearly half of all Americans run a balance each month. That's bad. But the more important number is this: Only about one in twenty Americans carry a balance of more than $8,000 each month. The extreme cases of $50,000 debts drown out the truth of the matter—half of U.S. households owe $2,400 or less to credit card companies, and in fact, many owe nothing. So those of you who like to think that America is dominated by families who outfit their living rooms with the latest technology using plastic to spend money they don't have—you're wrong. Yes, there are many of them. But they are a small minority. I thank personal-finance writer Liz Weston for her continuous efforts to correct this persistent misunderstanding.

I stress this point because I hear many irritating holier-than-thou things from pro-industry consumers who write in to my Red Tape Chronicles blog. The most irritating are those who argue that people who get hit with hidden fees from banks deserve them. "They should learn to manage their money!" is the constant theme.

Meanwhile, the exaggerated myth of the hyperconsuming American is used as justification for egregious bank behavior. Financial institutions regularly perpetuate this myth to distract people from these unfair tactics. There's a serious logic problem here, and to dispute it I'd like to invoke the wisdom of kindergarten teachers everywhere: Two wrongs don't make a right. Excessive consumption is not justification for predatory lending.

AVERAGE DAILY BALANCE— AND THE PAY-EARLY, BUY-LATER STRATEGY

I'm sure by now you are well aware of the basic principle at play here. Banks hire mathematicians to spend a lot of time trying to cook up formulas that are extremely advantageous to the banks. Every last tenth of a percentage point means a lot to banks. It might not sound like a lot to you, but it adds up to millions of dollars for the bank. Remember the plot of the movie *Office Space*, in which a computer programmer skimmed off fractional percentages of pennies from thousands of payments? When an employee does that, it's called stealing. Oddly, when a bank does that to consumers, it's called a business plan.

You might be inclined to just roll your eyes at all this, throw up your hands, and pay up. But you don't have to. Knowledge is power. Adjusting your payment strategy to account for bank mathematics can save you a lot of money, whether you run a balance all the time or almost never. But you have to know the rules first. And the most important rule is the "average daily balance."

Human nature dictates that people pay their bills at the last possible moment. On the other hand, people spend money erratically during the month. Some months, you might evenly spend $200 each week on charges. But the next month, perhaps you go on vacation and spend $2,500 during the last week.

If you are a bank, how can you make sure to maximize the interest you charge on all these purchases, given that people pay bills at the end of the month? More important, if you're a consumer, how can you reverse that effect?

The essential point to understand is the way card companies calculate interest charges. The method is called average daily balance. The bank takes the average of your outstanding balance each day during the current billing cycle, then applies a daily interest rate to it.

Here's a basic example. We'll start off with a simple case to show clearly how bad the effects are. Later, we'll use more realistic examples.

Say you make a single $3,000 purchase for plane tickets in a month during which you have no grace period because you are carrying a balance. To make life easy for now, we'll say that balance is one penny. If the purchase is made five days before the end of a thirty-one-day month, at a rate of 29 percent, interest charges will be $11.92. But if you make the charge five days into the month, the interest charge is more than *five times higher* at $64.36.

Putting off big-ticket purchases for twenty days can cut your interest charges by 80 percent! You'll never see that explained in those preapproved offers you receive in the mail.

Don't believe me? Confused? Here it is in chart form:

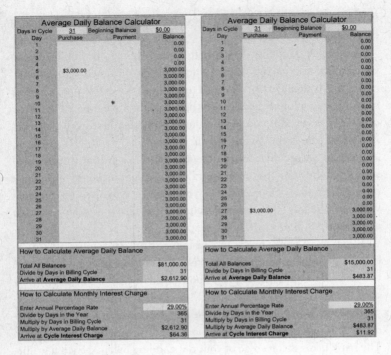

Left calculator:

Average Daily Balance Calculator

Days in Cycle	31	Beginning Balance	$0.00
Day	Purchase	Payment	Balance
1			0.00
2			0.00
3			0.00
4			0.00
5	$3,000.00		3,000.00
6			3,000.00
7			3,000.00
8			3,000.00
9			3,000.00
10			3,000.00
11			3,000.00
12			3,000.00
13			3,000.00
14			3,000.00
15			3,000.00
16			3,000.00
17			3,000.00
18			3,000.00
19			3,000.00
20			3,000.00
21			3,000.00
22			3,000.00
23			3,000.00
24			3,000.00
25			3,000.00
26			3,000.00
27			3,000.00
28			3,000.00
29			3,000.00
30			3,000.00
31			3,000.00

How to Calculate Average Daily Balance

Total All Balances	$81,000.00
Divide by Days in Billing Cycle	31
Arrive at **Average Daily Balance**	$2,612.90

How to Calculate Monthly Interest Charge

Enter Annual Percentage Rate	29.00%
Divide by Days in the Year	365
Multiply by Days in Billing Cycle	31
Multiply by Average Daily Balance	$2,612.90
Arrive at **Cycle Interest Charge**	$64.36

Right calculator:

Average Daily Balance Calculator

Days in Cycle	31	Beginning Balance	$0.00
Day	Purchase	Payment	Balance
1			0.00
2			0.00
3			0.00
4			0.00
5			0.00
6			0.00
7			0.00
8			0.00
9			0.00
10			0.00
11			0.00
12			0.00
13			0.00
14			0.00
15			0.00
16			0.00
17			0.00
18			0.00
19			0.00
20			0.00
21			0.00
22			0.00
23			0.00
24			0.00
25			0.00
26			0.00
27	$3,000.00		3,000.00
28			3,000.00
29			3,000.00
30			3,000.00
31			3,000.00

How to Calculate Average Daily Balance

Total All Balances	$15,000.00
Divide by Days in Billing Cycle	31
Arrive at **Average Daily Balance**	$483.87

How to Calculate Monthly Interest Charge

Enter Annual Percentage Rate	29.00%
Divide by Days in the Year	365
Multiply by Days in Billing Cycle	31
Multiply by Average Daily Balance	$483.87
Arrive at **Cycle Interest Charge**	$11.92

Courtesy: NCNBlogs.com

On the left: For the first four days of the month, your balance would be zero. Starting on day 5, your balance is $3,000. After thirty-one days, your average balance is $2,612.90. Multiply by the daily interest rate of about 8 cents per day per $100 and you arrive at $64.36.

Now, on the right: Your balance is zero until day 27, when it rises to $3,000. After 31 days, the average daily balance is $483.87. Multiply by the daily interest rate of about 8 cents per day per $100 and you arrive at $11.92.

Now you see the perils of the average daily balance. Perhaps you don't think much about these fractional interest charges when you buy things during the month, but the bank sure does. The penalty for not thinking like a bank is severe.

Now, let's start filling in the spreadsheet a little bit to make it more realistic. It's much more likely if you're paying interest that you'll start the month with a balance, you'll make a series of purchases during the month, and you'll make a payment. Let's flesh out the picture and see how the average daily balance could really be hurting you.

If you start the month with a $2,000 balance—all other things remaining the same from above—your finance charges will rise from $61.18 to $113.62 if you buy those plane tickets at the beginning of the month instead of the end.

Average Daily Balance Calculator

Days in Cycle	31	Beginning Balance	$2,000.00
Day	Purchase	Payment	Balance
1			2,000.00
2			2,000.00
3			2,000.00
4			2,000.00
5	$3,000.00		5,000.00
6			5,000.00
7			5,000.00
8			5,000.00
9			5,000.00
10			5,000.00
11			5,000.00
12			5,000.00
13			5,000.00
14			5,000.00
15			5,000.00
16			5,000.00
17			5,000.00
18			5,000.00
19			5,000.00
20			5,000.00
21			5,000.00
22			5,000.00
23			5,000.00
24			5,000.00
25			5,000.00
26			5,000.00
27			5,000.00
28			5,000.00
29			5,000.00
30			5,000.00
31			5,000.00

How to Calculate Average Daily Balance

Total All Balances	$143,000.00
Divide by Days in Billing Cycle	31
Arrive at **Average Daily Balance**	$4,612.90

How to Calculate Monthly Interest Charge

Enter Annual Percentage Rate	29.00%
Divide by Days in the Year	365
Multiply by Days in Billing Cycle	31
Multiply by Average Daily Balance	$4,612.90
Arrive at **Cycle Interest Charge**	$113.62

Average Daily Balance Calculator

Days in Cycle	31	Beginning Balance	$2,000.00
Day	Purchase	Payment	Balance
1			2,000.00
2			2,000.00
3			2,000.00
4			2,000.00
5			2,000.00
6			2,000.00
7			2,000.00
8			2,000.00
9			2,000.00
10			2,000.00
11			2,000.00
12			2,000.00
13			2,000.00
14			2,000.00
15			2,000.00
16			2,000.00
17			2,000.00
18			2,000.00
19			2,000.00
20			2,000.00
21			2,000.00
22			2,000.00
23			2,000.00
24			2,000.00
25			2,000.00
26			2,000.00
27	$3,000.00		5,000.00
28			5,000.00
29			5,000.00
30			5,000.00
31			5,000.00

How to Calculate Average Daily Balance

Total All Balances	$77,000.00
Divide by Days in Billing Cycle	31
Arrive at **Average Daily Balance**	$2,483.87

How to Calculate Monthly Interest Charge

Enter Annual Percentage Rate	29.00%
Divide by Days in the Year	365
Multiply by Days in Billing Cycle	31
Multiply by Average Daily Balance	$2,483.87
Arrive at **Cycle Interest Charge**	$61.18

Average Daily Balance Calculator			
Days in Cycle	31	Beginning Balance	$2,000.00
Day	Purchase	Payment	Balance
1			2,000.00
2			2,000.00
3			2,000.00
4			2,000.00
5	$3,000.00		5,000.00
6			5,000.00
7			5,000.00
8			5,000.00
9			5,000.00
10			5,000.00
11			5,000.00
12			5,000.00
13			5,000.00
14			5,000.00
15			5,000.00
16			5,000.00
17			5,000.00
18			5,000.00
19			5,000.00
20			5,000.00
21			5,000.00
22			5,000.00
23			5,000.00
24			5,000.00
25			5,000.00
26			5,000.00
27			5,000.00
28			5,000.00
29			5,000.00
30			5,000.00
31		$1,000.00	4,000.00

How to Calculate Average Daily Balance

Total All Balances	$142,000.00
Divide by Days in Billing Cycle	31
Arrive at **Average Daily Balance**	$4,580.65

How to Calculate Monthly Interest Charge

Enter Annual Percentage Rate	29.00%
Divide by Days in the Year	365
Multiply by Days in Billing Cycle	31
Multiply by Average Daily Balance	$4,580.65
Arrive at **Cycle Interest Charge**	$112.82

Average Daily Balance Calculator			
Days in Cycle	31	Beginning Balance	$2,000.00
Day	Purchase	Payment	Balance
1			2,000.00
2			2,000.00
3			2,000.00
4			2,000.00
5			2,000.00
6			2,000.00
7			2,000.00
8			2,000.00
9			2,000.00
10			2,000.00
11			2,000.00
12			2,000.00
13			2,000.00
14			2,000.00
15		$1,000	1,000.00
16			1,000.00
17			1,000.00
18			1,000.00
19			1,000.00
20			1,000.00
21			1,000.00
22			1,000.00
23			1,000.00
24			1,000.00
25			1,000.00
26			1,000.00
27	$3,000.00		4,000.00
28			4,000.00
29			4,000.00
30			4,000.00
31			4,000.00

How to Calculate Average Daily Balance

Total All Balances	$60,000.00
Divide by Days in Billing Cycle	31
Arrive at **Average Daily Balance**	$1,935.48

How to Calculate Monthly Interest Charge

Enter Annual Percentage Rate	29.00%
Divide by Days in the Year	365
Multiply by Days in Billing Cycle	31
Multiply by Average Daily Balance	$1,935.48
Arrive at **Cycle Interest Charge**	$47.67

Now, let's add a payment. Say you pay $1,000 toward your balance that month. If you pay in the middle of the month, on the fifteenth day, and buy your ticket toward the end of the month, your interest charges will be $47.67. But if, like most people, you pay at the end of the month, and buy your ticket early, your finance charge will be $112.82. Notice that slight adjustments to your buying and paying habits, in this example, can cut interest charges by nearly two-thirds!

Finally, let's look at the most realistic example. I'll randomly sprinkle $300 worth of charges throughout the month—evenly through both examples. While this mutes the impact I've described, slightly, it's still quite apparent. Making the large purchase early in the month and the payment late in the month carries with it a staggering 128 percent interest penalty!

Average Daily Balance Calculator

Days in Cycle	31	Beginning Balance	$2,000.00
Day	Purchase	Payment	Balance
1			2,000.00
2			2,000.00
3	$30.00		2,030.00
4			2,030.00
5	3,000.00		5,030.00
6	20.00		5,050.00
7			5,050.00
8			5,050.00
9	30.00		5,080.00
10			5,080.00
11	20.00		5,100.00
12			5,100.00
13			5,100.00
14	30.00		5,130.00
15			5,130.00
16			5,130.00
17	20.00		5,150.00
18			5,150.00
19			5,150.00
20	30.00		5,180.00
21			5,180.00
22			5,180.00
23	20.00		5,200.00
24			5,200.00
25			5,200.00
26	30.00		5,230.00
27			5,230.00
28			5,230.00
29	20.00		5,250.00
30			5,250.00
31		$1,000.00	4,250.00

How to Calculate Average Daily Balance

Total All Balances	$146,120.00
Divide by Days in Billing Cycle	31
Arrive at **Average Daily Balance**	$4,713.55

How to Calculate Monthly Interest Charge

Enter Annual Percentage Rate	29.00%
Divide by Days in the Year	365
Multiply by Days in Billing Cycle	31
Multiply by Average Daily Balance	$4,713.55
Arrive at **Cycle Interest Charge**	$116.10

Average Daily Balance Calculator

Days in Cycle	31	Beginning Balance	$2,000.00
Day	Purchase	Payment	Balance
1			2,000.00
2			2,000.00
3	$30.00		2,030.00
4			2,030.00
5			2,030.00
6	20.00		2,050.00
7			2,050.00
8			2,050.00
9	30.00		2,080.00
10			2,080.00
11	20.00		2,100.00
12			2,100.00
13			2,100.00
14	30.00		2,130.00
15		$1,000	1,130.00
16			1,130.00
17	20.00		1,150.00
18			1,150.00
19			1,150.00
20	30.00		1,180.00
21			1,180.00
22			1,180.00
23	20.00		1,200.00
24			1,200.00
25			1,200.00
26	30.00		1,230.00
27	3,000.00		4,230.00
28			4,230.00
29	20.00		4,250.00
30			4,250.00
31			4,250.00

How to Calculate Average Daily Balance

Total All Balances	$64,120.00
Divide by Days in Billing Cycle	31
Arrive at **Average Daily Balance**	$2,068.39

How to Calculate Monthly Interest Charge

Enter Annual Percentage Rate	29.00%
Divide by Days in the Year	365
Multiply by Days in Billing Cycle	31
Multiply by Average Daily Balance	$2,068.39
Arrive at **Cycle Interest Charge**	$50.94

Clearly, there are times consumers cannot control the timing of purchases—emergency auto repairs, for example. Delaying plane-ticket purchases can carry other financial risks—namely, the price may go up. Real life can intrude on this example in many ways. But that's not my point. My point is, banks use this spreadsheet, and you don't. Banks write the formulas and do a terrible job of explaining their impact on you. Spreading interest-rate charges over the maximum amount of days is a clever way to increase bank revenue. Making slightly smarter choices about when you buy things and when you pay for things can save you a whole lot of money.

Your most important takeaway from this discussion is, time matters. When you buy things matters, and when you send payment matters. For example, don't wait until you receive the bill to make a payment! Sending payments two weeks early every month would save you $150 a year.

CLEAN-CARD STRATEGY

Naturally, you can't always control when you make credit card purchases and payments. If you could, you wouldn't be using credit cards in the first place. If you are like 50 percent of Americans, you run a balance each month. And if you are like 99 percent of Americans, when you run a balance, you keep using that credit card, keep racking up interest charges, and pay up thinking there isn't much you can do to pay less. Well, there's a lot you can do—you can use the clean-card strategy. Put simply, you should always have one "clean" credit card in your wallet or purse; a card that you know you can pay off in full every month. Here's why.

Recall the "fall from grace" that occurs the moment you don't pay your credit card bill in full on time. The lure of credit cards is the free thirty-day loan you get when you buy something with plastic. As long as you pay up by the due date, you pay no interest charges. This is called the grace period. But the first time you are late, the grim reaper appears. Interest charges now accrue *immediately* on all future purchases. Roughly speaking, you pay $1 per day for every $1,000 you borrow with a high-rate credit card, or about $30 per month and $360 per year (based on about a 32 percent interest rate).

Scenario 1: You have a card with a $100 balance and a second, "clean" card. You make a $1,000 purchase on the first day of the month with the clean card and pay the card off thirty days later. Interest charges: Card 1 = $3; Card 2 = $0.

Scenario 2: You have a $100 balance on your credit card. You make a $1,000 purchase on the first day of the month and pay off the entire card on the last day of the month. Interest charge = $33. That's a $30 difference! Now, spread that impact out for an entire year and you'll hit $360.

Once again, I've oversimplified the math to show the impact, so let me make the scenarios a little more realistic. In this case, however, you'll see how the clean-card strategy can save you even more than the pay-early, buy-late strategy.

What I really want is for you to have two credit cards that you use in very different ways.

Card one is a "charge card." You make all your workaday purchases with this card. You vow to whatever God you believe in that you will pay off this card in full every month on time. To make sure you do that, you sign up for electronic bill pay at your bank and send a payment to the credit card firm automatically every month five days before the due date. You make the payment for your average budgeted amount; you can always manually adjust the amount.

Card two is a "line-of-credit card." You pull it out for big, emergency purposes that you can't pay off in full within thirty days. Then you put it back in your wallet, purse, or holster, with the safety latch on.

This will have two important effects on your credit card spending. One immediate improvement: You will have a much better grasp on your debt. Revolving debt, where you are constantly adding to and subtracting from the total, tends to get murky for users. When things get murky, your financial brain checks out and gives up.

When you are a serial revolving-credit user, you lose track of what you owe, and more important, you lose grasp of when you will pay it off. A single credit card with a $3,500 balance that never grows is manageable. You know that paying about $100 a month, you'll pay it off in about three years. On the other hand, a card with a $3,500 balance that is used to make $300 in purchases this month, then $50 next month, then $254 the following month, while you make $125 payments each month, except last month when you only paid $75 . . . well, I'm not going to tell you how long it will take to pay that off. I want you stop living like that. Dividing your purchases up into "charge cards" and "line-of-credit cards" will help you get your head around your debt and your financial situation.

But that's just a by-product of the strategy I'm pushing here. Remember, I want you to nickel-and-dime the credit card company. I want you to make math work for you. I want you to save a lot of money by making small adjustments, just as banks do. Watch what happens when you take those everyday purchases off your credit card balance sheet.

Let's say you use your card for everything, perhaps in pursuit of airline miles, for example. To make the math easy, say you spend $1,000 every month on lunch, dinner, gas, etc., using your card. That's $12,000 in spending each year. Of course, you use it for big-ticket purchases, too, and you can't pay it off every month. Let's say you could afford to pay off the workaday $1,000 in charges every month. But because you put all those charges on one card, you are borrowing $1,000 for thirty days every month. Remember that simple $1-a-day formula? Using your card this way costs you close to $365 every year—just for the everyday purchases you make.

Now, I've been quite generous in my calculations. In reality, you'll probably wait forty-five days to pay off those everyday purchases, thanks to the whims of billing cycles, meaning you'll be paying closer to $500 in unnecessary interest charges every year.

Of course, you will still have to pay interest on that line-of-credit card. But you'll be saving a sizable chunk of money just by picking your plastic wisely, and not borrow money for every purchase you make.

A special note to mileage addicts: Now, I know many of you love the miles or points you rack up by using that same card over and over. I'm sorry to say that many of you have been hoodwinked. Any benefits you receive from a mileage card are *completely nullified* the moment you run a balance and start paying interest charges. In all likelihood, you've already paid a yearly membership fee. We all know points aren't what they used to be, with all the restrictions the airlines put in place. Now consider my math above: Just by removing your daily charges from your card, you save enough money each year to buy a plane ticket! Unlike points, cash never expires!

The moral of the story: Always have a clean card. If financial Armageddon strikes and your "clean" card becomes dirty, use the exceptional tool of getting a third card and make that your clean card. But end the game there. If you feel a need to get a third clean card, you're in an entirely different financial place, and you need emergency help with debt relief. We'll discuss that in the "regular revolver" advice section.

Now, on to the type-specific advice. Feel free to skip to your profile.

YOU ALWAYS PAY YOUR BILLS IN FULL ON TIME

You are the sophisticated credit card consumer. You have it all figured out. You always pay your bill, you always get that free thirty-day loan, you pile up airline miles at no cost. You are sitting pretty—or so you think. But you should know, dear deadbeat card user, that the credit card industry is on to you. You are the reason sneaky late fees were invented.

Obviously, you're terrible for the banking industry. Banks make money by lending people money and making them pay it back with a penalty. That penalty generally takes the form of interest charges. But starting a decade ago, fierce competition for the easy profits of credit cards led to the elimination of annual fees.

These have been replaced by tricks. In 1990, the average late fee was $9 each month, according to the Philadelphia Fed. By 2006, the average fee was 350 percent higher. Meanwhile, the grace period, customarily one month, has continually shrunk and can now be as short as twenty-two days. Card issuers regularly change their billing due date to nudge a few thousand customers into the "late" column and collect $35 or more each time. Yes, this can happen to you. When it does, sophisticated card user, you will be stunned to find a fairly reasonable $11.89 finance charge on your bill, along with a $39 late fee. This, of course, is totally unreasonable. No one is perfect. When you make a mistake, or you are nudged into one, it's perfectly fair to charge you something for the right to borrow money. The common situation, however, that sees consumers paying more in late fees than interest charges is unfair and insane. The fee is made up out of thin air. But that's the reality of using credit cards today. That's the game of roulette you play. I want you to get out of the game.

For you, avoiding late fees is more important than avoiding interest charges. There's a simple solution. Use an online bill-paying service to automatically send your credit card company a payment every month, several days before the due date, to make sure you don't slip up one month. This way, you'll never pay a late fee.

YOU OCCASIONALLY CARRY A BALANCE

Let's call this group the generous Christmas-gift givers. Ten months out of the year, you pay your bills on time without fail. But once or twice a year, perhaps during December, and again during summer vacation, you fall behind. Here's what to watch for.

Naturally, all the perils that apply to the above group apply to you, too. Watch for the accidental late payment. Avoid that by automatically sending a minimum payment to your bank every month.

If you aren't familiar with the sneaky ways of banks, you might be surprised to find that if you are *very* generous some Christmas season, you can actually spend more than the stated credit limit on your card, and you'll get hit with a big fee when you do. The nominal credit limit is really just a fee trigger. Banks now approve transactions that exceed credit limits and charge up to $39 for the favor, called an "overlimit" fee. Soon, banks will be required to ask your permission to enroll you in their overlimit program—DON'T DO IT! There is no advantage whatsoever to paying $39 for such a short-term loan. Make sure you don't unknowingly agree to such "protection." If you're not sure, call your credit card company and decline the overlimit service by name.

If you are a responsible card user who rarely spends anywhere near your credit limit, you might not even know what it is. That can lead to a costly mistake. Also, card issuers reserve the right to slash your credit limit at any time for any reason. During the credit crunch of 2008, many consumers saw their limits cut in half. For some, that meant surprise overlimit fees—and a card that was suddenly useless, with no credit left for new charges. The lower limits also meant those consumers suffered hits to their credit scores, too. Even if the fees are less of a risk now, the credit-score hit is still the much bigger problem.

It's important to sneak a peek at the credit-limit field every month when you pay your credit card bill. During those occasional expensive months, log in or call to make sure you don't run out of headroom while you're buying the kids' Christmas toys.

You should also know that running up a tab that's anywhere near your credit limit can have a serious impact on your credit score, even if you only do it for a month or two. That's a good reason to avoid a new-car purchase the month after Christmas. A lower credit score could also lead to a higher interest rate on your credit card balance. Remember, try to never use up more than 50 percent of your credit limit, and it's best to keep the balance down around 10 percent.

Finally, since you are fortunately not very familiar with the inner workings of credit card interest-rate calculations, you might want to reread the earlier portion of this chapter. If you can't pay your January bill in full, there is no need to wait until the next bill comes to catch up. Make the payment as soon as you can. A full month's interest on $3,000 at 29 percent is $74. Make the payment two weeks early, and you'll only pay $33.37. By habit, many people just wait until the next statement comes to pay off their credit cards, but you don't have to.

YOU ARE A REGULAR REVOLVER

Revolving-credit customers are every card issuer's favorite segment. Thanks to the debtors'-prison mentality of American society, which equates owing money to a crime, banks often have their way with these borrowers. Those who carry credit card balances from month to month should know that card issuers have them right where they want them; and fairness is simply not part of the equation. Plan for that.

First off, whenever possible, take your big-balance credit card and put it in the freezer. Remember, find a second or third card you can use and pay it off every month—my clean-card strategy.

But perhaps you simply aren't in a position to do that. You have balances on all your cards and you've maxed out your credit so you can't get new cards. If that's your situation, you are in personal fiscal crisis. You'll need to embark on a serious debt-reduction program. There are plenty of models to follow. Dave Ramsey's popular "debt snowball" plan suggests paying off the smallest debt first, so you experience success and get some momentum before taking on bigger debts. The Debt Avalanche theory suggests that you pay off your highest-interest debt first, a more mathematically sensible strategy. Many of these programs work equally well, as long as you stick to them. I'm not here to tell you which one is best; I'm here to tell you how to avoid getting screwed as you climb out of the hole.

One suggestion you'll often hear is to switch from credit to debit cards for everyday purchases. Because debit transactions are immediately deducted from your checking account, this will help impose budget discipline on you and prevent you from paying interest on everyday transactions. That's true; but debit cards come with their own expensive traps. These are dealt with in detail in the previous banking chapter, but the short version is this: Casual debit card users are at risk of causing costly overdrafts on their checking accounts. Many consumers don't realize that it's possible to "overspend" with a debit card; banks will approve transactions that exceed the checking-account balance and will treat the transgression as if it's a bounced check. Consumers get dinged $30–$40 for each transaction, and debit card overdrafts often come in bunches. A weekend's worth of debit purchases can easily come with a $200 price tag in fees. For that reason, I don't recommend that consumers use debit cards this way. Cash is safer. (*Consumer Reports* came to the same conclusion in 2007.) Even judicious use of credit cards is safer than buying things with a debit card.

If you still like the idea of debit cards, try this: Open a new account at a small bank or credit union and decline "overdraft protection." Get assurances that transactions that exceed your balance will *never* be approved. Then, every month transfer an allowance onto that debit card. Use only that card for purchases. This is a great way to give yourself a budget ceiling, but it will also simplify balancing your checking account because you won't have twenty or thirty small transactions mucking up your main-checking-account statements. Generally, it's the "velocity" of transactions in a checking account that overwhelms consumers and leaves them in the dark about their balance. You should be able to say roughly how much money is in your checking account at all times. Breaking out your monthly purchases in one lump sum will make that much easier.

One common tactic for overwhelming credit card debt is to play the balance-transfer game. Because nearly all adult Americans who want credit cards have them, it's very hard for card issuers to increase market share. They are left with raiding each other's customers. To entice consumers from competitors, banks offer low- or no-interest balance transfers. As you might have guessed, these are traps. Used with extreme caution, they can be a onetime get-a-fresh-start trick for high-balance card users. Sadly, many consumers find themselves attempting to use the trick multiple times, which eventually leads to disaster. But if you want to try a balance transfer, it's important to know that they are rarely free. Fees attached to the transfers can be high, sometimes 3 percent of the balance. Second, card firms have traditionally applied payments to the least-expensive debt on the card first; that means new charges incur a much higher interest rate. For example, if you transfer $5,000 in debt to a card promising 5.99 percent interest, and the following month you make $400 in payments and charge $400 in new purchases, your account will have a $4,600 balance at 5.99 percent interest, and a $400 balance charged at the full rate—perhaps 19.99 percent. Within a few months, almost all that cheap old debt is now expensive new debt. New rules prevent card companies from being that blatant about applying payments in the least-advantageous way for consumers. But I'd watch carefully as card companies develop new strategies on this issue. That's why balance transfers should only be part of a real change in spending habits.

If you are a serial revolver, you should always keep close tabs on your interest rate. It can change for any reason at most banks. When changed, you'll be given a chance to close the account and pay off the balance at the lower rate, which is an option you should take if it's at all possible. How do you get a lower rate? Sometimes, you can just ask. Let's close this tricky discussion with a success story.

Kevin McPhail of Austin got his Texas-size rate increase lowered in 2008 by calling to complain—but only through old-fashioned persistence. His story highlights an important lesson for credit card users: If at first you don't succeed, try, try to lower your rate again.

McPhail, 43, called Citibank to complain as soon as he received a notice that his interest rate would climb to 15 percent. He was told the rate was the lowest available.

"Three times [the bank representative] told me there was not a lower rate," he said.

Undeterred, McPhail at last said the magic words that got Citibank's attention.

"I asked her to close the account," he said. Immediately, McPhail was transferred to an "account specialist," who was able to knock 5 percent off his rate. He even got a temporary discounted rate of 1.9 percent for the next six months.

A critical element to McPhail's success was this: When he called, he was holding an ad for a competitor's card. While he negotiated with the credit specialist, he read off the competitor's terms, giving him great bargaining power.

McPhail had a happy ending, but it left him with a bad taste in his mouth.

"I don't think I should have to threaten quitting to get their best rate," he said. "I felt like there was some level of dishonesty at the first [customer service] tier. I wonder how many people just walk away at that point."

He sent a letter:

Why is it your company's practice to literally lie to your customers about what rates are available to them? Why should a customer have to threaten to close their account to get a better rate, which they are actually qualified to receive?

Don't forget the power of negotiating when this happens. It is always worth calling the bank to ask for a lower rate. Often, you'll be rejected. Call again one month later. Ask what you'll have to do to get a lower rate. Ask, ask, and ask again. Never suggest you are looking for hardship assistance, which can give the bank an excuse to raise your rate. Just sound like a savvy consumer. And be prepared to hear a lot of no's first.

Card-rate bargain hunters will always encounter resistance and must be ready to threaten to close their accounts. "The people who answer the phone, they are being paid to get people off the phone as fast as possible. They might not know about all the options you have," says credit-score expert Liz Weston.

But you do know the options. And you will get a better deal.

Finally, one more note on clean cards. Know that a bank's definition of a clean card is very different from yours. If you call and ask what your balance is, you may be told the "balance" amount from your previous statement. That's fine as long as you aren't revolving credit. But if you are, the bank will lie to you. The true "payoff amount," which is the amount that would zero out your balance, including any finance charges, is something else entirely. It includes up-to-the-minute purchases. Most card issuers don't even make this amount obvious to their own telephone operators. At any rate, people ask for it so rarely that many operators won't even know what you're talking about. Just keep asking, "What is the amount I'd have to pay to have a zero balance today." If you don't, you might pay "in full," but still be paying interest charges an extra month.

Don't Get Screwed by Credit Card Companies

- Watch for new fees as new rules kick in during 2010.
- Try not to spend more than 10 percent of your credit limit.
- When you buy on credit, and when you pay your bill, both matter. If you can, buy big purchases later in the month and send payments early.
- If you occasionally run a balance, pay it off as soon as you can. Don't wait for the bill to come. Call the credit card issuer and get the exact payoff amount.
- Always have at least one credit card with no balance.
- Use automated online bill pay to avoid late fees.
- Check, check, and recheck your credit limit.
- Don't buy things with a debit card.
- Beware of balance-transfer fees.

3

Buying a Car

When you negotiate, this sheet should be covered with
numbers. . . . It should be like a battleground. And I don't
want to see the price dropping five hundred dollars at a
pop. Come down slowly, slowly. Here, I'll show you how.

—CAR SALESMAN, *from*
Edmunds.com undercover investigation

Sometimes it's easier to explain things by describing their
opposite. So here's a fictional account of a perfectly terrible
way to buy a new car.

John Nay-Eve has been driving a 1997 Ford Mustang from his
college days for about ten years. About every six months he drops
$500 on repairs, gets mad, but then gets his car back from the
mechanic and goes on with his life.

But one Friday night, as he's about to go on a date with a coworker—who he's been eyeing for months—the car starts making a
hideous knocking noise on the way to her apartment. For a moment,
John ignores the sound, as he's running late. But the noise gets
louder, and louder, and louder, until finally the car lurches a few
times and shuts down. John coasts to a stop on the shoulder, and
smoke starts to billow out from under the hood. He calls up Jill and
makes his apologies. From the sarcastic sound of her voice, John figures he won't get another chance with her.

"Great," he says to no one in particular. "That's it. Tomorrow I'm getting a new car."

So Saturday morning, he grabs his latest *Mustang Lovers* magazine and his checkbook, and he takes the bus to the nearest Ford dealership. As he hops off the bus, which conveniently stops right at the dealer's front door, he sees a flurry of activity. Men in white shirts and ties scurry about. At a table in the middle of the showroom a couple are sitting and signing papers. Near the front door are a line of convertibles in so many colors it looks like a fruit stand. John drifts right over to the red one. "Jill will go out with me if she sees me in this," he thinks. Within a few seconds, he hears a friendly voice.

"Beautiful, aren't they?" says a man in a raspy, cigarette-aided baritone. John whips around to see a burly man with a receding hairline, hairy arms, and overpowering cologne. "That one's a chick magnet. You're a smart man. If I was your age, I'd have to have one of these."

By now, Mr. Salesman has already spotted John's checkbook, popping out from the top of his shirt pocket.

"We only have one of those," Mr. Salesman says. John looks around and sees perhaps a dozen red Mustangs nearby, but says nothing. "In fact that couple over there was just looking at it. We can take a test-drive, but I'm not sure it'll be for sale by the time we get back."

They hop in the car. Mr. Salesman drives first. He rolls down the windows, cranks up the radio, and floors the gas.

"That's 190 horses of power!" he shouts. "And the biggest rush you'll ever feel outside of, well, you know what. But we can help you get that, too!"

They get to a parking lot a mile from the car lot. Mr. Salesman tells John it's his turn to drive.

"Wow," John thinks. "This is such a nice guy. He trusts me with this $28,000 car and his life! He must be a good man." John slips into the driver's seat and holds the steering wheel tight, like a child holding on to a Ferris-wheel guardrail. Then he steps on the gas and grins unabashedly.

While the two men drive back to the dealership, John hears a soliloquy about the benefits of the "all-new" Mustang. Leather steering wheel. Sport rims. New, ergonomic dashboard. Four cupholders. And power, power, and more power.

When they get back to the showroom, Mr. Salesman asks John to pull the car right up to the front door. When they park, he says simply, "C'mon inside," and walks into the showroom without looking back. John, not wanting to be impolite, follows. A cute girl in a tight skirt sitting at the front desk smiles at him as he walks by. "Nice wheels," she says, and smiles, before answering the phone.

John sits at a round table nearby. The salesman offers him a Coke, which he accepts. A flurry of announcements blare over the loudspeaker. The cute girl makes one: "Mr. and Mrs. Monohan, your neeeeeeew car is ready." Just as she says that, a big blue Ford Escape comes slowly rolling into the showroom, backward. A valet gets out, hands the couple the keys, and they get in. Sales staff gather round and applaud. The couple drive out through the huge double doors.

Mr. Salesman reemerges and breaks the moment. "That's lucky, kid. She talked him out of the Mustang. Be glad you're not married. Ha! You can have that sweet baby if you want it. You'll need to act fast, though. What can you afford each month? Let's figure out how to get you into that car."

John thought about his finances a little on the bus. He makes about $3,500 per month. After taxes, he takes home about $600 each week. After rent and the other basics, he has maybe $800 left over each month. He figures he can spend maybe half of that on a car payment.

"About $350 each month," John blurts out. He figures he's bargaining hard. "And I have a trade-in."

Mr. Salesman, meanwhile, isn't looking at John. He's banging away at a calculator, then putting numbers on a piece of paper. In one corner he writes $30,040. In another corner he writes $745.33. In another, $8,000. Then he looks up.

"Tell me about your trade-in, kid. I noticed you took the bus."

John tells the long story about the date with Jill, and the smoke, and the tow truck, from the night before.

Mr. Salesman hardly looks up. "You know, we might only get $200 for a car like that at auction. But I'll give you a break." He writes down $1,000 on his piece of paper. Then he crosses out $8,000 and writes $7,000. Then he shows the sheet to John.

"Okay, simple. You come up with $7,000 and this car is yours today. And there's your monthly payment. Can you write a check for $7,000?" Mr. Salesman points a pencil right at John's checkbook.

John, who has about $3,000 in his checking account, swallows hard. Questions he knows he's supposed to ask swirl around his head. What is the interest rate? Why is the price more than the $28,000 he saw on the sticker? What happened to $350 a month? But he can only muster one thing:

"No, I can't. That's too much."

"Hmmm. Too rich for you, eh? Well, I like you, kid, let me see what I can do for you."

At that point, Mr. Salesman disappears and leaves John sitting at the table, his new red Mustang in full view. And he waits. And waits. Ten minutes, fifteen minutes. Several people walk by his red car and size it up. Twenty minutes. Finally, Mr. Salesman returns.

"Great news. This just in. There's a $3,000 factory rebate on that car beginning Monday. But if we write the paperwork correctly, we can give it to you now and apply it to the down payment. That brings the down payment down to $5,000. What do you say, kid?"

By now, the reality of a $745-per-month payment has set in. With insurance and gas, transportation would take up nearly half of his take-home pay. He just can't do it.

"Well, the down payment I can hit," John says, imagining he can use a $2,000 credit card cash advance to supplement the $3,000 he has. "But I can't make that monthly payment. I thought we were going for something closer to $350 per month."

"Umm, $350 a month? Up to what?"

"Up to, ummm . . ."

"Because all that would get you is this white Ford Focus over here." The salesman interrupts, pointing to a two-year-old compact car sitting by the car wash.

"Up to, I guess, $450. Maybe, maybe $500," John says.

The salesman pencils $500 down on his sheet. "Okay, let me talk to my manager. But you're putting me in a tough spot."

Another long pause. Now, it's lunchtime, and John is starving. All he can think about is pulling up to a drive-through McDonald's in that red Mustang and ordering a hamburger. Another twenty minutes pass.

"Great news. I think we have a deal," Mr. Salesman says. "Your new payment is $650.44. It took a lot of talking, but I got my manager to come way, way down on his price, almost $100. Do we have a deal? Just initial here."

John slumps. His stomach growls. He still can't afford that. "Isn't there any way to get that closer to $500 per month?" he asks sheepishly.

This time, Mr. Salesman has another answer. "Well, there is one thing. We could spread you out a little." He grabs his calculator and taps away.

Suddenly, the salesman's face lights up. "Oh, you're going to like this." He scribbles a number on the sheet. "Look at this!" He passes the paper over to John.

It reads $549.43/60.

"If we spread the payments out over sixty months, you can drive away in that baby for $549.43 a month."

John looks over at the car.

"Now c'mon, John. We are right in the middle here. You said $350, we said $750, and $550 is right in the middle. You're never going to get a better deal than that."

THE PERILS OF car buying are familiar to nearly everyone; and nearly everyone has a car-buying horror story. Hopefully, the one you have will be your last. Thanks to the Internet, the balance of power in car shopping has really shifted toward consumers. It's so easy to get pricing information, making it so hard for dealers to get premium prices.

Buying a new car lands you in a rare marketplace that is about as pure as any you'll find. The Internet has made it possible, as with air-line tickets and books, to compare prices for essentially the same product from dozens of retailers nearly instantly, creating what economists call a "flat" market, or a race to the bottom on price. Sellers, understandably, hate this, and they aren't standing for it. Retailers in these deeply competitive environments have fought back like wounded animals. In 2008, we saw the airline industry add one absurd fee after another, as if they were engaging in a strange competition for the deepest irony. Finally, some airlines were charging for water and pillows (yup, JetBlue had a $7 pillow fee).

But that's child's play compared to the way car dealers have lashed out in response to the Internet. The overriding principle you should keep at hand as we discuss car buying is that, thanks to intense competition, dealers really do make little profit through the straightforward sale of a car at a price you can find through the Web. In some cases, they make only the "dealer holdback," a bonus given to the dealer by the automakers at the end of the year. That's a meager way to run a business. This necessitates stealing from consumers in other ways. Car dealerships simply wouldn't stay open if they didn't trick buyers into overpaying during some other part of the deal.

So the image you should keep in mind is this: Car salesmen have one job, and one job only. They want to "up" you at every turn and grab money out of your wallet. Their survival depends on it. Your job is to stop them.

By the time we're done, I hope you will be wondering to yourself why you are being asked to rescue such an industry. Not only does it constantly border on fraud, but it's the poster child for the problems of a market that's run on the Gotcha Capitalism system. Fairness isn't only good for consumers; it's good for companies, too. Industries that survive on lies eventually implode. That's the fatal flaw behind the failed U.S. car market.

YOU PROBABLY KNOW what happens next in John Nay-Eve's story. If John still balks, he's told his only remaining option is to lease the car;

but that's an even better deal! For only $2,000 down and $439 a month, he could lease the red Mustang for three years. That sounds so much better than the original $7,000 and $745 per month that John's defenses are completely worn down. He gives in and drives away in the car, then decides he can only afford a 99-cent burger at McDonald's.

Many negotiating techniques in this story will be familiar to you. Salesmen will often try to slowly worm their way into your good graces, then gradually sweeten their deal with add-ons such as undercoating or extended warranties. This is sometimes called the Foot in the Door strategy. The hope is—like a frog that doesn't notice the water it is in slowly being brought to the boiling point—the shopper will go in looking for a $15,000 car and leave buying a $20,000 car.

The opposite strategy—lovingly called by economists the Door in the Face tactic—is also present here. In fact, it's a bit more obvious. The salesman aims high—very high—going for shock value. After a $745-a-month payment is put on the table, almost anything would sound good to our Mustang buyer.

John, of course, has engaged in a long comedy of errors. Unluckily for him, he's encountered a professional salesman who knows every trick in the book. If John had a little larger bank account, for example, you can bet he would unknowingly have surrendered part of the $3,000 rebate that mysteriously appeared. As it is, John didn't balk at the salesman's "arithmetic error" and was about to give away $1,000 without batting an eye. As careful readers, you probably thought I'd made a mistake when the salesman dropped a $7,000 down payment to $5,000 after applying a $3,000 rebate. Instead, I simulated a common money grab that dealers frequently employ. I have purchased four new cars in the last ten years. Every one of the negotiations has included such an arithmetic error. In one case, a dealer tried to absorb an entire $1,500 rebate for himself by "miscalculating" my monthly payments. In another, lease payments were off by $30 each month. I assure you, these are not errors.

Let's look at some of the other basic mistakes John made:

- He went shopping for a car when the need was urgent. You always want to buy when you don't *have* to buy.

- He bargained on monthly payments instead of purchase price. This is the biggest mistake car buyers make. Notice the dealer reached the "compromise" of $550 per month by simply making John take out a longer-term loan. That's a terrible way to "make the numbers work" when buying a car. John will be on the hook for this bad deal for five years!

- He hadn't done the math before he left his house. Always arrive at a dealership with broad numbers in mind—a $10,000 car loan for forty-eight months at 6.5 percent costs about $200 per month. A $20,000 loan costs about $400 a month, and so on. When scratching out a rule-of-thumb calculation, work in sales taxes and fees, too. That's about another $25 per month for every $10,000. Such rough guideposts will keep you from getting severely screwed.

- John let the dealer do the math for him and unknowingly agreed to a *12 percent interest rate*. Even with the stolen rebate and other hideous terms, John could have paid nearly $100 less each month with a prevailing-interest-rate loan.

- Here's another cardinal sin: He let the dealer arrange the financing for him. Always show up at the dealer with pre-arranged financing from your bank or credit union. That will make it a cash deal and take away one major area for potential mischief during negotiation.

- He muddied his deal with a trade-in when he had no idea what the value of his car was. In this case, $1,000 sounds like a good price, but in reality, the dealer just overcharged him in another part of the deal. Many people know that they will get much more money from a private sale of a car than from a trade-in at a dealer. That's true, but my chief concern is not your trade-in profit: It's avoiding confusion. Car sales staff will tell you that trade-in shenanigans are one of their biggest profit centers. Everyone likes to think they got a good deal from the dealer on their trade-in. When they do, it almost always means they were overcharged for the car.

- John didn't shop around on price and accepted the "second sticker." He actually paid more than MSRP. The second sticker is merely the amount an auto dealer marks up a car above MSRP—the sticker price, the manufacturer's suggested retail price—in the hopes of skimming extra profit. In rare cases, a car is so popular and in such demand that dealers can actually charge premium prices—for example, the Toyota Prius hybrid during the 2008 gas-price crisis. But generally these are mere wishful thinking, and part of the "aim high" strategy many dealers follow, the "numbers framing" we described in the introduction. When you throw out a high number, it raises the "middle ground" number that becomes part of the bargaining later. Ignore second stickers when negotiating. Remember, if a car is actually sitting on the lot, it's not really in high demand.

- John went shopping on a busy Saturday. Generally, you'll do better when you go during a slow weekday. Yes, it is worth a vacation day—or two, or three—to get a good deal on a car. Often, you can get a better deal by shopping at the end of the month, too, when sales bonuses and other incentives are on the line for dealers.

- And John planned on using a credit card cash advance to supplement his down payment. That's a terrible idea! If you're struggling to make monthly payments, you'll obviously struggle to make credit card payments, too. And the interest rate on those could be three or four times higher!

Here's the bottom-line tragedy of deals like the one John made. A fair price for the Mustang he bought would have been fairly close to his original offer. At prevailing market prices of $26,000, plus the full rebate and another $5,000 down (a combination of cash and trade-in value), John could have paid $385 per month for forty-eight months.

But how would John be sure to get the best price?

Now that we know all the things people shouldn't do when buying a car, here's a recipe for doing it right. As with many other financial transactions, the most important steps are keeping it simple and sticking to your guns.

1. Get your own financing. Always show up at a dealership with one of those bank-loan checks that you can use to buy the car outright, in cash. You might be able to get a better financing deal from the dealership, and you can listen to their offer. After you're finished negotiating on price, you can say something like this: "Here's the bank deal I have. Can you beat it?"

2. Give yourself a lot of time. Maintaining your current car, and being realistic about its future, is one of the most important things you can do to get a good new-car deal. You never want to be a desperate shopper. Always shop before your car is about to leave you stranded. This is essential if you are going to follow strategy 3.

3. Be ready to leave. Deals always change along the way. In many cases, you will think you have a deal when you don't. If you feel mistreated, get up and leave. Far, far too few buyers tell dealers to shove it when they start playing games. Personally, I would rather pay a little more and deal with an honest salesman than fight over every penny with a thief. But even if you don't agree, leaving will be the most powerful negotiating tool you ever use. Last time I walked out on a dealer, I received no fewer than twenty phone calls in the subsequent days from the dealer begging me for my business.

4. Always negotiate over the total price, never the monthly payments. By *total price,* I mean the "out the door" price. That includes all taxes, title charges, and other fees. Don't negotiate down from the MSRP sticker, or even up from the "invoice" price you now hear so much about. Dealers fudge both numbers. The real price is the out-the-door "market" price, which leads to my next point.

5. Price compare. Car shopping can be simple. Call or e-mail seven dealers and get price quotes. Then email all of them each other's quote. When you're finished, you will have a true picture of the real market price. You may have one outlier that's either very low or very high. You should probably ignore either (why would one dealer undercut the others by $750? Probably because the dealer is better at scamming the $750 in another part of the deal). Car-buying sites such as Edmunds.com, which offers its own "true market value price," can help a lot. But every local market is different, and what really matters is what people near you are paying for that car. Competitive bids are the *only* way to get the real market price for a car. In fact, that's the definition of a market.

6. Expand your local area. Don't be afraid to drive an hour or two when buying a car to get a better deal. Hey, it's a once-every-three-year purchase. Thanks to the Internet, it really does make sense to shop long distances for cars. Make sure at least one of your seven price quotes is from a dealer that's out of your market. I know people who have happily purchased cars a state or two away. But notice I said "drive an hour or two" to buy a car. I don't recommend long-distance purchases made sight unseen over the Internet. Even Craigslist offers this blunt assessment of long-distance auto sales: "OFFERS TO SHIP CARS ARE 100 PERCENT FRAUDULENT."

7. Sell your old car separately. You want to take away the variables the dealer can play with. Many a neat-and-clean deal gets ruined by a bad trade-in deal. It is easy to use Craigslist to sell your old car. Price it reasonably—say, a few hundred below market—and you'll sell it in a day or two. Again, I'm not trying to get you top dollar for your used car; I just want to take booby traps out of your new-car purchase.

8. When signing paperwork, bring a friend who will help you say no. This final point is often overlooked. Many a disaster occurs in the back room, after it seems as if all the dealing is done, when signing papers with the "closer." That's where unnecessary extended warranties are added (these are *never* a good deal), or bogus under-coating gets layered on. The back room is where math can go horribly wrong. Have a friend who's not emotionally invested—or hungry—sit with you and read everything. It will also make a dealer less likely to do something that's outright illegal.

If you are a visual person, there's a fantastic five-minute testimony on how to buy a new car, from an expert named Rob Gruhl, easily found on YouTube and many other places online. His main point, however brutal it may be, is that you have to prepare to "feel like an asshole." This is the magical skill that all sleazy car sales staff have. One time when I stormed out of a dealership I felt wasn't being honest with me, I was followed into the parking lot by a sales manager who was yelling, "You don't get to call me a liar." He was. But these people are so self-deluded (remember the assertion in *The Sociopath Next Door* that one in twenty adults is a born liar) that they have to fight hard to keep up their self-delusion. If you are at all normal, you will feel like a jerk while negotiating with such sleazeballs. When you get up to walk out, for example, you will hear that you've wasted their entire day, or that you are literally keeping them from sending their kids to college. Really, that's okay. They shouldn't be selling cars and mistreating people.

NEW OR USED?

One clear way to save money buying a new car is not to buy a new car. You probably know that new cars lose up to 20 percent of their value the moment you drive them off the lot. That's a severe price punishment for getting that new-car smell. In some segments—certainly the under-$7,500 price range—buying used makes a lot of sense. But buying a new car in the days of the Web has some major advantages, so let me try to convince those among you who are serial used buyers to at least consider buying new.

Buying a new car and buying a used car are fundamentally different.

Buying new is akin to shopping for a new television—they're everywhere, they're easy to compare, and if someone buys the set you were about to pull off the rack, there's always another. And most important, price comparisons are part of the game. You can tell a salesman, "Hey, the guy across the street is charging $100 less on the exact same model," and you will likely get a discount.

Buying a used car is more like shopping at an antiques store. When you find that old Tiffany lamp, there's only one. If you don't buy it, it might be gone tomorrow. "Buying panic" is likely to take hold of most consumers in this situation. Without question, the buyer has less leverage. It's normally impossible to play one antiques dealer off another to get a better price.

That's how things work in the used-car market. Sure, you can find similar models with similar odometer readings. But two used cars are always different—one is more of a cream puff, one has obviously worn brake pedals that hint at aggressive use, one has a cigarette burn in the backseat, and so on. It's hard to play dealers off each other because by the time you travel to a competitor, the car you want could really be gone.

So when you shop for a used car, you are surrendering the most powerful bargaining tool you have: competition. Nowadays, the Internet has really tipped the scales of comparison shopping toward consumers.

Before we leave the arena of car shopping, here are a few other expert tips you might consider:

- Given the complicated and often twisted nature of car-sale commissions, end-of-month incentives are common. If you buy your car toward the end of the month, you might get a better deal.
- You will almost certainly get a better deal on "dealer stock." Look for cars that are at the edges of the lot or that look a little dusty. Keeping a car on the lot costs the dealer—they have to pay insurance, for example, and often they finance their inven-

tory. Taking a slightly older model off their hands will work to your advantage.

- Many credit unions offer free or inexpensive car-buying services. Because they buy in bulk, they can often negotiate better deals. More important, they are used to haggling and dealer tactics. Using one might let you skip all this trauma.

- For hassle-free window-shopping, figure out the one or two days each month when the dealership is closed and wander the lot then. You'll be able to do a much better job of keeping your head without being hassled by obnoxious salesmen.

- Rebates. It's nearly always better to take the cash than those enticing zero percent loan rates. The only exception would be for very large loans ($25,000 or more) and very long loan terms (forty-eight or sixty months). Several "Should you take the rebate?" calculators are available online. Obviously, "free money" has a cost. Here's one way to look at it: writer Tom Evslin has a calculator that expresses the higher cost of the car (sans rebate) as an annual percentage rate. Here's an example: Say a dealership will sell you a car for $29,000 financed at zero percent, or paid with a bank loan at 6.5 percent for $25,000 (with a $4,000 rebate). The zero percent deal costs an extra $21.82 each month, or an APR of 8.77 percent. Obviously, the bank loan is the better deal.

- One new way dealers turn you into cash is to keep you coming back for $450 worth of unnecessary repairs every fifteen-thousand miles or for pricey oil changes. Yes, your warranty still applies even if you go elsewhere for service. Do that. Again, don't muddy your deal with expensive or confusing extras, like one year's worth of oil changes at $50 a pop.

- Finally, the usual "I know a guy . . ." advice applies. Take everything your friends say with a grain of salt. Everybody thinks they got a good price on their new car. That's part of every car dealer's magic. Many manage to convince buyers that they "stole" the car, then laugh all the way to the bank. Listen to your friends, but listen more to your gut and your research, and make the decision for yourself.

Don't Get Screwed Buying a Car

- Buy when you want, don't need, a new car.
- Never negotiate over monthly payments, always the purchase price.
- Come with your own money—cash or a bank loan.
- Do the math before you arrive. Know what your payments should be.
- Sell your used car separately.
- Shop around . . . way around. Include distant cities in your search.
- Use email to get price quotes.
- Bring a friend when you sign the paperwork.

4

Buying a Home

Imagine the following conversation, overheard inside a hospital waiting room:

"Well, maybe the doctor misdiagnosed that tumor, but the patient really should have looked at the biopsy results himself and asked more questions. You know what they say, buyers beware! It's not like it was brain surgery!"

"Yup. It's his fault. Too bad they amputated. But he did sign the contract!"

If you've never bought a home, you might think a comparison between reading closing documents and reading X-rays is a bit absurd. But talk with a few brain surgeons who got screwed on mortgages or closing costs and you'll know better. America has, for decades, cast consumers into the abyss of home buying and left them there to suffer alone. We've allowed clever bankers and brokers to talk people into incredibly self-destructive behaviors, the likes of which we would never tolerate in other industries. Who would knowingly let people eat poisoned food, buy a car with brakes that are sure to fail, or live in a San Francisco apartment that couldn't withstand even small earthquake tremors? That's what we've done in the world of home buying. Even if you are a staunch believer in people's right to hurt themselves, the societal cost of these mishaps is staggering. After all, who pays for the costs of treating all the poison victims, all the earthquake victims, and the housing meltdown?

You do.

Let's set aside for a moment the problems of the families who get kicked out of their homes because they can't afford their mortgage. Foreclosure hurts you, too. Every time a bank takes possession of a property, the surrounding fifty homes lose $3,000 in equity. The effect is compounding, too—the more foreclosures in a neighborhood, the bigger the equity drain on nearby homes. At a certain point, I would argue, the empty homes stop being an equity drain and start being something much worse. If you live on a block where four or five homes are for sale—particularly if the bank owns them—that doesn't just hurt your equity, it can darn near make it disappear. A house on that block simply won't sell. It has, at least temporarily, no market value. Dealing with the fallout from the 2007–9 housing collapse will ultimately rob Americans of some $500 billion in equity in their homes. Unfair and deceptive housing-market practices are everyone's problem—a problem that could be solved by a return to common sense and a little respect for mathematics.

In early 2009, one in five Americans were living in a home that was underwater—meaning the money owed to the bank was more than the market value of the house. In the hardest-hit areas, some home-buyers had seen their home values drop by more than 40 percent.

But in most of the country, the dip was on the order of 15 percent. That's an important number. As I've mentioned before, some of the things I write about in this book make me so angry that my hands literally shake while I type. This is one of those times.

For decades, a simple provision had been in place to prepare for just such a housing downturn—the 20 percent down payment. Twenty percent was seen as an important threshold that demonstrated potential home-buyers had the financial wherewithal and discipline to afford a home. That's nice, but it's not the most important reason for the large deposit. The reason was, and is, simple: It gives the lending bank a 20 percent cushion in case of a market downturn. It's simple: If you buy a $500,000 home and borrow $400,000, the bank's risk only kicks in when the price of that home falls to around $400,000. Until then, it still holds an asset that's roughly as valuable as the loan.

That's one heck of a cushion, and had it been in place from 2002 to 2007, there would never have been a housing bubble, a recession, and very likely few if any housing-related bank busts. Twenty percent down payments would have ensured a safe landing in nearly all housing markets in America. During 2008, the worst of the housing-bubble burst, only California, Florida, Nevada, and Arizona suffered more than 20 percent declines. The economic disaster could have, and should have, been contained. Instead, disaster struck, and American families were forced to spend $2,000 each just on the bailout of AIG.

Often, things that are made to sound complicated are really very simple. In fact, complexity is one of the best indicators that you're on the wrong track. Remember Stevie Wonder (or for that matter, Einstein): Don't believe in things you don't understand.

Now, I hope I've convinced you that the crazy way we buy and sell homes in America has got to end. Every year, Americans spend $110 billion buying and selling homes—and that doesn't include the price of the homes! That's just the fees associated with the transactions. The median commission paid to real estate agents was $11,558—for a total of $80 billion annually. That's one more reason the time to reform home purchasing is now.

It would be grand if the government took decisive steps to stop allowing consumers to buy mortgages that are the equivalent of cars without brakes. It should be obvious that the federal government needs to set some national lending safety standards. But that's unlikely given that the financial industry is the single largest donor to Congress. Instead, we will talk about the problem for several years, ensuring the discussion takes just long enough to allow for a market recovery. Then, thanks to our collectively short memories, we'll enact embarrassingly shallow improvements, such as greater disclosure by banks and brokers.

What we'll get, I'll bet, is one more piece of paper to sign at the closing table. It'll be another warning notice that will be ignored, the equivalent of a disclosure notice like this from a car dealership: "The brakes on this car might fail within six to twelve months."

Industry reform is the sensible route. It's easier to train a few thousand market professionals than several million consumers. But knowing that this sensible route is unlikely, I want you to take matters into your own hands. I want you to fix the housing industry by yourselves, one Gotcha fighter at a time.

BUYING A HOUSE is probably the most perilous transaction in any consumer's lifetime. The potential to get screwed is orders of magnitude larger than in any other transaction you'll ever undertake. As we saw during the great housing meltdown, screwing up a housing purchase can cast a shadow over family finances for years or even decades. That's the lesson I want you to take away from the housing collapse; your primary goal when buying a home should be this: Don't ruin your future. With that in mind, let me introduce my blasphemous rule for the home-buyer:

The loan is more important than the home.

People go about home shopping in a bass-ackwards way. They might spend months looking at dozens, even hundreds, of properties. They read up on schools. They hunt for grocery stores. They look up crime data. One thing they often never do: They never buy the first house their Realtor shows them. And they don't move right into a condo that their friend Larry at work said he heard about from his friend Jennifer. Yet when it comes to pledging the largest amount of money they'll ever spend—when it comes to pledging one-quarter to one-third of their monthly earnings for thirty years (let me say that again, thirty years!)— people often take the first piece of advice they get.

People often spend five hundred hours or more shopping for a home and thirty minutes shopping for the loan. That's nuts.

Here's the lesson I hope we learned during the housing market meltdown: It's *much easier* to move out of a house you don't like than a mortgage you don't like. Getting out of a bad mortgage is such a nightmare that the Harvard law professor and bankruptcy expert Elizabeth Warren, co-author of *The Two-Income Trap*, gives this counterintuitive advice: You're better off taking a bunch of expensive vacations and blowing money on nice clothes than buying a house with a bad mortgage. You can always stop making the frivolous purchases when times get tough. But going deep into debt that can't be erased—even by a bankruptcy proceeding—can be an impossible problem to solve.

It's important to buy a house you love. If you love the home, and you can afford the monthly payments, then you should ignore all the talk about housing values. It is just noise. Even if you are underwater on paper, you needn't worry—if you have a nice place to live and there's no immediate concern that you'll lose your job or be relocated. Primary homes are not an investment and should never be chosen as one. The benefit of a mortgage is that you've locked in your housing costs for thirty years, and with only the rarest of exceptions, your housing payment will be a bargain if you stay in the home for more than ten years.

But it won't be a bargain if you get a bad loan. Even if you get a bad house, you can fix it up or redecorate. But a fresh coat of paint does nothing to improve your debt situation. This is why the loan is more important than the home, and I want you to spend your time accordingly.

WHY HOME BUYING IS SO HARD

You buy things every day. You make judgments, you bargain, you look for sales, you ward off aggressive sales tactics. All those experiences should prepare you for buying a home. But they don't. Why? Limited selection.

A buyer who sets out to buy a flat-screen TV, like a shopper who sets out to buy a home, has thousands of possibilities. TV buyers will usually find multiple copies of the item they seek, sold by competing retailers. Home-buyers, however, are at a serious disadvantage. When a shopper finds the perfect condo, there's only one. It truly is a once-in-lifetime opportunity. The supply represents the ultimate scarcity.

You don't need to know all about supply and demand to understand that when there is only one of something, the seller has a lot of leverage. There is often no time for buyers to think, as another buyer can swoop in and take the home away. That means the pressure on the transaction is immense.

This single fact makes home buying fundamentally different from almost any other transaction consumers undertake. Even a new-car purchase, hardly an easygoing affair, doesn't contain this kind of once-in-a-lifetime pressure. You can always go to another dealer and find the same car.

The intensity and unfamiliarity of these once-in-a-lifetime transactions make home selling ripe for abuse. I am generally a big proponent of the do-it-yourself approach. But when buying a home, you'll need to be represented by someone you can trust. There's nothing more important you can do when home shopping than picking good people to surround yourself with. Real estate law is local. In some states, an honorable agent is sufficient; in others, a real estate lawyer will be required. Picking an honest advocate is the most important bridge to a fair transaction.

Because people buy homes only about once every ten years, they are generally forced into questionable trust relationships with strangers, relationships that are similar to doctor-patient relationships. And they often misunderstand the true nature of these new "friends," who all stand to benefit economically from their bad choices. The truth is, when you are buying a home, no one is your friend. Not the agent, not the mortgage broker, not the bank, or the escrow company. For everyone involved, it's strictly business.

Yet, without the help of a professional, few people can make sense of the mysterious HUD-1 closing document, and that's only one of the pieces of paper you will have to sign when you buy a home. When the pile of papers shows up on closing day, most consumers have no idea that all the terms of their loan can change, even if those terms were presented in writing, in a Good Faith Estimate. Consumers are often hit with random extra charges (I've heard of brokers who add something they call a "dumb-ass fee" on closing documents). But that's not as bad as bait-and-switch stories, such as this one sent in by a reader to the Red Tape Chronicles, about a sale gone bad in Los Angeles.

The lender will tell you that you are getting a 30 year fixed rate loan at 6% with no points, no pre-pay penalty, and no fees. You're just so excited about the interest rate and terms that you don't ask for it in writing, and thus essentially you don't receive a "good faith estimate." So, when the time comes and your agent has removed all contingencies on the purchase of your new home, including the loan, you sit down to sign the loan docs that have been essentially prepared by your lender. This is where you become a victim of the "don't ask, don't tell, bait 'n' switch game." You come to find out that your loan is now 6.5% and you're paying 1 point, along with some other "administrative" costs. This makes your monthly payment increase by $500, no longer allowing you to afford the home at a comfortable monthly payment. Nor did you know that you were going to have to pay $5,000 or more just to get the loan. Additionally, since there is a pre-payment penalty, you cannot re-finance until the pre-determined time, without paying a hefty penalty. This could cost you thousand and thousands of dollars.

The above scenario happened to my client.

I want you to spend serious time picking an honest real estate agent and mortgage broker. Because in the end, no matter how clever you are, if you are dealing with the devil, you are going to end up in housing hell.

You should still understand, however, that the someone you trust—even if he or she is as pure as the driven snow—is helplessly subject to an economic bias that you need to understand. That wonderful neighbor who's helping you buy your first home may say he wants to get you the best price during a negotiation, but he gets nothing until you sign on the dotted line. Then, he makes thousands of dollars. Same for the seller's agent. Both really have only one incentive: they want to close the sale at any price. That means, in the end, you really are on your own.

Knowing how perilous the journey from idea to new home is, I want to lay out ten steps to help you safely swim the rapids of home buying.

The Ten Steps to Buying a House and Not Getting Screwed

1. Estimate your monthly payments and down payment
2. Get a preapproval letter
3. Pick an agent
4. Pick a home—make an offer
5. Get several GFEs
6. Fill out Bob's GFE
7. Consider backing out and renting
8. Read and understand a HUD-1
9. Stay involved during the interregnum
10. Get your HUD-1 early

1. ESTIMATE YOUR MONTHLY PAYMENTS AND DOWN PAYMENT

First things first. I want you to make an honest assessment of what kind of home you can afford. How do you do that? There are lots of formulas. Unfortunately, the half-crazed housing market of the past ten years has wreaked havoc with many of them. Still, they form solid guidelines.

Traditionally, home-buyers were given simple rules involving the number three. As in, buy a house that's no more than three times your annual salary. Or this: Your monthly payments shouldn't be more than one-third of your monthly take-home income. I'm sure you're gasping right now. After all, I don't know too many people with $100,000 salaries who live in $300,000 homes. Sometime in the last decade the number three became the number five. On average, the ratio of income to house value has risen from three to nearly five. By the same token, an alarming number of people pay 50 percent of their monthly income to the bank holding their mortgage. That's nuts.

You should find a happy medium. Obviously, the rest of your financial picture should weigh heavily in your calculations. If you hold no other debt, make $6,000 per month, and believe you have good prospects for future raises, perhaps you could take on a $2,400-a-month mortgage (40 percent) to buy a home. With a traditional mortgage, that would get you a home worth $450,000 or so—as long as you had about $50,000 in down payment and closing costs saved up. Still, a $450,000 home would be more than six times your annual income, putting you in pretty risky territory. Watch how quickly a mortgage obligation like that would strangle your finances. If property taxes and home insurance add another $600 to your payment (easy—if property taxes are $6,000 and hazard insurance is $1,200), you'll be paying half your *gross* salary to the bank each month. You'd have around $1,500 left for all other life expenses after taxes.

You should probably go shopping again.

In this step, a simple mortgage calculator and monthly budget spreadsheet will be your friend. Run several scenarios through this calculator. For someone who earns $72,000 a year, a $300,000 home (4.2 times income) is much more comfortable. Monthly mortgage payments would be closer to $1,500—closer to 25 percent of monthly income. You'd even have a shot at pulling together a full 20 percent down payment ($60,000) and avoiding private mortgage insurance or a second mortgage. And you'd generally have a much easier time sleeping at night.

The key at this step is making realistic choices. It's very American to feel optimistic about future job prospects, future earnings potential, investment success, and the like. I love optimism, but it doesn't pay the mortgage. Long-term commitments such as a thirty-year mortgage must account for the high probability of financial hiccups along the way. If both you and your spouse plan on contributing to the mortgage payment and figure that into your monthly budgeting, you should include in your calculations the reality that your family faces twice the likelihood of being hit by a job loss.

Before you leave this step, you want to arrive at a monthly payment you can afford. Then I want you to keep that number a secret and use a Web calculator to arrive at the house price you can afford. Working backward, a $2,000 monthly payment would get you about a $400,000 home.

It's important to arrive at your magic number before you talk to an agent because you don't want the agent unduly influencing your math. Agents can't help but push your price up because that makes their job easier. Don't tell them what you can afford each month, for the same reason you don't have that kind of conversation with a car dealer. If you let on your secret payment figure, you'll likely hear them recommend a friend who can help you with some creative financing. When talking to agents, stick with a grand total number instead.

2. GET A PREAPPROVAL LETTER

Before you begin seriously shopping for a home, you'll need a preapproval letter from a bank. This note will say you are a good candidate for receiving a mortgage up to a certain amount, based on stated income. You can get one from any bank or mortgage broker—they are usually eager to hand them out, as they carry no guarantees. You might as well get one from a lender who would be a serious candidate for getting your business when you actually apply for the mortgage. It might be nice to get preapproval letters from a few lenders, as a way of testing the waters for the actual loan application, but that would carry a risk—obtaining a letter will slightly ding your credit score because the lender will access your credit report. So stick with one letter.

Some banks offer a prequalification letter rather than a preapproval letter. But the preapproval process is a little more rigorous than a prequalification. Lenders issuing preapprovals will require more documentation—tax returns or pay stubs, for example. Preapproval letters carry more weight. So that's your better bet.

It's good to have the letter before you interview agents because then you won't be tempted to simply follow their advice and get a lender letter from their friend-of-a-friend, which could easily start you down the road to getting your mortgage from their friend. And if you show up with a preapproval letter, you will show prospective agents you really mean business.

3. PICK AN AGENT

Outside of picking the loan, the most important choice you'll make when buying a home is picking your real estate agent. This person will be with you every step of the way, knocking on doors, wandering around neighborhoods, negotiating with other agents. Choose carefully. This is no time to settle for Uncle Ernie or the out-of-work teacher you know. Or even your best friend's wife. You're picking the person who will be in the best position to cost you or save you tens of thousands of dollars.

You should interview at least three agents. You should listen to what they say and see if it jibes with what you learn from the rest of this chapter. You should trust your instincts about how honest the person is. You should get names and numbers of former clients and ask them if they were happy with the transaction. All agents will be some combination of biased salesman and unbiased adviser. Find someone who's not selling you all the time.

If you want a $350,000 home, you should be sure to pick agents who work in your price range. You don't want to be the low-commission client for someone who normally sells to millionaires.

You do want to visit your state's Department of Real Estate or similarly named entity to do a quick background check. There, you'll be able to verify that the agent's license is still valid and see any complaints that might be pending. A quick two-minute Web search can save you from hours—or perhaps years—of heartache later on.

Agents will probably require you to sign a contract that indicates you are exclusively working with him/her while home shopping. That's okay. The contract protects your rights, too. Be sure to check the conditions for dissolving the contract. If things go poorly, you want to be able to sever ties and start fresh with someone else. Contracts should include a clause that says something like this: "Can be voided with twenty-four hours notice by either party."

Once you've signed, you can start the fun part. House shopping.

4. PICK A HOME—MAKE AN OFFER

You know better than me how to pick your home. I'll just make one point. Buy a place you love, not a place that you think will make you money. Your goal should be simple—get a place you'll want to stay in for many years at a payment you can afford every month, and you'll never have to worry about the ups and downs of the housing market.

Making an offer is pretty straightforward. Your agent and you will submit a written proposal. It will include the price you are willing to pay, proof that you can pay it (generally, a copy of a preapproval lender letter), and a check toward the down payment, called earnest money. I know, you'll be told that more earnest money will show you are a "stronger" buyer. But there's really not much need for that. Remember, if you cancel the deal later, you'll lose this amount. Put down as little earnest money as you can.

The seller can accept or reject the offer. Expect offer number one to be rejected. But if it's accepted, the deal is legally binding, and you must begin the process of buying the home.

It is never smart to submit an open-ended offer. Always put a time limit on it; the quicker the better. Otherwise, the seller will simply use your offer to try to shake other offers out of the trees. Generally, twenty-four hours is an acceptable period. There's nothing wrong with asking for an answer by the end of the business day, however.

You will likely receive a counteroffer, which instantly voids your first offer. Now, they are on the legal hook. If you accept, you get the house. You can make another counteroffer. Then, a few more counteroffer rounds may follow.

Either way, the offer will have contingencies. These can put the brakes on a deal even after an offer has been accepted. The most common involves a home inspection. Houses have flaws that are invisible to the untrained eye. No one should buy a home without getting it inspected by a professional. That can cost up to $500 for a typical home, and the buyer pays, but it's always worth it. Even if the inspector turns up nothing wrong, inspection reports always form the foundation for a great list of small, worthwhile projects to take on (the gutter should be turned away from the foundation, the roof probably only has five years left). Never agree to an offer that doesn't allow for contingencies such as home inspections.

5. GET SEVERAL GFES

Now, it's back to the bank. I mean banks. You'll have to act fast, of course, because picking a lender is part of the race of tying up the home. You don't have to select a lender before signing a purchase agreement, but you'll need one quickly after striking a deal.

At this point, you can force banks to be more specific with you. You ask for a Good Faith Estimate (GFE) on your potential purchase. That'll include precise numbers for closing costs, monthly payments, down payments, and many other details that would apply to your specific home purchase.

It'll look like this:

The Good Faith Estimate is a critical step in the process. You can't pick a bank without one. You should get at least three: two from banks and one from a mortgage broker. Conveniently, the GFE is simpler than the form you'll get at closing itemizing all your charges—the HUD-1 form, which we'll discuss in a moment—but it's relatively easy to compare the two. That will be important later on, when you want to make sure no sneaky charges have been added. But for now, the GFE has one purpose: to allow you to comparison shop.

All your requests for GFEs should be submitted on the same day, for the exact same kind of loan with the same number of points, to ensure you'll get an apples-to-apples comparison.

OMB Approval No. 2502-0265

Good Faith Estimate (GFE)

Name of Originator		Borrower	
Originator Address		Property Address	
Originator Phone Number			
Originator Email		Date of GFE	

Purpose

This GFE gives you an estimate of your settlement charges and loan terms if you are approved for this loan. For more information, see HUD's *Special Information Booklet* on settlement charges, your *Truth-in-Lending Disclosures*, and other consumer information at www.hud.gov/respa. If you decide you would like to proceed with this loan, contact us.

Shopping for your loan

Only you can shop for the best loan for you. Compare this GFE with other loan offers, so you can find the best loan. Use the shopping chart on page 3 to compare all the offers you receive.

Important dates

1. The interest rate for this GFE is available through _____. After this time, the interest rate, some of your loan Origination Charges, and the monthly payment shown below can change until you lock your interest rate.

2. This estimate for all other settlement charges is available through _____.

3. After you lock your interest rate, you must go to settlement within ☐ days (your rate lock period) to receive the locked interest rate.

4. You must lock the interest rate at least ☐ days before settlement.

Summary of your loan

Your initial loan amount is	$
Your loan term is	years
Your initial interest rate is	%
Your initial monthly amount owed for principal, interest, and any mortgage insurance is	$ per month
Can your interest rate rise?	☐ No ☐ Yes, it can rise to a maximum of %. The first change will be in
Even if you make payments on time, can your loan balance rise?	☐ No ☐ Yes, it can rise to a maximum of $
Even if you make payments on time, can your monthly amount owed for principal, interest, and any mortgage insurance rise?	☐ No ☐ Yes, the first increase can be in and the monthly amount owed can rise to $ The maximum it can ever rise to is $
Does your loan have a prepayment penalty?	☐ No ☐ Yes, your maximum prepayment penalty is $
Does your loan have a balloon payment?	☐ No ☐ Yes, you have a balloon payment of $ due in years.

Escrow account information

Some lenders require an escrow account to hold funds for paying property taxes or other property-related charges in addition to your monthly amount owed of $ _____.

Do we require you to have an escrow account for your loan?

☐ No, you do not have an escrow account. You must pay these charges directly when due.

☐ Yes, you have an escrow account. It may or may not cover all of these charges. Ask us.

Summary of your settlement charges

A	Your Adjusted Origination Charges *(See page 2.)*	$
B	Your Charges for All Other Settlement Services *(See page 2.)*	$
A + B	Total Estimated Settlement Charges	$

Good Faith Estimate (HUD-GFE)   1

Understanding your estimated settlement charges

Some of these charges can change at settlement. See the top of page 3 for more information.

Your Adjusted Origination Charges

1. Our origination charge
This charge is for getting this loan for you.

2. Your credit or charge (points) for the specific interest rate chosen

☐ The credit or charge for the interest rate of ⬚ % is included in "Our origination charge." (See item 1 above.)

☐ You receive a credit of $⬚ for this interest rate of ⬚ %. This credit **reduces** your settlement charges.

☐ You pay a charge of $⬚ for this interest rate of ⬚ %. This charge (points) **increases** your total settlement charges.

The tradeoff table on page 3 shows that you can change your total settlement charges by choosing a different interest rate for this loan.

A Your Adjusted Origination Charges — $

Your Charges for All Other Settlement Services

3. Required services that we select
These charges are for services we require to complete your settlement. We will choose the providers of these services.
Service   Charge

4. Title services and lender's title insurance
This charge includes the services of a title or settlement agent, for example, and title insurance to protect the lender, if required.

5. Owner's title insurance
You may purchase an owner's title insurance policy to protect your interest in the property.

6. Required services that you can shop for
These charges are for other services that are required to complete your settlement. We can identify providers of these services or you can shop for them yourself. Our estimates for providing these services are below.
Service   Charge

7. Government recording charges
These charges are for state and local fees to record your loan and title documents.

8. Transfer taxes
These charges are for state and local fees on mortgages and home sales.

9. Initial deposit for your escrow account
This charge is held in an escrow account to pay future recurring charges on your property and includes ☐ all property taxes, ☐ all insurance, and ☐ other ⬚

10. Daily interest charges
This charge is for the daily interest on your loan from the day of your settlement until the first day of the next month or the first day of your normal mortgage payment cycle. This amount is $⬚ per day for ⬚ days (if your settlement is ⬚).

11. Homeowner's insurance
This charge is for the insurance you must buy for the property to protect from a loss, such as fire.
Policy   Charge

B Your Charges for All Other Settlement Services — $

A + B Total Estimated Settlement Charges — $

Good Faith Estimate (HUD-GFE) 2

Instructions

Understanding which charges can change at settlement

This GFE estimates your settlement charges. At your settlement, you will receive a HUD-1, a form that lists your actual costs. Compare the charges on the HUD-1 with the charges on this GFE. Charges can change if you select your own provider and do not use the companies we identify. (See below for details.)

These charges cannot increase at settlement:	The total of these charges can increase up to 10% at settlement:	These charges can change at settlement:
■ Our origination charge ■ Your credit or charge (points) for the specific interest rate chosen (after you lock in your interest rate) ■ Your adjusted origination charges (after you lock in your interest rate) ■ Transfer taxes	■ Required services that we select ■ Title services and lender's title insurance (if we select them or you use companies we identify) ■ Owner's title insurance (if you use companies we identify) ■ Required services that you can shop for (if you use companies we identify) ■ Government recording charges	■ Required services that you can shop for (if you do not use companies we identify) ■ Title services and lender's title insurance (if you do not use companies we identify) ■ Owner's title insurance (if you do not use companies we identify) ■ Initial deposit for your escrow account ■ Daily interest charges ■ Homeowner's insurance

Using the tradeoff table

In this GFE, we offered you this loan with a particular interest rate and estimated settlement charges. However:

■ If you want to choose this same loan with **lower settlement charges,** then you will have a **higher interest rate.**

■ If you want to choose this same loan with a **lower interest rate,** then you will have **higher settlement charges.**

If you would like to choose an available option, you must ask us for a new GFE.

Loan originators have the option to complete this table. Please ask for additional information if the table is not completed.

	The loan in this GFE	The same loan with lower settlement charges	The same loan with a lower interest rate
Your initial loan amount	$	$	$
Your initial interest rate¹	%	%	%
Your initial monthly amount owed	$	$	$
Change in the monthly amount owed from this GFE	No change	You will pay $ **more** every month	You will pay $ **less** every month
Change in the amount you will pay at settlement with this interest rate	No change	Your settlement charges will be **reduced** by $	Your settlement charges will **increase** by $
How much your total estimated settlement charges will be	$	$	$

¹ For an adjustable rate loan, the comparisons above are for the initial interest rate before adjustments are made.

Using the shopping chart

Use this chart to compare GFEs from different loan originators. Fill in the information by using a different column for each GFE you receive. By comparing loan offers, you can shop for the best loan.

	This loan	Loan 2	Loan 3	Loan 4
Loan originator name				
Initial loan amount				
Loan term				
Initial interest rate				
Initial monthly amount owed				
Rate lock period				
Can interest rate rise?				
Can loan balance rise?				
Can monthly amount owed rise?				
Prepayment penalty?				
Balloon payment?				
Total Estimated Settlement Charges				

If your loan is sold in the future

Some lenders may sell your loan after settlement. Any fees lenders receive in the future cannot change the loan you receive or the charges you paid at settlement.

Good Faith Estimate (HUD-GFE) 3

Until recently, GFEs were incredibly flawed. Banks could literally change everything they entered on the form when closing day came, an invitation to lowball offers. But there's good news. Beginning in January 2010, lenders will have to use a new GFE form that should limit at least some of the bait-and-switch tactics. As you'll see on page 3 of the form, banks have to commit to some costs at this point, and others, such as recording fees, can only vary up to 10 percent. The new form is a vast improvement over the old GFE.

Still, GFEs should be viewed with caution, particularly because the changes are so new. It's unclear how many banks and mortgage brokers will play ball—or play around—with the forms. Use them to comparison shop, but take them with a grain of salt.

It's not my intention to make you paranoid, just wise. Even in the worst of times, not all banks lie. Some even operate on what's called an Up Front basis. That means they guarantee all loan costs before you commit. If you can find an Up Front broker or bank, you're ahead of the game, and you'll have one less thing to worry about. Regardless, the first questions you should ask when you get back a GFE are "Which items here are guaranteed?" and "Which can change?"

The next question is similar: "Which of these items can I shop around for?" Can you find a cheaper title-insurance provider, for example? The right answer is yes—and you should. But asking such questions of your lender can be a useful tool. If your bank is helpful in answering these questions, then you know you have a chance at a square deal. If you feel undue pressure toward one or another title company, for example, then you'll know the bank sees you as one big, fat dollar bill.

The other terrible trick with Good Faith Estimates is the apples-and-oranges problem. It's hard to compare a thirty-year, no points, fixed loan with an interest-only, 1⅛-point loan. Just don't do it. The best way to pick a bank is to have all three run the numbers on the most basic loan—a thirty-year fixed with 20 percent down—and compare those. That way, the amounts for closing costs will square up neatly, and the best deal will be obvious. Remember, however, that what looks like the lowest price might not actually be the best deal. The lowest *guaranteed* price probably is.

Notice that I have yet to mention interest rates in this discussion. There's a reason for that. I've seen too many consumers discuss interest rates the way men discuss horsepower in cars or megahertz in computer processors; or students compare grades in high school. Often, dickering over a one-eighth interest-rate point is penny-wise and pound-foolish. Many buyers waste much more money on closing costs or poorly structured loans than they do on extra interest charges. A one-eighth-point interest-rate difference on a $250,000 mortgage saves you about $20 a month, for example. That's nice. But I'd rather you spend your energy saving $3,000 at closing. When loan shopping, go to a website such as Bankrate.com and get a sense of the prevailing interest rates in your area. But don't get hung up on getting the most horsepower or the absolute lowest rate. Get the best deal instead.

Foreshadowing step number 10, be sure to make your lender promise that it can deliver your HUD-1 form to you seventy-two hours before closing, so you can hunt around and find those last-minute hidden fees.

Jack Guttentag, aka the Mortgage Professor, would tell you the receipt of Good Faith Estimates is the most important moment in a home purchase. He would have you focus nearly all your attention on the bottom line once you get the estimates. Guttentag, a professor emeritus at Wharton Business School, says that the average consumer cannot be expected to perform line-by-line comparisons of every element in a mortgage. Better to have people concentrate on the big number at the bottom—so long as that number is guaranteed.

"Borrowers should focus on the total, that is all that matters," he said to me while discussing mortgages. He's right, of course. The bottom line of the Good Faith Estimate is the moment of truth for the borrower. Banks might shift costs here or there to make things sound appetizing (to wit, there's no such thing as a "no cost" mortgage. The costs are just shoved into other parts of the loan). His site, MTG Professor.com, is full of additional free information.

I'm not disagreeing with Jack. I'm just priming you to be well-informed when the moment of truth comes. You should be prepared to question individual items in the Good Faith Estimate, and you should be ready to demand more from the quote the bank gives you.

6. FILL OUT BOB'S GFE

One missing element on the Good Faith Estimate is the long-term consequence of your loan. It should be obvious that I favor old-fashioned mortgages, but if you plan to dip into the world of adjustable rates, interest-only loans, low-down-payment loans, and the like, you should come armed with a boatload of additional questions. Let's call it the Good Faith Estimate extension. The Good Faith Estimate shows your loan expenses and can be used to generate costs for month 1.

I want you to see, in black and white, your estimated monthly payment for month 13, month 37 (three years), month 61 (five years), month 85 (seven years) and month 121 (ten years). I want you to build into black and white the guaranteed payment and average increases in real estate taxes (10 percent each year unless a better estimate is available) and homeowner's insurance. Then I want you to take a good hard look at the commitment you are making.

BOB'S GOOD FAITH ESTIMATE WORKSHEET

	Total Payment	Mortgage	Taxes	Insurance	Outstanding Loan Balance
Month 1					
Month 13			110%	110%	
Month 37			130%	130%	
Month 61			150%	150%	
Month 85			170%	170%	
Month 121			200%	200%	

7. CONSIDER BACKING OUT AND RENTING

Looking at this payment scale should be the best way for you to analyze a decision most people never even bother to make—should you rent or buy? The U.S. tax code is tilted wildly in favor of homebuyers over renters. If you're a renter, you can add about 25 percent to your rent payment to cover a mortgage payment and still come out even thanks to the tax deduction of mortgage interest.

Still, there are plenty of solid arguments for renting instead of buying (we all die, so aren't we all really renters?). There is no shame in not owning property. The single best reason to buy a home is to build relatively stable housing costs into your life. You will know precisely how much that mortgage will cost for thirty years. An expensive monthly payment in year one can, and usually does, look cheap in year fifteen, or even year ten. Of course, real estate taxes can climb and distort this simple rule of thumb. But it's easy to imagine the rent on your apartment doubling in the next ten years, isn't it? The best way to analyze a home purchase is from the point of view of long-term housing costs. Nothing helps a budget like predictability.

If anything tips the scales in favor of renting, other than a housing market in free fall, it's property-tax considerations. In areas where property taxes are oppressive, such as New Jersey (where some buyers need second mortgages to pay $1,000 a month in local taxes), renting often beats buying. The threat of mountainous property-tax hikes easily outweighs the threat of rental increases, particularly where rent controls are in place.

Still, mortgage-interest deductions can easily outpace property-tax considerations, nudging you back to the "buying" side. But if you are staring at the extended Good Faith Estimate and you're getting a queasy feeling in your stomach, DON'T IGNORE IT! It might be a normal case of nerves; or it might be your wallet telling you that danger lies ahead. I don't advocate voiding purchase and sale agreements lightly. It's better to face this reality check when you are at step 1, deciding on monthly payments. But you can still void a deal at this point, and if the numbers don't line up, you should. This is your last chance.

You might be able to cancel the deal over a dispute on the inspection, but you may have to just drop out and lose your earnest money. If that's the case, you'll be glad your earnest-money check was deliberately small. But even if you lose $5,000 or $7,500, it's still better than taking on a thirty-year obligation that's oppressive.

8. READ AND UNDERSTAND A HUD-1

Now, I'm going to give you some homework. The moment you agree to a deal to buy a home, the first thing you should do is the last thing most people do—you should look up a HUD-1 form. I know, that sounds a lot less exciting than picking out bathroom colors. But the HUD-1 is the only place you will see every cost associated with your home purchase. Consider it a cheat sheet for hidden fees. *If you want to avoid getting screwed, getting to know the HUD-1 form is the single best thing you can do,* and the single most overlooked part of a housing transaction.

The good news for you, dear reader—and it is fabulous news—is that starting in January 2010, major changes will be instituted to the HUD-1 form (just like that Good Faith Estimate form). Buying a home won't necessarily be easy, but it will be harder for you to get cheated. The form includes improved disclosures and groups many expenses together in a fashion much simpler than on the old form.

Still, the new HUD-1 form depressingly resembles a tax form and appears to have as many as thirteen hundred lines. Fortunately, I can boil it down for you to about ten important lines. This part might seem a bit tedious, but when we're done, you'll see how understanding the form helps at every other step along the way. And how it will make you the equivalent of a Jedi master of house purchasing.

The new HUD-1 form is available from the government's Housing and Urban Development website and from hundreds of other places online—and in the following pages of this book.

OMB Approval No. 2502-0265

A. Settlement Statement (HUD-1)

B. Type of Loan

1. ☐ FHA 2. ☐ RHS 3. ☐ Conv. Unins.	6. File Number:	7. Loan Number:	8. Mortgage Insurance Case Number:
4. ☐ VA 5. ☐ Conv. Ins.			

C. Note: This form is furnished to give you a statement of actual settlement costs. Amounts paid to and by the settlement agent are shown. Items marked "(p.o.c.)" were paid outside the closing; they are shown here for informational purposes and are not included in the totals.

D. Name & Address of Borrower:	E. Name & Address of Seller:	F. Name & Address of Lender:

G. Property Location:	H. Settlement Agent:	I. Settlement Date:
	Place of Settlement:	

J. Summary of Borrower's Transaction		K. Summary of Seller's Transaction	
100. Gross Amount Due from Borrower		**400. Gross Amount Due to Seller**	
101. Contract sales price		401. Contract sales price	
102. Personal property		402. Personal property	
103. Settlement charges to borrower (line 1400)		403.	
104.		404.	
105.		405.	
Adjustment for items paid by seller in advance		**Adjustments for items paid by seller in advance**	
106. City/town taxes to		406. City/town taxes to	
107. County taxes to		407. County taxes to	
108. Assessments to		408. Assessments to	
109.		409.	
110.		410.	
111.		411.	
112.		412.	
120. Gross Amount Due from Borrower		**420. Gross Amount Due to Seller**	
200. Amounts Paid by or in Behalf of Borrower		**500. Reductions In Amount Due to Seller**	
201. Deposit or earnest money		501. Excess deposit (see instructions)	
202. Principal amount of new loan(s)		502. Settlement charges to seller (line 1400)	
203. Existing loan(s) taken subject to		503. Existing loan(s) taken subject to	
204.		504. Payoff of first mortgage loan	
205.		505. Payoff of second mortgage loan	
206.		506.	
207.		507.	
208.		508.	
209.		509.	
Adjustments for items unpaid by seller		**Adjustments for items unpaid by seller**	
210. City/town taxes to		510. City/town taxes to	
211. County taxes to		511. County taxes to	
212. Assessments to		512. Assessments to	
213.		513.	
214.		514.	
215.		515.	
216.		516.	
217.		517.	
218.		518.	
219.		519.	
220. Total Paid by/for Seller		**520. Total Reduction Amount Due Seller**	
300. Cash at Settlement from/to Borrower		**600. Cash at Settlement to/from Seller**	
301. Gross amount due from borrower (line 120)		601. Gross amount due to seller (line 420)	
302. Less amounts paid by/for borrower (line 220)	( )	602. Less reductions in amount due seller (line 520)	( )
303. Cash ☐ From ☐ To Borrower		**603. Cash** ☐ To ☐ From Seller	

The Public Reporting Burden for this collection of information is estimated at 35 minutes per response for collecting, reviewing, and reporting the data. This agency may not collect this information, and you are not required to complete this form, unless it displays a currently valid OMB control number. No confidentiality is assured; this disclosure is mandatory. This is designed to provide the parties to a RESPA covered transaction with information during the settlement process.

L. Settlement Charges

700. Total Real Estate Broker Fees

Division of commission (line 700) as follows:

	Paid From Borrower's Funds at Settlement	Paid From Seller's Funds at Settlement
701. $ to		
702. $ to		
703. Commission paid at settlement		
704.		

800. Items Payable in Connection with Loan

801. Our origination charge	$	(from GFE #1)	
802. Your credit or charge (points) for the specific interest rate chosen $		(from GFE #2)	
803. Your adjusted origination charges		(from GFE A)	
804. Appraisal fee to		(from GFE #3)	
805. Credit report to		(from GFE #3)	
806. Tax service to		(from GFE #3)	
807. Flood certification		(from GFE #3)	
808.			

900. Items Required by Lender to Be Paid in Advance

901. Daily interest charges from to @ $ /day		(from GFE #10)	
902. Mortgage insurance premium for months to		(from GFE #3)	
903. Homeowner's insurance for years to		(from GFE #11)	
904.			

1000. Reserves Deposited with Lender

1001. Initial deposit for your escrow account		(from GFE #9)	
1002. Homeowner's insurance months @ $ per month $			
1003. Mortgage insurance months @ $ per month $			
1004. Property taxes months @ $ per month $			
1005. months @ $ per month $			
1006. months @ $ per month $			
1007. Aggregate Adjustment –$			

1100. Title Charges

1101. Title services and lender's title insurance		(from GFE #4)	
1102. Settlement or closing fee	$		
1103. Owner's title insurance		(from GFE #5)	
1104. Lender's title insurance	$		
1105. Lender's title policy limit $			
1106. Owner's title policy limit $			
1107. Agent's portion of the total title insurance premium	$		
1108. Underwriter's portion of the total title insurance premium	$		

1200. Government Recording and Transfer Charges

1201. Government recording charges		(from GFE #7)	
1202. Deed $ Mortgage $ Releases $			
1203. Transfer taxes		(from GFE #8)	
1204. City/County tax/stamps Deed $ Mortgage $			
1205. State tax/stamps Deed $ Mortgage $			
1206.			

1300. Additional Settlement Charges

1301. Required services that you can shop for		(from GFE #6)	
1302.	$		
1303.	$		
1304.			
1305.			

1400. Total Settlement Charges (enter on lines 103, Section J and 502, Section K)

Comparison of Good Faith Estimate (GFE) and HUD-1 Charges		Good Faith Estimate	HUD-1
Charges That Cannot Increase	**HUD-1 Line Number**		
Our origination charge	# 801		
Your credit or charge (points) for the specific interest rate chosen	# 802		
Your adjusted origination charges	# 803		
Transfer taxes	#1203		

Charges That in Total Cannot Increase More Than 10%		Good Faith Estimate	HUD-1
Government recording charges	# 1201		
	#		
	#		
	#		
	#		
	#		
	#		
	#		
	Total		
Increase between GFE and HUD-1 Charges		$ or %	

Charges That Can Change		Good Faith Estimate	HUD-1
Initial deposit for your escrow account	#1001		
Daily interest charges	# 901 $ /day		
Homeowner's insurance	# 903		
	#		
	#		
	#		

Loan Terms

Your initial loan amount is	$
Your loan term is	___ years
Your initial interest rate is	___ %
Your initial monthly amount owed for principal, interest, and and any mortgage insurance is	$ _____ includes ☐ Principal ☐ Interest ☐ Mortgage Insurance
Can your interest rate rise?	☐ No. ☐ Yes, it can rise to a maximum of ___%. The first change will be on _____ and can change again every _____ after _____. Every change date, your interest rate can increase or decrease by ___%. Over the life of the loan, your interest rate is guaranteed to never be lower than ___% or higher than ___%.
Even if you make payments on time, can your loan balance rise?	☐ No. ☐ Yes, it can rise to a maximum of $ _____.
Even if you make payments on time, can your monthly amount owed for principal, interest, and mortgage insurance rise?	☐ No. ☐ Yes, the first increase can be on _____ and the monthly amount owed can rise to $ _____. The maximum it can ever rise to is $ _____.
Does your loan have a prepayment penalty?	☐ No. ☐ Yes, your maximum prepayment penalty is $ _____.
Does your loan have a balloon payment?	☐ No. ☐ Yes, you have a balloon payment of $ _____ due in ___ years on _____.
Total monthly amount owed including escrow account payments	☐ You do not have a monthly escrow payment for items, such as property taxes and homeowner's insurance. You must pay these items directly yourself. ☐ You have an additional monthly escrow payment of $ _____ that results in a total initial monthly amount owed of $ _____. This includes principal, interest, any mortgage insurance and any items checked below: ☐ Property taxes ☐ Homeowner's insurance ☐ Flood insurance ☐ ☐ _____ ☐ _____

Note: If you have any questions about the Settlement Charges and Loan Terms listed on this form, please contact your lender.

To get you started, here are the things to look for on a HUD-1 form—also known as the real estate Settlement Statement.

Fortunately, for the purpose of hunting down hidden fees, you can just about ignore all of page 1. Those are calculations related to the price of the home, the payoff of previous mortgages on the home, taxes, and so on. The page is neatly divided into a description of the purchase from the buyer's point of view on the left, then the seller's point of view on the right. Of course, on closing day you should look at it to make sure there are no surprises.

The action, however, is on page two, under what are called "Settlement Charges." It begins with the juiciest part, the commissions. Here, I will digress. Please indulge me.

Unfair loans are the biggest problem facing home purchasing today. But a close second is real estate commissions. I hereby forgo any future Christmas cards from the National Association of Realtors.

Every day in America, real estate agents tell thousands of new home-buyers that their services are free. Yes, free. Now remember, on a $400,000 home purchase, the buyer's real estate agent and his/her office will receive a $12,000 commission. That's right, free = $12,000. This practice, by the way, is not only condoned, but encouraged by the National Association of Realtors Code of Ethics:

"Standard of Practice 12-2—Realtors may represent their services as 'free' or without cost even if they expect to receive compensation from a source other than their client provided that the potential for the Realtor to obtain a benefit from a third party is clearly disclosed at the same time."

Here's the "out." For accounting purposes, all real estate commissions are paid by the seller. On the HUD-1 form that's signed on closing day, it appears that the buyer is paying no commission. That's ridiculous, of course, and proven wrong every day by smart buyers who negotiate their agent commission down to 2 percent. The difference comes right off the price of the home. Yes, it's that simple. If your agent drops his or her fee from a 3 to a 2 percent commission, that $400,000 home becomes a $396,000 home. Imagine if you had the following thirty-second conversation before you bought your first home.

You: "Would you take two percent instead of three percent?"
Agent: "Grrr. Okay."

You would have earned yourself $4,000 in thirty seconds. Not bad! Probably the most valuable thirty seconds of your life. When you begin such a negotiation, don't think you are starting a revolution. Your agent will have heard your gripe before. A *Consumer Reports* survey of its readers (who are admittedly more savvy than average) revealed that 46 percent had tried to negotiate a lower commission when selling their home, and nearly three-quarters of them succeeded!

The problem is much more serious than your $4,000 gain or loss, however. This is an enormous structural problem with the buying and selling of homes. Buyers' agents make about $40 billion each year in the United States, and there is virtually no market pressure of any kind put on those commissions. Buyers are told they are getting free services, so they don't bargain. Sellers can't bargain because they have no relationship with the buyer's agent. This is a supremely broken market. Third-party transactions that break the relationship between buyers and agents are by definition unfair. They are adding wasteful costs to our system of buying and selling homes, and that puts undue pressure on our real estate market. If ever there was a time to correct this market inefficiency, it would be now. In the meantime, be a good capitalist, and a good American, and find a buyer's agent who will at least discuss discounting his or her services.

Notice, by the way, I did not say buy or sell your home by yourself (okay, I am still working on those Christmas cards after all). I am not a big believer in for-sale-by-owner transactions. Buying or selling a home is the most important and most complicated transaction you will ever engage in. I want you to get it right. Some people are qualified and clever and patient enough to do this without professional help. But many sellers who try this route find they have big trouble marketing their homes, and that limits their pool of buyers which in turn hurts their sale price.

Let's use eBay to make this point. Many sellers hate it, but they keep using it. Why? Because the second-largest auction site is so much smaller than eBay, it's a far inferior market, and that leads to far inferior prices.

Buyers face many, many unforeseen elements in real estate transactions—this block is having roadwork done next year, that school has a new principal who's fantastic, and so on. These are well handled by honest, professional real estate agents, and such agents do exist. You will recognize them by their willingness to bargain with you over lower commissions. As long as you are paying a fair, negotiated price for the service, I'm a believer in real estate agents for most folks. I just don't believe in extortion or nonnegotiated third-party payments.

One more special note before I leave this section about friends, cousins, co-workers, and the guy around the corner who sold your babysitter's parents' home three years ago. I've made this point several times, but it bears repeating: So many unhappy stories about personal finance begin with the phrase "But he was a friend/cousin/co-worker . . ." Just because you know a person mows his lawn every week does not mean he is good at buying or selling homes, and it does not mean he is willing to put your interests above his—or that the firm he works for is honest. Listen to friends' suggestions, but find your own agent. It's a business transaction, not a backyard barbecue. Keep it that way. You will be happier in the end.

There, I'm glad I have all that off my chest. Now, on to the rest of the form.

There's a lot of lines, but only six sections, and they boil down to a few straightforward things. Here's a guide to where you should slow down and read up. Areas where I've indicated a green light mean a lie or mistake would represent outright fraud and you wouldn't have a hard time getting your money back. Yellow and red lights, on the other hand, are areas where banks or brokers often pad the items and steal from you without much recourse. But note that this new form has easy references to the corresponding line on the Good Faith Estimate. That'll make it easy to check some of the fees for fairness.

HUD-1 Sections

800s—Bank fees. Red light.

900s—Prepaid items such as a few days' interest. Green light.

1000s—Reserves for upcoming near-term tax payments, etc. Green light.

1100s—Title charges. Red light.

1200s—Recording fees. Yellow light.

1300s—Additional charges. Yellow light.

All right, let's dig in to those yellow and red items now.

800s—Bank Fees. Red Light

801—Origination charge. This is a flat fee your bank charges to close the loan. You should agree on this amount early on. Some banks will actually give you a "no-fee" loan and enter zero here. Don't worry, they make money in other places. Make sure there's no surprise here. The amount can change right up until closing.

802—Points and yield-spread premiums. Points are a fee you pay to reduce your interest rate, or as credit you receive for accepting a higher rate. This number should be static and safe—as long as it's precisely what you expected. Yield-spread premiums are a fee you pay a mortgage broker to shop around for you and find a better interest rate. These are controversial and should be studied carefully, but it is possible for a broker to get a better loan rate for you, even when the cost of the broker is figured into the deal.

803—Adjusted origination charges: 801 plus 802.

804—Appraisal fee. An appraisal is mandatory, but the price can vary widely. Make sure you know how much your bank will charge for this appraisal before closing day. You can haggle over this price and suggest a cheaper appraisal.

805—Credit report fee. Mandatory. Your bank pays a few pennies for this. It could charge you up to $50. It'd be nice if you could negotiate this, but you really can't. Small potatoes in the end. Fight over larger items.

806—Tax service fee. A onetime amount paid by the lender to make sure you pay your property taxes on time.

807—Flood certification. A concern only for those in a federally designated flood zone.

808—Here's where the trouble begins. This area is for "extras." Lots of goodies can appear here. The yield-spread-premium fees used to appear here, and it's unclear if other broker- or agent-related fees might find their way onto this line, such as the "CLO access fee." What's that? It's just another way to give a kickback a fancy name. CLO stands for Computerized Loan Origination systems. Sounds great, right? But here's the problem. The Real Estate Settlement Practices Act bars Realtors from getting kickbacks from banks for steering business their way—a practice that's sometimes called naked referrals. Again, such kickbacks are wasteful and add unnecessary expense—as well as a decided lack of transparency—to the system. Real estate agents, however, set about finding their way around this clear limitation on their abuse of the privileged relationship they have with you as a buyer. Here's the loophole: Taking money for nothing is illegal, the Housing and Urban Development Office has ruled. But taking money for additional service is okay. So agents who sit buyers down in their office in front of a computer and review loan possibilities with them can say they've offered a service to buyers: CLO access. Now, if nearly all those buyers end up going to the same bank, well, that's just good business. And if that bank pays the broker, well, that's just America.

Naturally, you don't need to pay for loan advice from your real estate agent. Make sure you're not paying for CLO access.

Other junk fees you might find in this area include a mortgage processing fee (aren't you already paying the bank a fee?), a broker origination fee (this is fine as long as you have agreed to the amount ahead of time), an escrow waiver fee (if you decide to pay your own taxes. Ask for it to be waived), and courier fees (yes, even FedEx makes money on home closings).

1100s—Title Insurance fees. Red Light

Title insurance is one of the most misunderstood, and therefore most abused, parts of a home transaction. Aside from the agent fees and the hidden mortgage costs, title insurance is also the most expensive part of the transaction. Every year, home-buyers spend about $16 billion on title insurance, which is in place simply to make sure no one else can lay claim to property you are buying. Almost all of that money is a waste. In traditional insurance, such as auto insurance, firms pay out about 80 percent of what they collect in premiums. There are so few title claims, however, that the title-insurance industry pays out only around 5 percent of what it collects.

Nevertheless, you can't live without it. Banks won't give you a loan without it. You can buy additional title insurance to protect yourself, but you don't have to (though most consumers do so anyway). The best thing you can do is to get at least three quotes from three different firms before closing. Don't just take your agent's recommendation. Direct kickbacks are forbidden, of course, but most real estate firms have figured out ways around this law and benefit from referrals.

You can save big money by asking a title firm to reissue the old policy held by the prior owner rather than writing you a brand-new policy—sometimes 20 to 30 percent. Always ask for a reissue.

Here are more details on the form:

1101—Title services and lender's title insurance. This is the total cost of title insurance, document preparation, and everything else that the settlement agent does for you.

1102—Settlement or closing fee. The fee for the settlement agent to prepare documents for closing, etc. It's worth shopping around and getting a bid from at least a couple of settlement agents. You'll have to do that right after you agree to a sale, so don't wait!

1103—Owner's title insurance. This is insurance you can buy to protect yourself from a title issue. In many cases, it is not mandatory. Its value is debatable, with basic and premium policies offered. If it helps you sleep at night, buy insurance, but there's little argument for the premium policy. Buy the cheapest possible, and be sure to shop around.

1104—Lender's title insurance. This is the amount you pay to protect the lender from a title problem. It's required. Pay as little as possible, as described above.

1105—Lender's title policy limit. The amount of insurance coverage—that is, the total the insurance company would pay if there's a claim.

1106—Owner's title policy limit. The amount of insurance coverage.

1107—Agent's portion of the total title insurance premium. The commission the agent receives for selling you the title insurance. Will be shockingly high.

1108—Underwriter's portion of the total title insurance premium. The amount that the insurance company receives.

1200—Government Recording and Transfer Charges. Yellow Light

The critical thing here is to make sure the amounts match the amounts promised on the GFE. The recording fees should be small potatoes, so most of your energy should be focused elsewhere.

1300—Additional Settlement Charges. Yellow Light

This is the wild-card section. I've heard horrid tales of mortgage brokers dropping $1,000 "sucker's fees" into this section. You might see a "funding fee" here, which could be a charge to receive a wire transfer. You might see a flood-certification fee to determine if the home is in a flood zone. Pest inspections or other structural inspections will also land here.

People who are signing closing documents are so incredibly amped up that they often don't see items like these. That's why your best defense to getting screwed at the closing table is to get a preliminary HUD-1 form from your lender seventy-two hours before closing. You want to take that form and spend a few hours in front of a computer double-checking all the math. You want to leave time for questions—and not five minutes before you are scheduled to close. The only way a mere mortal—or for that matter, a twenty-year pro—can catch mistakes or cheats is to have plenty of quiet time to study the documents. If a bank says it cannot honor this request, you have the wrong bank.

Digging through the HUD-1 might seem tedious, but now that you've read this section, you've become a top 1 percenter. You'll know more about your coming real estate transaction than 99 percent of your peers. And you'll be ready for closing day.

9. STAY INVOLVED DURING THE INTERREGNUM

After the long, winding road to picking a home, and the longer, windier road to picking a lender, have been run, most home-buyers will consider their work finished. But you know better. The interregnum—

literally, "time between kings," but in your situation, the time before you become king of your castle—is when all the action happens. That's when a series of companies converge and do their best to take your money. While you're busy picking out drapes and paint colors, they're busy giving each other kickbacks for your business. Make sure you get at least two bids for title insurance, one of the largest closing costs that'll hit you; pick an inspector you trust, and carefully observe the home inspection; ask for a discount on the bank's appraisal fee, you just might get it; pester your agent for other ways to keep costs down. Don't just let these thirty to forty-five days pass; stay involved.

10. GET YOUR HUD-1 EARLY

Finally, closing is three days away and you have your hands on that HUD-1. Put on a big pot of coffee. Then, sit down with this book, and the Internet. Go over every line, make sure you understand every entry. If you don't, call your broker or lender and get a good answer. By now, they'll know you mean business. They'll know you've done your homework. You'll have served notice that you won't put up with getting screwed. And you'll end up in a good home at a fair deal.

If you feel still feel underqualified and overwhelmed, you can get inexpensive, professional help from an expert. For $45, the National Mortgage Complaint Center (866-714-6466) will review your HUD-1 statement and call out too large fees.

Don't Get Screwed by Your Mortgage Company

- The loan is more important than the home.
- Don't dis renting.
- No one is your "friend" during a house purchase.
- Pick from among at least three lenders, using Good Faith Estimates.
- Get a realistic sense of future cost using Bob's Good Faith Estimate.
- Study a blank HUD-1, then get yours early.

5

Cell Phones

I have an 18-year-old mentally disabled daughter who I
bought a phone for over the summer. I blocked all Internet
access and added unlimited texting to protect myself. I
knew nothing of [premium text] services. She discovered
them in a magazine ad, and ran up $10,000 in charges in
just one month. She had no understanding of the reper-
cussions, and I received no alerts from the phone company of this escalating bill. When I opened the bill, it was
just pure shock. There were pages and pages and pages of
things on there.

—SEAN CLARK,
profiled in the Red Tape Chronicles

A fictional account:

Joan Richer was about to, finally, give in. And her kids knew it.
They were practically squeaking in the backseat of the minivan, they
were so excited.

As the car bounced down the dirt road from their home toward
town, the three girls shot coordinated glances back and forth. Karen,
the teenager, led the assault.

"So, Mom, remember that time I was out at Jennie's and it started
snowing and the power went out and you couldn't get ahold of me?"

"Yeah, you were pretty upset, Mom," piped in Cassidy, the little one.

Mom shot a look in the rearview mirror with matronly disapproving eyes. "Oh, now I see why you were all so anxious to come with me to get *my* new cell phone," she said, struggling to force down a wry smile. She, of course, was ready for this line of attack. She'd heard it before. "And here I thought you all ran to the car to help me with the grocery shopping."

"But, Mom, Dad never lets you leave the house without a cell phone," said the ten-year-old, Morgan. "I'm sure he wants the same for us."

"Yeah! Yeah!" they all chanted.

Mom then turned up the motherly tone. *"Silence!"*

The squeaking stopped suddenly.

Five seconds later, the car erupted in laughter.

"Look, you guys know the rules. We'll get you one of those for-kids cell phones when you turn fourteen, then a real phone when you're sixteen, and that's that!"

The girls smiled. They'd read the advertisement in the paper. They knew they had Mom exactly where they wanted her.

Joan's cell phone was a relic, three years old, cracked screen, ink on the numbers all but gone, battery life barely two hours. It worked for her, but her husband was insistent. By the time they headed for vacation next week, she must have a new cell phone, he said. The family was going on a cruise. They were going to be separated for several days while he went to a conference. They needed a reliable way to stay in touch.

"CAN I HELP you?" said the smiling young man in the crisp, red shirt. He began to hand lollipops to the girls, but stopped abruptly and looked straight in Joan's eyes. "Oh, only if this is okay with you?"

Joan nodded, then quickly spat out, "I want the simplest new phone you have, something kind of like this." She brandished her old phone.

The salesman grabbed it from her. "Aha, this is just like the phone Ronald Reagan used to call Nancy right after he said, 'Mr. Gorbachev, tear down this Wall.' "

Karen laughed out loud, then the other girls followed. Cassidy tugged on her sister's shirt and said, "What wall?"

"Well, you are in luck. We have a fantastic deal going on right now. You won't believe this, but I can probably get you a new phone for free. We love taking customers from our competitors. In fact, since you will be new customers, I can get phones for the whole clan for free!"

By now, Karen was already playing a video game on a smartphone nearby.

"No, no, all I need is a basic phone and a very basic plan," Joan forged on. But the girls could see her breaking.

"Your daughter has fabulous taste," said the salesman, walking over to Karen. "That's our brand-new, VRY-NCE smartphone. It comes with free television programs, Microsoft Push email—"

"I just want a regular phone."

The salesman ignored Joan. "Even GPS monitoring for the kids. Get them this phone, you will always know where they are." As he said this, he motioned to a computer screen running a whizzy demo of the GPS software. It showed a map of the United States, then zoomed in to a map of their town, then zoomed in to the block they were standing in. A blinking light indicated the child's location.

"Wow," said Joan. "That's pretty amazing."

All three kids were lined up on one side, with the salesman. Joan was on the other side.

"We can have that service working for you in fifteen minutes, miss. And I'll tell you what. I'll give it to you for free for three months. You don't like it, just cancel it." He then grabbed the smartphone handset that Joan had unconsciously picked up near the display. It had a small keyboard, a 3.2 megapixel camera, a touch screen . . . and was far from the end of the display counter, where all the cheap, basic phones were nearly hidden from sight. As he walked toward the register, the group drifted behind him en masse. He whipped out a sales contract.

Joan was still trying to muster a fight, but it wasn't working. "Now, is that the best phone for me? Is it simple?"

"Simple?" He lit up again. "Well, it was rated number one among our consumers last month. And, it'll only cost you forty-nine dollars. And you can get email on it. Now, does your husband need one, too? Because if he does, I have an even better deal for you."

"Ummm . . . well, his phone contract is up, too."

"Our family-share plan—two thousand minutes per month for only one hundred dollars. And you can call each other for free. You've got to get four phones, though."

Morgan shrieked. Karen stepped on her foot. The salesman was busily scribbling away.

"Four phones? But I don't need four phones. I only wanted one. Rick is going to kill me."

"Okay, what's your name? Morgan?" the salesman said, completely ignoring Mom. "Here, Morgan, which phone number do you want? You get to pick your number. And, look, you can have a pink case if you want."

"I can pick? Wow!" She winked at Cassidy, confirming their earlier bargain to share the fourth phone. For now.

"Just sign these forms here," the red-shirted man said, turning back to Mom. "I know there's a lot of paperwork, but just pay forty-nine dollars each for the four phones and you will be on your way. In fact, you know what, we'll just bill you for them. Don't pay anything."

THREE WEEKS LATER.

"Well, it worked great during the trip, and on the cruise. I don't understand why it's not working. Here, you try it."

Rick had just hit redial for the eighth time. He was on his way home from school, and he wanted to let Joan know he'd picked up the girls.

"C'mon, Dad, everyone knows this service doesn't work around here," said Morgan. "I knew that before we got the phones. As soon as we pass this set of trees on Main Street, it stops working."

"What? Then why didn't you tell your mom?"

"Only texting works. That's why I keep texting my friends."

"Well, easy there, kiddo. I read the plan and you only get 250 messages a month. That sounds like a lot to me, but I don't want you running out."

Morgan checked her sent folder and showed it to Karen. It read 1,312. She didn't say anything.

"Criminy," Rick said as he pulled into their driveway. "Her car's gone. She's already left for school to pick you all up."

FIFTEEN MINUTES LATER.

"Morgan! Karen! Come down here right now."

Dad had a pile of mail in one hand. In the other, he was gripping about twelve pieces of paper in a fist. They knew the look in his eye. He'd had it last summer when they drove the rider mower around the lawn when he wasn't home.

"This bill says I owe YourWireless $595.21. See that? $595.21 What have you been doing?"

While the girls muttered their defense, Joan burst into the house.

"Thank *God* you are here. I've been calling you for half an hour. Why didn't you pick up?" she said.

"Mom, the phone doesn't work around here, everyone knows that," Morgan said.

"*Morgan!*"

After a curt hug, Rick whisked Joan into the study.

"Joan, what is all this? Thirty-five-dollars activation fee. Thirty-five-dollars activation fee. Thirty-five-dollars activation fee. They are all over the place!"

"The guy at the store told me the phones were free."

"And what are all these things? Ringtones America . . . $24.99. Then look at this: Txtr datr . . . $232.34. What is that?"

"I don't know, I don't know. It looks like it's only on Morgan's phone."

"Well, whatever it is, I know I can't even call you on my commute home. What are we getting for $595?"

"YES, MS. RICHER, that's a third-party text-message service," the cell phone customer-service agent said. "They call it 'premium text messaging.' Txtr datr is a text-message-based dating service. An adult had to authorize that charge. Maybe your husband did?"

"No, he didn't authorize it and I demand a refund. Two hundred dollars for a dating service? How could that possibly happen? I want a refund!" Joan was feeling stupider by the minute.

"I'm sorry, but you'll have to contact the third party for that. I can give you their number. It's 1-555-DATR-TXT."

"Forget it. The signal doesn't work anyway. Let me just pay the bill and get rid of these phones. They've been nothing but trouble."

"You want to cancel the phones?"

"Yes, cancel the phones."

"Okay, how would you like to pay the eight-hundred-dollar cancellation fee, by credit card?"

"The *what*?"

"Well, you have agreed to two-year contracts on each of these four phones. Canceling them before the end of the contact requires you to pay an eight-hundred-dollar cancellation fee."

"You want me to pay eight hundred dollars to cancel service on four phones that don't even work at my house?"

"Miss, you had fourteen days to test the phones. If they didn't work, you should have brought them back during the fourteen-day period. Now, your contact says you must pay eight hundred dollars. The other choice you have is to keep paying for the service."

Joan felt her heart race in her chest. Her one-morning trip to the cell phone store was going to leave her with an angry husband and without $1,300. And now, her kids would hate her if she canceled the phones. But she couldn't bear paying for a service that barely worked.

"Is there anything I can do to make the phones work better at the house?"

"Well, we do sell a new product called a signal booster, which you can install yourself in your house. It only costs three hundred dollars. . . ."

POOR JOAN RICHER. She made a host of missteps on her way to the wireless store. You probably spotted a lot of them, but I'll bet some of them would have fooled you, too.

The first, of course, was shopping with her persuasive children. But close behind was signing up for a new cell phone service right before her family went on vacation. Many, many elements go into providing a reliable signal for cell phone reception. No one can tell you, definitively, that your phone will work in the places you need it most often—on your back deck, in the car along your route to work, at Grandma's nursing home. The best you can do before you sign up for a new service is talk with friends in these various locations and ask how reliable their service is. But even their thumbs-up is no guarantee the service will work for you. For that, you must conduct a test-drive. The most important thing cell phone consumers can do is run their phone through the ringer in the first few days after purchase. Try out the phone along your commute route, at Grandma's house, in your basement rec room, or anywhere else you'll really need it. Free return periods can be as short as fourteen days. After that, cell phone contracts are harder to break than most marriage licenses. That fourteen-day window is a very short honeymoon, so take advantage of it. Never get a new cell phone service right before you leave for vacation, or at any other time when you can't put it through the paces of your normal work/play routine.

Unwieldy text-message plans are the bane of many parents' existence today. Kids can send far more text messages than most parents could possibly imagine. The average young teen sent 1,742 texts each month in 2008. That's nothing compared to the 14,528 texts sent by thirteen-year-old Reina Hardesty of Silverado, California, during a single month in 2008. In case you're wondering, that's 484 messages per day. She would have blown past a 250-message limit by lunchtime on the first of the month.

Fortunately, Hardesty's dad had an unlimited text-message plan, but don't be fooled by that name! Unlimited text messaging refers only to standard texts. An entirely different type of texts, called premium texts, can cost $1 or more per message. Online game shows use them, seedy ringtone subscription services use them, and strange teenager dating services use them. As you read in the quote at the beginning of this chapter, I once interviewed a man whose daughter had rung up nearly $10,000 in text charges in a single month before he discovered the problem—and he was paying for unlimited texts at the time. Obviously, that's incredibly unfair. No gadget should give a teenage child the ability to spend thousands of dollars of their parents' money without consent. But this is the reality of our time. Many providers will now allow you to turn off premium text-messaging services, and you should. If not, give your kids a stern talking to when they get their hands on a phone.

As a general rule, remember that cell phone companies are constantly trying to shrink the distance between the cell phone in your front pocket and the wallet in your back pocket. Here's one Joan Richer never thought of. When she called up her previous cell phone provider to cancel the service, the company would have insisted that she pay for nearly an extra month of service. Why? That's standard policy. Cell phone providers bill customers in advance. That means you pay March 1 for your March service. So even if you cancel on March 4, and even if your phone is deactivated that day, you must still pay clear through until March 31. That's an extra twenty-seven days of revenue the company collects, a kick in the pants on the way out the door. It's wrong, of course—how can they charge without providing service?—but right now, no one is stopping them.

One fee the Richers didn't have to pay, but they will in the future, is the "upgrade fee" charged when consumers get new phones for the same service. Think of it as a loyalty fee. When people decide to stay with their cell phone provider and get a new phone, the provider will charge an $18–$36 upgrade fee—over and above the price of the phone. To make things even more murky, the fee often appears two to three months after the phone purchase.

Why isn't the upgrade fee simply part of the price? That question should also be asked about those $35 activation fees, too. After all, the phone companies have no desire to sell phones that don't get activated. It's deceptive not to include the price of turning on the phone with the price of the phone. You should ask about it; ask for it to be waived; and at least make sure to include the price—normally $35—in your computations when deciding on the best deal.

The central trouble with cell phones is the ridiculous nature of their pricing, which boils down to this: "We'll charge our best customers the highest prices!" Customers pay for an arbitrary amount of calling minutes during arbitrarily picked times. Then, they are extorted an outrageous amount for excesses. "Excess" minutes are typically charged at a 600 to 800 percent higher rate than in-plan minutes. This is a game consumers can't win because in most services, unspent minutes go into cell phone never-never land. That leaves the most practical advice for consumers at this: When picking a plan, you are safer taking the "insurance"—the most minutes you'll need. Yes, you will essentially be paying extra for "protection." But at least this way you'll have a steady bill, and you'll avoid the surprise $400 cell phone bill.

Some cell phone providers offer a little-known feature to combat this kind of minute waste. Verizon, for example, will let customers call in the middle of the month to upgrade their plans . . . then allow a downgrade later on. This feature comes in handy if you have a family crisis and suddenly find yourself making fifteen hundred minutes of calls. It's always worth calling and asking about a temporary plan change if you are in a situation like that.

The rules for international travel are similar. A two-week trip to Canada, for example, could cost you $500 in international calling—or $20 for a one-month upgrade to a North American Calling Plan. Always call to see if your cell phone provider will make short-term plan changes. Providers don't advertise them (why would they?), but they do exist.

When asking for such a change, be extremely careful about your intentions, however. Make it clear you don't intend to renew your two-year contract with the company. Many firms will take any excuse to lock you up for another two years and will even engage in unethical behavior to do so. You should always end every conversation you have with a cell phone operator with the question "When does my current contract expire?" Then you should double-check the expiration date on every bill that's sent to you.

Richard Branson, head of the massive Virgin empire, discusses various misleading cell phone company tactics in his book *Business Stripped Bare*. While designing his popular prepaid service, Virgin Mobile, he realized that most cell phone companies were engaged in what he calls "confusion marketing." The real price of the phone is unduly cheap, but the real money is in hidden fees and oppressive contracts. The monthly price is obscured by still more fees (have you ever got the same cell phone bill twice?) and leaves consumers always paying either too little or too much. Consumers rarely understand what they are buying and end up suffering with shoddy service because they have no alternatives. Half of U.S. cell phone users say they don't use all their minutes every month, and 20 percent say they have never used all their minutes in any month, meaning they are all wasting money. Finally, the best customers—the ones who are most loyal and use the service most often—pay the highest prices. Exceed your thousand-minute-per-month plan? You'll pay forty or fifty cents per minute extra. No other business penalizes its best customers like that.

Meanwhile, the industry's watchdog, the Federal Communications Commission, is asleep at the switch. What happens if you file a formal complaint with the FCC about that final-month charge for leaving a cell phone company? You land in what the agency calls its "informal mediation" process. Here's a brief recap of an encounter with that kangaroo court I had in 2009. I closed my account and was forced to pay an extra half-month's service. The company refused to refund me, so I filed a complaint with the FCC. I got an acknowledgment of receipt but heard nothing for six weeks. When a response arrived, it actually came from Sprint, an email from an "analyst" in Sprint's Executive & Regulatory Services department. She asked me to repeat my complaint. I replied to her email explaining my situation and got this deflating response:

"If services are terminated before the end of the billing cycle, we do not prorate monthly service charges. . . . We regret that this may not have been explained to you; however, this information is provided in our Terms and Conditions of Service."

But that wasn't all. There was also this troubling conclusion:

"In addition, based on my research, your account is currently in an active status and was not terminated. If you would like to terminate your account, it will be necessary to speak with you directly."

Soon after, I received a new email from Sprint: a bill for $104! The customer service agent who insisted that I pay $48 to close my account had never closed my account.

The Sprint analyst and I swapped emails for the next two weeks. She said I had to speak directly to her on the phone to cancel my account, but I was busy working and missed her calls. Then she didn't answer mine, and she went on vacation for a week.

During this stretch, on February 11, Sprint replied to the FCC with a simple message and sent me a copy: "Please be advised that Sprint advertises and provides services in monthly increments. . . . The monthly charge is valid." The letter was signed by the analyst I'd been communicating with. It said she had tried to contact me on "three different occasions" but was "unsuccessful."

At this point, unlike in my first encounter with the FCC, the agency responded with incredibly efficient haste. Within two days, a follow-up letter was mailed to me.

As I opened it, I was hoping my government stood at the ready to fight for my rights. I hoped for a tough-as-nails reply. I was disappointed:

"The information in the company's response appears to address the issues raised in your complaint. Therefore, we are closing your case."

If you're wondering why cell phone service is so poor, and customer service even worse, that's why. Cell phone companies get to be judge and jury whenever a dispute arises.

BRANSON'S VIRGIN MOBILE was among the first to offer a cell phone alternative that more consumers should consider—prepaid, or pay-as-you-go service. These phones give consumers far more control over their bills. You buy minutes up front. You use them. When they're gone, the phone won't work anymore, until you buy more minutes.

The savings come from two directions: First, there's no overpaying for cell phone bill "insurance." You'll never pay for 1,400 minutes per month but only use 175. It's really a good deal for low-minute users.

Second, as we learned earlier, consumers always spend less when they pay as they go—rather than through some automated method. It's much easier to keep track of your calling habits, and to make better choices ("I'll wait thirty minutes and call after nine p.m. because I'm out of daytime minutes").

Plenty of folks could save a bundle by dumping their contracts and switching to prepaid. The average cell phone user pays $63 each month for service, yet nearly half of cell users spend less than two hundred minutes a month yakking on those phones. That means lots of people are overpaying. It's not hard to find prepaid services for $30 a month that provide two hundred minutes of talk time . . . with no contracts. You can buy a new phone, or switch providers, at any time. If you talk less than two hundred, or even three hundred, prime-time minutes per month, you should seriously consider a prepaid plan.

For years, the major cell carriers pushed their long-term-contract phones with ferocity and exclusivity. But since 2008, all the big mobile providers—Verizon, Sprint, T-Mobile, and AT&T—have come up with their own prepaid phone plans and marketing strategies. When Virgin Mobile and a host of smaller companies started offering really competitive prices—such as $50 a month for unlimited minutes, with no contract—the big providers had to follow suit.

As is customary, however, the beautiful simplicity of month-to-month phones is being disrupted by the complexity-loving,

Gotcha-creating sales teams at the big four. For example, Verizon has a great-sounding pay-as-you-go plan that charges consumers only 99 cents per day for a no-contract phone. Calls outside the Verizon network cost 10 cents per minute, though. For $1.99 per day, you can call anyone for free during nights and weekends, or for $2.99 per day, you can call anyone—really, anyone—for free. That's about $90 per month, however, which is a pretty standard price for unlimited calling plans. And don't forget: There's a $5-a-month charge for two hundred texts, a 99-cent-per-day fee for mobile Web access, and a $25 activation charge. And don't forget: Minutes you buy can expire in as little as thirty days.

Deciding between all these prepaid plans is at best a hassle, but at worst a new Gotcha minefield. As always, I favor simplicity over all else. Pick a plan that has a clear cost that you understand, and you'll be happy. There are some great tools on the Internet to help. My favorite is the PrePaid Cell Phone Plan Chooser, maintained by About .com. Users answer questions about their typical behavior, and the quiz spits out appropriate plans. Similar plan choosers can be found all over the Web. As an example, I imagined a light-use caller I know and told the About.com quiz that she makes only three to four calls per day, uses fifty-one to a hundred minutes per week, makes about half her calls at night and on weekends, and sends more than ten text messages per day. Here are some of the options the finder spat out to me. Plans change all the time, but this gives you a good idea of the savings you could be enjoying.

For sixty minutes per week:

Net10
Refill card: $30 at least every sixty days
Average monthly cost: $26.08

Virgin Mobile—Pay by Minute
Refill card: $20 at least every ninety days
Average monthly cost: $33.08

T-Mobile—T-Mobile To Go
Refill card: $50 at least every ninety days
Average monthly cost: $33.92

For eighty minutes per week:

Net10
Refill card: $30 at least every sixty days
Average monthly cost: $34.75

Virgin Mobile—Pay by Minute
Refill card: $20 at least every ninety days
Average monthly cost: $41.75

Verizon Wireless—EasyPay
Refill card: $50 at least every thirty days
Average monthly cost: $59.08

If you can't use your cell phone during work hours anyway, prepaid plans are a great option (are you listening, teachers?). Steer your calling to nights and weekends and you can get pretty solid service for around $30 a month and change phones at any time. That's why the smartest cell phone users I know use a prepaid service instead of a contract.

Don't Get Screwed by Your Cell Phone Company

- Never buy a phone with a new service before a vacation. Always put new phones through rigorous real-life tests right after you get them.
- Watch your bill for "upgrade" fees if you renew your contract. Call and ask that they be waived. Same with activation fees.
- If your firm provides them, get text-message alerts when you get dangerously close to an overage in calling minutes.
- Always know your contract termination date. That'll make it more fun to shop for a cell phone.

- Consider paying more up front for the handset to avoid a two-year contract.
- Know your company's early-termination-fee policy. Most fees are $150 to $200, but many providers now prorate the fees, so you'll only pay about half if you're halfway through the contract.
- Turn up the parenting restrictions when you give your kids a phone. Turn off premium text messaging, for example. Consider a limited-use phone for kids that only lets them call a few friends or shuts off after a certain number of minutes.
- Consider prepaid phones with no contract. They can be best for light phone users who call three hundred minutes or less each month. Terms on these phone vary wildly, however, so proceed with care.

6

Pay TV

After reading Bob's [Red Tape] article, I decided to take
the plunge. I got an antenna. . . . A week and some elbow
grease later I was walking into the Comcast office to drop
off my HD DVR. We're saving $80/month now and getting
90% of our favorite shows that we watched on Comcast,
but now they are completely free. . . . I hope to get cable
back someday after the cable and satellite companies are
brought to their knees and forced to do honest business to
stay afloat.

—ADAM, *from Monument, Colorado,
a Red Tape Chronicles reader*

Watching television is the ultimate passive activity. Soon
after the word *television* was invented, the term *couch
potato* was coined. Today, about four in five households pay for the
right to be couch potatoes, and we donate $53 billion to the cable
industry every year.

As I'm sure you've absorbed by now, being a passive consumer
makes you easy prey for the world of Gotcha Capitalists. That's why
pay TV is such a lucrative business. I don't care which company
you're talking about: DirecTV, Comcast cable, Verizon FiOS—they
all count on one thing. You sign up, you pay up, and you forget about
it. A great $29-per-month deal turns into a not-so-great $50-a-month

deal after a few months, then turns into a horrible $100-a-month deal a few months later. Suddenly, you realize you are spending 10 percent of your disposable income on television—even though you only watch six or seven of the three hundred channels piped into your home.

Their strategy is simple: Pay TV providers expect you to forget when your teaser-rate deal expires, and you're automatically put on the oppressive plan. After all, it's easy to lose track of the extra movie channels you pay for, or which channels come with which tiers of service. Channels change all the time, too. Before you know it, you are wildly overpaying to sit on the couch in your living room and watch the same five shows over and over. I'll bet you don't know how much your cable bill was last month, but if you are average, it was $98.75, at least in 2007. The price is up 77 percent since 1996, according to the Bureau of Labor Statistics, an increase that far outpaces the rate of inflation.

But I have excellent news for you. After years of monopoly-laden service and unfair treatment, change is coming. Where once you had only a single choice of ESPN or MSNBC, slowly but surely choice is arriving. Most Americans (at least those who don't live in apartments) now have at least two choices, thanks to the proliferation of small-dish satellite TV. Soon, many will have three choices or more, thanks to fiber-optic technology that's being pushed by Verizon. Endless studies have shown how quickly customer service improves, and how quickly rates go down, when competition appears. But even more choice is careening down the information superhighway as I write this.

Thousands of TV shows are now available for free on the Web, and the technology needed to watch online is getting cheaper and easier all the time. That's partly why cable companies started to see a grand exodus of customers, beginning in 2008. Time Warner, for example, lost 119,000 subscribers in its fourth quarter that year. It should be no surprise that TV providers are fit to be tied by their coaxial cable. Hey, you'd be scared, too, if you ran a business and someone suddenly started giving away the product you sell for free.

But as a consumer, you should feast on that fear. Finally, you have bargaining power, and I'm going to show you how to use it. First, we'll discuss lowering your current price for pay TV. Next, I'll show you how to shrink that bill to zero.

BARGAINING: JUST ASK!

Maybe you like throwing away money every month. Maybe you enjoy paying $1,200 every year for television. If you do, you should skip this section. But here's a question: When you pay $659 to sit in a cramped middle seat of an airplane and find out your seatmate paid $309, don't your nostrils flare? If you are paying $100 a month for television, I guarantee you have a neighbor paying half that. You should be angry. You should be so angry that you should grab your cable or satellite bill and find the billing department's phone number. Go ahead . . . why are you still reading?

Okay, now that you have the phone and the bill, don't dial just yet. First, check your pile of recent junk mail to see if you've received any ads from competitors. If not, go online and hit all their websites—DirecTV, EchoStar, Comcast, Cox, Verizon. Enter your zip code to make sure the firms offer service in your area and read through the offers. Find a package that closely matches your current programming package. Don't forget to include your current provider in this research. I know the ad will say, "New customers only," but ignore that.

Now that you know the real market price of pay TV, smoke might be coming out of your ears. But do one more thing before you call: Get yourself into the frame of mind that you are committed to switching providers if you don't get an answer you like. Pick a deal from an alternative company that you know will work for you and firmly install that in your head as plan B. This step is essential. Only by having a real option in your mind—and not merely a bluff—will you be guaranteed a successful exchange with a customer service operator.

I know changing cable or satellite providers sounds like a hassle. Getting a dish installed on the roof might seem prohibitive for some. Taking a day off to wait for the cable guy seems like a real headache. But remember that many firms make switching exceedingly easy, given the enormous incentive they have to do so. It's only after you sign up that you are neglected as a customer.

Many consumers don't have to actually change services to take advantage of competition. Often, the mere threat of defection is enough. By properly using the leverage you have, courtesy of competition, you'll be delighted by the results. Every American who pays for TV—all 85 percent of you—should take thirty minutes every six months and shove a competitor's ad in the face of your current provider. Here's what happened when personal-finance writer Jeffrey Strain used this formula:

> I don't know why people don't like to call the different companies that give them services to try and get a better price, but there are a lot of people out there. My mom is one of them. I wrote last September that we shaved my mom's cable bill from $65 to $39.95 a month last September. After doing so, I specifically told her that she needed to call back every 3 months to get a better rate, which she promptly failed to do. Even worse, she decided to upgrade her account to a silver level to get some of the premium movie channels and I found she was paying $79.20 a month for cable.
>
> That was ridiculous when there were other competing firms offering a free month and $29.95 a month after that for similar service. So I gave a call to the cable company today to see if we could get a better deal for her. I simply called like I always had done in the past and went directly to the cancel service option. I explained I had a better deal from one of their competitors (they asked which offer and I gave the company name and the offer), but really didn't want to go through all the hassle of changing if they could give me a similar deal. While they didn't match the deal, they did drop the rates significantly over what she had been paying.

They actually came back with a number of different options and I ended up taking the one that offered the exact same service (including the premium channels my mom likes) for $39.95 a month rather than the $79.20, which is good for 6 months—that's a nearly a 50% savings a month and a total savings of $235.50 over the 6 months of the offer. Certainly not bad for a 15 minute phone call.

For this "just ask" strategy to work, you must be willing to threaten to cancel your service . . . and be willing to follow through. Frontline operators for many pay TV companies do not have the authority to give you a discount on your current rate. But if you are transferred to the "cancellation department," i.e., the "customer retention department," you will be playing a new ball game. Operators in this part of the company have all sorts of magic powers to keep you as a customer. You may not get the rock-bottom teaser price in the end, but you'll almost certainly end up with a better price than what you currently pay. Sure, all this might take an hour of annoying phone calls. But remember, saving just $20 each month means you are saving $240 a year. Who among us could turn our nose up at a $240-an-hour job right now?

FREE TV

Now, what if you found out that the person sitting in the window seat on that expensive flight you were taking paid nothing? Nada. Zilch. You'd certainly ask a few questions about how he or she pulled that off, wouldn't you? This is the question that every television watcher should be asking right now. The real revolution hitting pay TV these days is the possible end of the word *pay*.

As they said in Washington, D.C., an awful lot during the 2008 presidential campaign, change is coming. Cable and satellite companies long resisted the notion of à la carte programming, which would allow consumers to pay for only the channels they watch (rather than packages of one hundred useless channels and five good ones). Now, entertainment providers are offering this service on their own, through the Internet. If you are a consumer who buys cable or satellite only for sporting events or Comedy Central programs such as *The Daily Show,* the Internet has a deal for you. Many shows can now be purchased directly from their maker, or on iTunes.com. Others are free, as long as you sit through some advertisements— usually far fewer than you'll watch on television you pay for. The website Hulu.com—part-owned by the corporate parents of NBC, ABC, and Fox—offers instant access to many popular shows, including *The Colbert Report, The Office, Heroes,* and thousands more. Subscribers to the popular movie-rental firm Netflix can view archives of thousands more shows on their computers instantly. The list of networks is impressive, including ABC, NBC, CBS, Fox, Discovery Channel, and many more. All the major sports leagues now have Internet pay plans or, at the least, highlight packages. Purchasing programs directly from the source, you'll save money and you won't feel that you're paying for things you don't want.

This news is incredibly important to the 30 percent of the U.S. population that lives in multifamily units, such as apartment buildings, where dishes are difficult if not impossible to install. So far, many of these consumers have had absolutely no choice in pay TV service. Until now.

Connecting a laptop computer to your flat-screen TV might seem like a bridge too far for some. Internet-delivered TV comes with a long list of caveats: No one wants to watch TV on a computer; it can be hard to find the show you want; some shows are only available after the initial viewing on "real" TV; sports fans have severely limited options; the quality isn't as good; it's really difficult to make Web TV work on multiple TVs around the house; and the kicker: "I don't want to trade in my remote control for a keyboard!"

All these things are true, but are becoming less true over time. Netflix, for example, now sells a $100 set-top box named Roku, which makes its service work just like traditional television, remote control included. Meanwhile, most flat-panel televisions now have easy connections for PC video. Just sit your laptop next to your TV and beam it there.

It's true, the signal is not as good as cable. But would you be willing to accept 80 percent of the quality for 20 percent of the price? That's what Internet-based TV is currently offering.

Afraid you'll miss out on the most popular programs? Don't be. In 2009, complete episodes of nine in ten prime-time network-television shows and roughly 20 percent of cable shows were available online. A small but fervent Internet movement was growing, led by websites such as CancelCable.com, that made it easier to cut the cord. CancelCable.com even offers a *TV Guide*–style listing called Showfinder of programs available for download or streaming.

But what about that $1,000 forty-two-inch flat-screen TV you just purchased? Isn't it a waste of good technology to watch shaky, pixelated TV shows on it? Not if you add one small piece of *really* sophisticated new technology—an antenna. The changeover to digital-television was a confusing hassle for many people, but it did come with a gift-wrapped present. The new free digital-television signals are fantastic. In most markets, there are now more channels, in much higher quality, than ever before. For about 90 percent of television watchers, only an old-fashioned antenna is needed to capture the latest digital channels from your local broadcasters. You might even get channels that are unavailable on your dish or cable service. Most TV watchers are stunned by what's available for free over-the-air, and how good it looks on an HDTV. In fact, videophiles claim that over-the-air HD is actually better than cable or satellite TV, because the pay providers must compress their signals for delivery. You probably won't notice the difference—except in the price.

I recommend that every consumer take a cable-free day about once every six months and explore free offerings over the air. Supplement those channels with Internet broadcasts and you will rack up some serious savings. CancelCable.com has a tool to show TV watchers how much they'll save for their industriousness. At $95 a month, assuming 5 percent annual interest earnings, those who cut the pay TV cord will save nearly $1,200 in one year, or almost $40,000 in twenty years. Or, as the site likes to say, paying for cable is the equivalent of buying a fifty-inch flat-panel television and throwing it in the trash every year.

I realize that laptop TV and rabbit ears aren't for everyone. But here's my point: Finally, you have a choice when it comes to pay TV, even if it doesn't seem so. Once you realize you do have options, you'll be a much better negotiator. No one should be paying more than $1,200 per year to watch television. And now you don't have to. You can stop being the passenger in the middle seat.

BEFORE WE LEAVE the subject of pay TV, here are a few other things to watch out for on that monthly bill, if you decide to keep it. With the advent of HDTV, a whole new set of fees are in play. Many consumers are paying an extra monthly fee for HD service and to rent set-top boxes. Only pay for boxes you need! If your TV is already HD-ready, you don't need to rent a converter box, for example. Some upgraded digital-cable networks might require a cable box anyway, but don't assume you need one. Ask. Don't expect the cable provider to tell you that you can live without it. If you sign up for service with the promise of free installation, watch your bill for several months to make sure installation charges don't creep onto there. And if you expect a huge refund or rebate as part of a sign-up package, make sure you understand the terms. Many rebates are cleverly disguised early-cancellation fees: You only receive them as service credits if you continue to pay for the service.

Finally, cable customers shouldn't forget that they can file complaints about service and billing problems with their local government's "cable franchising authority," a surprisingly effective way to get satisfaction. The phone number is on your bill. Satellite customers aren't so lucky and can only file complaints with the Federal Communications Commission.

Don't Get Screwed by Pay TV

- Call and ask for a lower rate every six to twelve months. Watch competitors' ads and ask that your provider match the price.
- If you switch providers, beware of long-term contracts with early-termination fees. They are a harbinger of unfair treatment to come.
- Investigate "free" options on the Internet.
- Take advantage of great new over-the-air digital signals. Old-fashioned antennas will actually get you newfangled, free TV.

7

Student Loans

Live like a student while you are in school so you don't
have to live like a student after you graduate.

—MARK KANTROWITZ,
student-loan expert, FinAid.org

tacey dreamed of teaching children. She followed that
dream by earning a master's degree at a great Northeast-
ern private school, Quinnipiac University, in Connecticut. Her
dream, however, has turned into a nightmare. In her words: "My education has ruined my life."

Quinnipiac isn't cheap—tuition is more than $30,000 per year—
and Stacey didn't qualify for federal help. On the advice of school
counselors, she used a mix of private loans to pay for school. "It will
be worth it," they told her. "You need an education to succeed."

On the surface, Stacey's counselors were right. She quickly
landed a decent-paying job at a good elementary school, making
$45,000 a year—$48,000 if she works during the summer. After
health-insurance copayments, state taxes, and other unavoidable
expenses, she goes home with $1,090 every two weeks.

Sallie Mae, her student-loan company, expects her to send $700
to them every month.

Even at that oppressive rate, it will be thirty years before she is
finished repaying the $98,000 she borrowed from the company.

Other loans gave her a grand total of $120,000 in loans, which had swelled to $150,000 by the time we talked.

"After I get paid and pay Sallie Mae, I have $740 left that has to last me two weeks. Consider that I haven't accounted for car insurance [$125 a month], rent, food, gas, electric, phone . . . and everyday life in general, I'm basically negative," she says. "I'm not even twenty-eight years old and I feel as though the chance to make a good living and good life for myself has passed me by. It's no longer an option. I'll never own a home, I'll never be financially comfortable, I'll never be able to retire. My financial life is effectively over and I've got no recourse."

Natalie's situation is a little bit better. She borrowed $75,000—evenly split between private and federal loans—to pay for a degree in environmental science at a top school in Ashland, Wisconsin, called Northland College. Her loans would have been larger, but she worked two and sometimes three jobs at school, knowing she wouldn't be making big bucks after graduation.

Her degree also paid off. She landed a $27,000-a-year job at a nonprofit, working in her chosen field—no small success. But there's hardly anything left over at the end of each month to pay her loans. She pays what she can. Her federal loans are temporarily in forbearance, so she can concentrate on paying her four separate private loans, some at 10 or 11 percent interest. She pays $200 to Wells Fargo and about $75 to American Education Services every month. In each case, she is paying the absolute minimum—the amount covers only interest. The principal on those student loans is exactly the same as when she left school.

"If I was making full payments on all my student loans, it would equal about six hundred to seven hundred dollars a month, which would be a third of what my take-home pay is," she said.

OUTSTANDING COLLEGE DEBT is a ticking time bomb for America. Total student debt is about half the amount of total credit card debt, but terms of repayment can be much more oppressive. There is virtually no way to discharge student debt, even in the case of serious illness or personal bankruptcy. Borrowers such as Stacey and Natalie, if they fall behind on payments, face the real prospect of garnished wages, income-tax-return seizure, even Social Security–check seizure later in life.

To many former students of high-priced colleges, Stacey's story will sound mild. She has a decent job and is managing to make her payments, for now. But the fragility of her situation is obvious. Annual 4 percent raises will do nothing to help her get ahead. Any mild misfortune—an illness, a layoff, a dispute with her superiors—could easily push her over the edge.

"At the time apparently I was young and naïve or simply didn't research enough about the effects of living with a large student loan, because now I am suffering," she says.

Thousands of tales like Stacey's are collected every year by the website StudentLoanJustice.org, which chronicles the plight of millions of former students and their trials of dealing with a life of unforgivable loans.

One in ten college students graduates with more than $35,000 in debt. Many leave school owing much more. The thousands who find their way to StudentLoanJustice often have complicated life stories. Some have unexpected children or illnesses; many took out ill-advised loans at high interest rates to pay for nontraditional schools. Some completely misunderstood their rights as borrowers, and the rights of lenders to exact high interest and fee penalties when they erred. The litany of their mistakes is heartbreaking, but many are avoidable. We'll discuss them here.

The first and most common mistake, however, is misunderstanding the value of a college education.

The cost of college is up about 450 percent since 1982—a rise that's double the increase of skyrocketing health-care costs and dwarfs both inflation and income growth. College costs at a four-year public school—the cheap kind—now take up 25 percent of a median middle-class family income, up from 18 percent just a decade ago. The numbers just don't add up. In many cases, the cost of a college education is far, far greater than the economic value of that education. Wages for college graduates haven't risen nearly enough to justify the rate of increase in college expenses; in fact, inflation-adjusted wages are essentially flat since 1990.

The biggest hidden fee of all is buying into the mythology that a pricey degree is essential to life success.

This is not an argument against education. It's an argument for economically rational decisions about education. The seduction of impressive-sounding schools or exciting athletic programs has, for too long, blinded people to the truth about school.

FinAid.org is the world's leading source of student-loan and educational-finance information. The man who runs the site, Mark Kantrowitz, is a former college financial-aid officer and probably the nation's leading expert on student aid. His rule of thumb is simple: Don't borrow more for all college expenses than you can honestly expect to earn in your first year of employment.

Here's an example: A handy calculator on the FinAid site estimates that a young worker with a $400-a-month loan payment needs to earn about $48,000 a year to comfortably afford that payment.

A student such as Natalie, who borrowed $75,000, would end up with a $572-a-month payment under the best of circumstances, assuming a low 6.8 percent interest rate and a generous twenty-year repayment schedule. To afford those payments, Natalie should earn $68,000 per year, FinAid estimates—roughly 2.5 times her current salary. No amount of graduated payments or deferments can compensate for a gap like that. She'll either have to leave her profession for a higher-paying industry or find some other source of income.

My review of thousands of complaints from former students like Natalie and Stacey reveals a pattern of mistakes. Among the most common: trusting the math provided by school counselors and private lending firms. Many graduates say they were told their loan payments would be "around three hundred dollars a month," when they are ultimately closer to $500 or $600.

In many cases, this is not fraud, but excessive optimism. Those calculations didn't include interest that accrues during four years of school, or during forbearance periods, a process known as capitalization. For example, consider a single $10,000 loan taken out at the beginning of a student's freshman year with an interest rate of 8 percent. Interest capitalization on the loan adds more than $3,700 to the size of the loan by the time the student graduates—it would be $13,727 after forty-eight months—and that's on graduation day.

The mathematics of student loans and the punishing power of capitalized interest are oppressive, so here is a rule of thumb. For every $1 a student borrows during freshman year, that student owes $1.40 by senior year. Ten years later, each $1 costs more like $3. Throw in a few financial accidents such as late payments or deferments, and the costs can easily climb toward $5 for each $1 borrowed.

So it's very important to do your own math and know exactly what your monthly obligation will be at graduation and beyond, and to relate that to a realistic assessment of earning potential. The calculation should include all four years of expenses and should also include estimates of yearly tuition increases, to provide a realistic financial picture. Many colleges cost 20 percent more by the time senior year rolls around.

Fair-minded colleges and lenders would provide tables akin to mortgage amortization schedules to students, so they would know how long their monthly payments would last and what the full price of their education would be. The $120,000 that Stacey borrowed would ultimately cost her $280,000 at about $780 per month for thirty years, assuming a low 6.8 percent rate. Paying that loan would require nearly a $100,000-per-year salary.

But students usually pay for college one year at a time, with a patchwork of loans that feel as if the parts are less than the total. One relatively affordable $15,000 loan to pay for freshman year can easily turn into four or five loans that total closer to $75,000 by graduation day.

Borrowing piecemeal also makes record-keeping harder, which exacerbates an already bad arrangement that has teenagers taking out loans that are essentially the size of small mortgages. Another com-

mon complaint to StudentLoanJustice is confusion over the total outstanding debt, and in some cases disagreement over what's been paid,
and which interest rate is applied to which loan. With help from parents and counselors, students should keep detailed records of every
loan balance and payment terms before and after graduation.

Other common complaints involve pricey nontraditional schools,
such as technical colleges or cooking schools, that offer too rosy predictions about postgraduation job placement and salaries. Technical
training is a great resource, but would-be students should know that
the rise of the private, for-profit student-lending industry has neatly
paralleled the rise of for-profit training schools. Such schools are
often not worth the deep debt their students must live with.

Inexpensive community colleges often offer similar programs and
far cheaper prices. Many students find they learn just as much from
a two-year school as they would have during their first two years at a
big-name college. Transferring to the high-reputation school for the
final two years can literally give a student a college degree at half-
price. The savings can be a lifesaver. Turning a $700-per-month loan
payment into a $350-per-month loan payment can be the difference
between surviving and declaring personal bankruptcy before a thirtieth birthday party; and the difference between following a dream
and taking a high-paying sales job just to survive.

In short, Kantrowitz often reminds collegians that they should live
by this simple rule:

"Live like a student while you are in school so you don't have to
live like a student after you graduate."

Here are a few other booby traps to avoid, designed with help
from StudentLoanJustice's Alan Collinge.

BEFORE LEAVING SCHOOL

Barter with the school's financial-aid department. Loans are not
the same as grants; far from it. Many students never consider asking
for more aid after they receive their initial package, but it's entirely

possible. Turning even $5,000 worth of loans into $5,000 worth of grants will ultimately save a borrower more than $10,000 during a twenty-year loan.

Use federally guaranteed loans first. The private student-loan business is a sea full of sharks. Avoid private loans. Private, adjustable-rate loans can end up tagged with credit-card-like interest rates. While federal loans are no picnic, their rate is fixed by federal law. For the neediest of families, interest on federal loans is suspended until graduation.

Know where your debt is. Because financial institutions such as banks can offer both private and federal loans, many young people end up confused about precisely what loan they have. Collinge says that only two out of ten students know where their loans are coming from.

Shop around. Don't assume that the university is looking out for your financial interests. Many schools have financial relationships with lenders and may even hint that you must deal with their preferred lenders. That's illegal. Always get bids from at least three lenders when pricing out student loans.

Don't use cosigners. Many private lenders advertise attractive teaser loans of 7 or 8 percent, but the small print indicates cosigners are required. That means you're essentially borrowing on your parents' (or other relative's) credit score. But cosigning opens the door for a whole host of potential problems within the family down the road.

Nickels and dimes are expensive. Many banks offer valuable discounts, such as a half percent off the interest rate for those who pay through automatic payment or who demonstrate reliable payment histories. These are great, but often come with severe limitations. One late payment can cause the student to lose the discount for years, or forever. Check the penalties *before* taking the loan. Ditto for late-payment fees, which can be severe and are often hard to compare. Sallie Mae late fees can range from 4 to 10 percent of the outstanding monthly payment, and that amount is added to the principal, meaning the fees accrue interest. Go with lenders that don't charge high late fees.

AFTER SCHOOL

Carefully research your options for combining multiple loans. Most students end school with a smattering of loans at different rates. Loan consolidations are often a good idea; having one bill makes it easier to pay on time, and easier to keep track of precisely what's owed. Generally, consolidations can result in lower overall interest rates, too. But students must choose their lender carefully. As mentioned above, a good interest rate can turn bad very quickly with a lender who has oppressive fees and penalties. Know the penalties—and the reputation—of the bank before giving all your loans to one institution. Also, different types of loans cannot be mixed in a consolidation. A federal student loan and a private loan can't be consolidated together; a parent PLUS loan and a student loan can't be consolidated.

Keep careful watch of your monthly statements. Many StudentLoanJustice users report payments not being credited in a timely manner, unfair tiering of multiple late fees, additional payments not being credited toward the loan principal, and other game-playing with loan payments.

Consider joining the Income Based Repayment plan. Beginning in 2009, a new federal law called the College Cost Reduction and Access Act gives graduates the option to enroll in a new program and cap their federal loan payments at 15 percent of their discretionary income (salary, minus 150 percent of the federal poverty line). After twenty-five years of paying 15 percent, any remaining balance on the loan is forgiven. It's a good program for those who graduate and want to work in a high-reward, low-pay field such as social work.

Work for the government. Not enough students find their way into loan-forgiveness or loan-deferment programs by working at government jobs, or teaching in at-risk schools. Many of these programs are very generous. Students who feel the weight of their debt crashing in upon them during junior and senior year should take a good, hard look at such programs. Multiple options exist for teachers who work in poor areas, for graduates who work in the Peace Corps or AmeriCorps, and for federal employees at many agencies, such as the National Institutes of Health. Most of these programs, however, apply only to federal loans—not private loans. FinAid.org offers a long list of options at its website, http://www.finaid.org/loans/forgiveness.phtml.

Do not let your loan be placed into default by the lender. Lenders have a perverse financial incentive to place loans into default. Once default is declared, they have access to a long list of onerous methods for recouping their money from you, potentially including wage garnishment of up to 15 percent of your paycheck. If you apply for a forbearance or deferment, send it certified mail, and don't without confirmation just assume that the lender received it, warns Collinge. And don't assume the deferment was granted.

Work with the Department of Education. If you do default on your federal loans, contact the loan guarantor and insist that it transfer your loans directly to the Department of Education (the true guarantor of federal student loans). Other "guarantors" are nothing but extremely expensive collection entities that survive on the penalties, fees, and collection costs put onto defaulted debt. Also, do not agree to "rehabilitate" a loan after a default. This is really nothing more than a clever ploy by the industry to legitimize the massive fees and penalties attached to the debt in the form of a newer, much larger loan after the default. In some cases, borrowers who begin repayment plans say they have been assessed thousands of dollars in "collection fees," which are added to the principal payments.

For common problems with loans after graduation, you can seek answers at the Department of Education's website. For more complicated subjects, such as hardship loan-deferments, borrowers can directly contact the department's ombudsman. That's much better than working with a collection agency.

8

Insurance

Our car and home insurance has increased dramatically in the last two years, in conjunction with our credit scores dropping. We have not had claims, tickets, etc. We are good drivers and I cannot remember the last time we had claims on any of our policies. The insurance company advised that they base premiums, at least partially, on credit score. What does that have to do with my insurance, either car or home? I think, especially with the increasing number of "normal folks" having economic problems and credit score problems, that they have found a new way to get away with increasing premiums on good people.

—DAVE LAUFFER,
Red Tape Chronicles reader

Everyone hates insurance. You hate talking about it. You hate shopping for it. Most of all, you hate paying for it. Until you need it. Then . . . well, you might still hate your insurance company, depending on how it handles your claim, and how much it punishes you later. But in the moment, you'll be glad there was a safety net in place when you took that fall.

The average American consumer spends about $4,000 each year collectively on auto, life, home, and health insurance. Yet most of the time, buying insurance feels like you're getting nothing for something. For example, only about one in fourteen drivers make a claim on their comprehensive insurance every year. That means you could easily pay $10,000 in auto premiums from age twenty-five to age thirty-five and feel as if you've got absolutely nothing for that money.

But when your day comes, you will likely be glad you paid up. The average comprehensive-claim payment is about $4,000. Those $65-a-month payments will sound like a bargain when that $4,000 bill gets paid. Of course, if you elected to pay $55 a month and picked a high $1,000 deductible, you will probably kick yourself when you walk away with $3,000 instead.

If all this sounds a bit like gambling, well, it is. No one can predict the future, and few people are good at even having hunches about the future. Yet you pick your premiums for auto insurance, life insurance, and homeowner's insurance based on some vague notion of the likelihood that you'll need it someday.

Naturally, insurance companies are much better at these predictions than you could ever be. They have years and years of data for comparison, they have big computers that crunch the numbers, and they have salespeople who are good at scaring you with visions of disaster.

All these factors make buying insurance one of the most mystifying choices a consumer has to make. As a result, most consumers are either overpaying or underinsured.

So I'm going to simplify insurance purchasing for you. Here are two things you need to remember, no matter what kind of insurance you're talking about:

1. Insurance isn't really a product you buy. It's a concept.
2. Insurance is about preventing an unexpected catastrophe. It's a safety net for large disasters, not small ones.

Knowing these two things can save you a lot of money when shopping for insurance. It will also simplify your choices when the confusing sales pitches come. Now, let's work through these two points.

NO. 1: INSURANCE, THE CONCEPT, NOT THE PRODUCT

It's often said that insurance was born thousands of years ago, invented by Chinese merchants who would plan for potential shipping disasters by instructing captains to distribute the merchants' goods among numerous ships. That protected a merchant from being ruined if a single vessel was shipwrecked. The odds that all shipments from a single merchant would fall to ruin were extremely low.

By adding slightly to their costs, and sharing risk, merchants dramatically decreased their odds of complete disaster.

Another subtle aspect of the tale, however, is the social contract. Insurance embodies a notion that society is better off absorbing the risks and consequences of catastrophes, rather than allowing individual victims to be devastated by them. In China, when there was a shipwreck, each merchant suffered a manageable loss, rather than allowing the ruin of one.

This is generally referred to as the pooling of risk. Modernizing the idea is easy. Nearly every homeowner purchases homeowner's insurance for a few dollars per day. A tiny percentage each year have a tree fall on their house. When they do, the insurance company builds them a new house . . . paid for, essentially, by everyone else.

It might sound socialistic to you, but it plays an important role in capitalism, too. Anytime you reduce someone's risk, you encourage the person to invest. Merchants might quit the shipping business if one storm could end their career. With that risk minimized, more merchants are emboldened to join the business.

So insurance—the pooling of risk—is an important concept that evolved simultaneously with the evolution of societies and markets. The Code of Hammurabi, the first known codification of law, actually includes provisions for insurance.

In the United States, government agencies often mandate insurance. In most states, it's illegal to drive without insurance, for example. Certain levels of insurance are even prescribed. Yet, insurance is bought and sold by for-profit companies in a kind of pseudo–free market. Obviously, the market isn't free if consumers have no choice. Imagine how easy it would be for insurance companies to conspire with one another to keep prices artificially high.

To prevent this kind of abuse, the insurance industry is subject to heavier regulation than other industries. State insurance regulators try to keep up with insurance firms and make sure they don't gouge customers. As a very general rule, insurance companies pay out 80 cents in claims for every $1 of premiums they collect. After costs for marketing and overhead, the difference is their profits—which are enhanced by the investment income the insurance firm makes during the year on the "float," money held after collecting premiums and before paying out claims. If an insurance company is too profitable— meaning it's paying out much less in claims than it's taking in with premiums—regulators may step in and demand a price change.

Now, see how far we've traveled from a normal for-profit industry?

INSURANCE COMPANIES DO well when they attract a lot of customers. The larger the pool, the easier they can absorb losses by individuals. They do even better when they attract the "right" kind of customers—good drivers, healthy people, homes in areas not prone to natural disasters. They constantly work to separate out good customers from bad.

One method for skimming off the cream is price. Higher-risk consumers are charged more. Smokers, risky drivers, people who live in floodplains, all pay more. That way, they are either discouraged from signing up or pay so much that they are ultimately profitable. How much more? How are those calculations made, and how can you get on the right side of the equation? That's the question the rest of this chapter is about.

One factor that makes buying insurance maddening is that insurance firms use complicated formulas to determine the price of their products. These formulas are a carefully guarded secret, and you'll never know what they are. Oh, your agent might throw some terms at you such as *collision* and *comprehensive*. You might hear that rates go down when you turn twenty-five, or when you get married. But basically, you will never know the reason why you pay the price you pay for insurance.

That means you have only one way of knowing if you are overpaying for insurance: quotes. You have to comparison shop. You've got to bid out your insurance costs every year. You must do this even if your rates don't go up, because some competitor might have a new discount formula you don't know about. Your credit score might improve, for example, and at some companies that might mean lower rates. Or you might have reached an age that puts you into a new "bucket" of safer drivers. But you'll never know unless you try. More than for other kinds of purchases, you must regularly pit companies against one another to find out what's a fair price. Remember, you are buying a concept rather than a product—you are buying a little piece of risk protection. The only way to get a fair price while dealing with the concept of insurance is to be a pesky guppy in the pool of risk.

NO. 2: CATASTROPHE VS. CONVENIENCE

Insurance is there to prevent you from losing everything in one unlucky event. It is not there to make your life perfect, or to make you 100 percent whole after a disaster. It's there to prevent a complete catastrophe. So principle number two is this: Always buy high-deductible insurance.

If your car is stolen, you'll be glad you paid for comprehensive insurance. It will help you get the $15,000 you need to plunk down for a new car and help you keep your life in order.

But you shouldn't see insurance as a tool for making everything perfect and risk-free. If someone steals a $300 GPS from your car, you should just chalk it up to experience and know to park your car somewhere else. You shouldn't expect someone else to pay for that. The biggest mistake insurance consumers make is overpaying for "make everything perfect again" insurance with low, low deductibles.

You should always buy auto insurance with a $1,000 deductible, and you should be ready to pay the first $1,000 to recover from a theft or fender bender. Raising a deductible from $200 to $1,000 will save about 40 percent on the cost of comprehensive insurance—roughly $100 a year for the average driver.

But how will you pay that $1,000 should something happen? You'll think big. You will self-insure, the way all the big companies do. That means they are big enough to set aside money to cover unexpected disasters and don't need to pay for insurance. Of course, you can't do that. But you can self-insure against your deductible.

You'll put $1,000 into a special account (or set aside $1,000 in your normal savings) that will act as your "deductible" across all your various insurance products. You'll build this kitty with the money you save by not overpaying for a low deductible. Then once every ten years when you have an insurance claim, you will use your own money to pay the high deductible. In the meantime you will have:

- Earned interest on that $1,000 during those ten years (better you than the insurance company).
- Saved yourself an additional $1,000 in insurance payments.
- Avoided making small-time claims with your insurer that could negatively impact your rates and led to a paperwork hassle.

WHEN YOU NEED IT

So far, we've talked about the expense of monthly premiums, but that's only one element of buying insurance. At some point, you will actually need it. Images of Hurricane Katrina victims screaming near their ruined homes should give you pause about the claims process. Sometimes, it's refreshingly easy. Sometimes, it's a nightmare. The distance between these two things can merely be bad luck, but it's important to consider a firm's claims record when buying insurance. Because most claims adjusters are local, and other elements of the claims process are local, service can vary from company to company and area to area, so it's always worth talking to friends who've made claims. Naturally, anecdotal information is of limited use. But there is a little-used government database that contains detailed information on insurance-industry complaints and breaks them down in a way that makes it easy to compare one company to another—called a complaint ratio. It's a calculation based on complaints per $1 million in policies, which allows apples-to-apples comparisons of large and small firms. Not all states maintain complaint-ratio data, but about half do. You should never purchase insurance from a company without visiting your state insurance commissioner's website and looking up the company's complaint ratio to see how it compares to competitors.

Now, on to the individual types of insurance, and how you can start to shrink that annual $4,000 expense.

AUTO INSURANCE

Automobile insurance is the most familiar insurance product for many consumers, and as a result it's the most competitive. Prices have remained relatively flat for about a decade—the average auto bill in 1998 was $703, while in 2006 it was $817, a rise that's roughly in line with inflation. What wonders competition can do!

Still, many consumers overpay for insurance because they don't have a great grasp of what they're buying. Some consumers pay extra because their credit score is less than perfect, for example. No one knows what this credit-score penalty might be because insurers do not reveal this information, and each company prices credit scores differently. But you can find out if you are being overcharged in general by comparison shopping.

When getting multiple quotes, it's important to lobby for maximum discounts. Many firms give discounts for multiple family members, low annual mileage, good driving records, good grades, loyalty, and so on. Any competent agent or website should ensure you get them, but always double-check. Ask for such discounts by name, or don't be afraid to ask the simple question: "Are there other discounts I qualify for?"

Naturally, auto insurance firms are constantly questing after more data to accurately asses the potential risk of drivers. One newfangled —and unnerving—way they do it is to track driving habits. Progressive, for example, will offer drivers the chance to install computer chips inside their cars that calculate how far consumers drive, how frequently they stop and start abruptly, and what time of day they log miles. The chip also includes a cell phone, and it "phones home" once each day to tell Progressive how its customers are doing. Then, it adjusts premiums accordingly.

Progressive does not track car-location information, but technology to do so is readily available, and certainly some auto insurance firm will soon try that.

Low-mileage drivers might see discounts, and some consumers enjoy knowing they are getting a break for driving mostly during safe daylight hours. But others feel this level of tracking is spooky. You'll have to decide for yourself if you believe the savings are worth the loss of privacy.

ESSENTIALLY EVERY STATE requires drivers to carry automobile insurance. Most drivers must consider two major things, then a host of minor things. We'll start with liability, where many consumers are underinsured, then look at theft and fire coverage, where most overpay.

Liability Insurance

This is the basic form of auto insurance that covers people you might hurt (including you) or damage you might cause while driving. Each state sets minimum standards. These are easy to find on the Web, or at your state's insurance commission's office. These are not to be confused with minimum insurance requirements recommended by your insurance company. In many cases, it is a good idea to buy more liability insurance than your state requires, but it is often not a good idea to purchase the minimum recommended by an insurance agent. When getting price quotes, always ask for the state minimum, then make a judgment about the value of buying additional coverage.

You will often see liability insurance expressed as a series of three numbers, such as 25/50/10. That indicates $25,000 in coverage for a single person's injury in an accident, $50,000 in coverage for all people who might be hurt, and $10,000 coverage for any damage.

Note that who gets paid by your insurance company after an accident varies based on whether your state is a "tort" state or a "no-fault" state. In tort states, the responsible party's insurance firm pays. In no-fault states, your insurance will pay you no matter whose fault the accident is. So if you skimp on coverage, you might actually be skimping on your own compensation.

How does an average driver decide if it's a good idea to buy more than state-required minimums? Much of it has to do with net worth and how appetizing a target you may be for a lawsuit. If you have a lot of money, you probably know that a victim in a car accident might sue you to get some of it. *Consumer Reports* recommends that consumers with decent-size bank accounts consider 100/300/100 coverage. But if you don't have that kind of money, you don't really need that kind of coverage.

Comprehensive and Collision

Hopefully, these are the only two kinds of insurance you will ever really use. A great deal of confusion surrounds them and a great deal of overpaying goes on. In short, collision pays for repair/replacement of your car after an accident. Comprehensive pays for repair/replacement in the event of a host of other disasters, such as fire and theft. These cover the vast majority of auto-damage incidents; liability coverage generally kicks in only with major accidents that cause serious injury.

Many people pay for this coverage when they don't need it; most pay too much for it.

According to the National Association of Insurance Commissioners, 77 percent of drivers bought comprehensive in 2006, and 72 percent bought collision. The decisions they make show little appreciation for a correct balance of risks and rewards. Collision and comprehensive generally make up 30 to 40 percent of a policy's price. It's money that's often wasted.

Consider, for example, this typical scenario: You buy a three-year-old compact car for $11,000, and you purchase collision and comprehensive coverage with a conservative and costly $200 deductible. Your "cadillac" insurance costs $1,300 per year. Five years pass. The eight-year-old car now has a book value of $2,300 and a real replacement value of $1,650. You never change your policy. You are now paying $1,300 per year for coverage that would gain you, at best, a check for about $1,450 should the car be damaged or stolen. That's bad math. Dropping the collision and comprehensive on this car would drop the annual premiums to about $750.

Many, many drivers could drop collision and comprehensive coverage today. Instead, maintain a savings account that matches your car's replacement value. You could apply this simple formula: As soon as you wouldn't spend a few thousand dollars on a major repair for your car and would instead simply buy a new car if such a bill arrived, drop your collision and comprehensive. Or, if you'd like a more complicated formula, drop collision and comprehensive when your annual premiums for those coverages multiplied by ten exceed the replacement value of the car. In other words, if you are paying $400 a year for collision and comprehensive, drop the coverage when the car is no longer worth at least $4,000. That'll put you on the right side of the insurance equation.

When making this calculation, don't let an exaggerated notion of the value of your car get in the way of levelheaded economics. Remember the endowment effect in the introduction? People tend to exaggerate the value of things they already own. You might think your clunker is worth $3,000, but you probably wouldn't get $3,000 from the insurance company if it were totaled in an accident.

So each year, when rebidding your auto insurance, look up the real value of your car on a site such as Edmunds.com or Kelley Blue Book.

If you're still too timid to drop these supplemental coverages, at least consider changing to a high deductible, something we've already addressed in this chapter; moving from a $200 deductible to a $1,000 deductible can save you up to 40 percent on collision or comprehensive. If you don't, you'll be throwing away money.

Other Notes

Many auto insurance companies now load up policies with other unnecessary expenses, such as roadside assistance or rental reimbursement. These luxuries aren't necessary and can confuse the purchase. Unless your firm gives you a great deal on roadside assistance—so good you can drop your Triple-A membership, for example—just skip it.

One other note: When buying a new car, it really is worth making a quick call to your insurance company to ask about the impact it will have on your premiums. The cost to insure one car over another can vary wildly; the difference can easily erase any "good deal" you may have received from the car dealer. In fact, a high cost to insure may be the reason you're getting that good deal. You don't want to be the last to know. Always ask before you buy and avoid any big surprises.

Finally, it's nice to know your insurance company will be efficient, fair, and helpful the day you really need it. After checking complaint ratios at your state insurance commissioner's office, ask your auto mechanic or a nearby body shop for general impressions. Do their customers complain about the insurance claims process? Does anyone have nice things to say about their insurance company? Those kinds of anecdotes, while not foolproof, can offer the best insight into the value of an insurance company. Price shouldn't be the *only* factor when you pick.

HOMEOWNER'S INSURANCE

Consumers shop around even less for homeowner's insurance than auto insurance, though their annual costs are roughly the same. The average homeowner's premium is about $800 per year. Home claims are slightly more rare than automobile claims—each year about 6 percent of homeowners file a claim.

For most homeowners, getting insurance is simply part of getting a mortgage, because all banks require homeowners to have insurance. This protects their investment in the property; in effect, you are buying insurance for the bank as much as for yourself. Many consumers even allow the banks to pay their premiums for them, sending in monthly chunks as part of a normal mortgage payment. Once the mortgage payments start, homeowners rarely give their insurance another thought, until they move, refinance, or file a claim.

Big mistake.

Homeowner policy prices can vary as much as those of auto policies. When you do your annual "bidding," get a quote for home insurance, too. Just as with auto insurance, a host of surprising factors can impact your home insurance rates, factors you aren't privy to. Your credit score will impact it, for example. So will the history of insurance claims in your neighborhood, and at your property. Even claims made years before you purchase a home can impact your rates, meaning you could be paying a much higher price than your next-door neighbor. That's why it's essential when considering a home purchase to get a quote before you head to the closing table. Surprisingly high rates—perhaps because a tree fell on the home seven years earlier—could make an affordable monthly payment unaffordable. You should also check a database of claims made against the property that's maintained by data-collection firm ChoicePoint Inc. The database is called CLUE (Comprehensive Loss Underwriting Exchange), and what you'll get is like a credit report for the building. Every year, when you get your home insurance quote, get a CLUE report, too—they're free. That way you'll ensure there aren't any errors factoring into your rate, just as you want to be sure there are no errors in your credit report that hurt your credit score.

Buyers can lower their premiums using some of the methods described for auto insurance. Remember, you have insurance so you can rebuild your home in case it burns down, not to fix the damage when your neighbor's kid hits a home run over the hedges and into your window. You want to keep your CLUE report clean. Raise your deductibles, then set aside that money and fix the ticky-tacky problems yourself. Generally, you'll also save money if you have auto and home insurance with the same company, but don't let that keep you from checking for cheaper prices at other companies every year.

Also, when deciding how much insurance you need in case of disaster, don't confuse the price you paid for the house with the cost to rebuild. It could be much lower—you'll only be rebuilding the structure, the property will remain after a fire. Or it could be higher if you've lived there a long time and construction costs have soared.

Lots of factors go into pricing your home's risk of fire or theft. Security systems, location of the nearest fire hydrant and fire station, even the employment status of the occupants, can all figure in (for example, retired couples, who are home more often, are less likely victims of theft). It's important to keep your insurance company updated on any changes that might impact your insurance formula. If a fire station opens nearby or you install a sprinkler system or you retire, call and ask for a discount. While you're at it, ask if there's anything else you can do to lower your premiums.

Finally, weather disasters such as Hurricane Katrina have been a sober reminder that flood damage is not covered by homeowner's insurance. That seems crazy, given that 90 percent of all natural disasters in the United States involve flooding. But remember, insurance is a concept, not a product. Flood damage is so severe and costly—but at the same time, so geographically targeted—that property owners in most of the country don't want to be part of a pool that pays for flood damage. Flood insurance is available to anyone, but those who live in flood-prone areas, as defined by government maps, are generally required to buy into a separate insurance pool from the

National Flood Insurance Program. After a hurricane or other weather-based disaster, homeowners without flood insurance can spend years trying to squeeze money out of their insurance company—often claiming that wind, not water, was the cause of the damage. They usually lose. It's a fight you'd be better off avoiding.

A quick note about condo/renter's insurance. Both are relatively inexpensive investments. Rental insurance, which can cost as little as $15 per month for small apartments, can generally be added as a "rider" to automobile insurance policies. Go with a high-deductible plan that you would invoke only if someone stole all your belongings. Condo insurance costs a little more because you might have to pay to rebuild the inside of your unit if a fire struck. While the condo association holds insurance on the structure as a whole, you would be responsible for replacing your inner walls, floors, and ceiling. Make sure to purchase only the amount you'd have to spend to rebuild the inside of your condo. Insurance companies notoriously overestimate this amount. You can ask your building inspector on inspection day for a rough estimate of rebuilding costs. Of course, you should try to keep that estimate current—if construction costs soar, you might have to bump up your coverage.

LIFE INSURANCE

Insurance, you'll remember, is a concept and a safety net. It is not a convenience. And it most certainly is not an investment vehicle.

But many well-intentioned parents get caught up in fanciful sales pitches from commission-hungry insurance salespeople and turn a very simple purchase of life insurance into a very complicated investment/insurance proposition. As with any complicated financial tool, a small set of experts who want to play numbers games are welcome to do so. But complex life-insurance/annuity/investment tax-shelter accounts should be left to them. You, responsible parent, simply need to pay a little each month to make sure your spouse and children are cared for in case the unthinkable happens. For most people, that means buying term insurance, which covers the untimely death of the main wage-earner during the critical years of child rearing. Later on, you need considerably less to make sure your spouse is cared for in old age. As your investment savings rise, Social Security kicks in, and your obligations fall, you can eventually stop paying for life insurance altogether.

The good news is that life insurance rates overall are plummeting. Premiums dropped 50 percent from 1994 to 2007 according to the Insurance Information Institute, thanks to better risk-assessment formulas and, naturally, competition.

The main trick to purchasing life insurance is deciding on the death benefit. The key question is, how much money would your family need to survive without you? That's a very personal question. There are a number of online calculators designed to help you find the answer. For example, you might consider the cost of a four-year education at a private college for each child, along with the cost of replacing your annual earnings. This is sometimes called a capital-needs analysis. Among the better tools is the LifeHappens.org tool at http://lifehappens.org/life-insurance/life-calculator.

A more common rule of thumb, which is good for a back-of-the-envelope estimate, is to use simple multiples of annual income. A thirty-five-year-old head of household should have a benefit equal to twenty times his or her annual income. That means a $100,000-a-year earner should have $2 million in coverage. The younger the earner, the greater the multiple, like this:

Age	Life Insurance Coverage
25	25 times annual income
35	20 times annual income
45	15 times annual income
55	10 times annual income

The most common mistake people make when conducting a capital-needs analysis is ignoring other sources of income available to the surviving spouse, such as Social Security benefits, when making the calculation.

When pricing life insurance, it's a good idea to set a few different levels—$1 million, $1.5 million, $2.5 million—and price each one to get a good idea of the cost of the death benefit.

Even simple term policies come with a few complexities, however. Among the things you'll need to consider are the term of the policy; the death benefit (sometimes called the face amount); should the benefit remain constant or slowly decline; and monthly premiums, which can also remain level or increase.

The best way to make sure you aren't overpaying for life insurance is to shop around, which has never been easier, thanks to the Internet. Websites that offer multiple quotes abound. After your initial purchase, it does pay to occasionally rebid your business, but be careful. Life insurance is not like auto insurance or homeowner's insurance. The price can go up as you age or your health changes, meaning there could be financial punishment for switching providers.

Another great way to cut life insurance costs: Be healthy. Smokers get killed on life insurance premiums. Other at-risk groups, such as those with high cholesterol or high blood pressure, also pay more. So do workers in risky professions, such as firefighters.

When shopping for term insurance, be sure to ask about convertibility and renewability. When policies expire, it's an advantage to have an option to renew the policy for another ten or twenty years without having to submit to a physical; or to be able to convert it to permanent life (explained ahead).

Insurers will often give discounts to customers who submit to a physical. But if you don't get one, don't think that you can hide your bad habits. Buying health insurance means giving your supplier access to something called the Medical Information Bureau, kind of like a credit report for health issues. It's a clearinghouse of information on consumers who have applied for life insurance with participating companies in the last seven years. In your application, the insurer generally receives permission to obtain information from your doctors.

Finally, don't overlook the obvious. Many employers offer free or discounted life insurance as a perk. Term life insurance you buy should only fill in the gaps.

Because life insurance can be a complex product, and because of so much misbehavior by those who sell it, many states offer strong consumer-protection laws, including "free look" periods—similar to regret laws covering health club memberships. In many states, insurance-policy purchasers have ten days to reconsider their purchase and return the policy for a full refund. That's good, because as you'll see, once you get into the realm of combo insurance/investing products, you're in a dragon's lair.

Other Kinds of Life Insurance

As I've mentioned, life insurance agents have slowly evolved their product far beyond the simple safety net that is was designed to be. In most cases, these products are not appropriate for average consumers. But in the interests of completeness, here's a quick summary of other life/investment insurance products available for purchase.

Return-of-premium life insurance (ROP term). Provides both a death benefit and a refund of premiums if the benefit isn't used. It's aimed right at one of the greatest objections to term-life plans: "I am probably not going to die, and my money will have been wasted." These policies cost more than normal term, of course, and most consumers would be better off buying term and saving the difference themselves in an investment account.

Permanent. A life insurance policy that's in place until the benefit is paid. Permanent insurance also builds a cash value that the buyer can access by withdrawing money, borrowing the cash value, or surrendering the policy and receiving the surrender value. The main feature is that insurance companies invest the premiums, theoretically with the attractive goal of growing the cash value. But insurance firms are notoriously expensive investment firms—their annual costs tend to exceed even the pricey fees of mutual funds. The monthly premiums are more expensive than term. And often, elderly consumers don't need the large death benefits (sorry, kids). Comes in two flavors: whole life and universal life.

Whole life. Half insurance, half investment. When the consumer signs up, he or she pays something for a death benefit, and something extra to build "cash value." Whole-life provides a fixed death benefit, a fixed monthly premium, and the possibility of monthly income later in life. Premiums are also fixed for life. Like annuities, whole-life plans can offer guaranteed minimum values. The cash value of the plan is also available to consumers as a loan during their lifetime, similar to loans against 401(k) retirement plans. In whole-life plans, the insurance company does the investing. In some plans, investment earnings grow tax free, making these plans attractive to high-net-worth individuals as a tax shelter. But for most, whole life is an ill-conceived marriage of insurance and investing, where the investment account has excessive fees and unclear investment earnings.

Universal life. Similar to whole life, but more like one-quarter insurance, three-quarters investment. The consumer has more control over where the money is invested. Premiums can be split between investments and death benefits, with the ratio changing as consumers get older and need less insurance. Some offer guaranteed benefits and values, like annuities. One main benefit over whole life: Fees, expenses, and investment gain are broken out and made clear to the consumer. Whole-life policies disclose much less to buyers. Still, universal-life investment fees are high and the investment options limited. Buy term life and invest the rest yourself.

Limited pay. Another kind of whole-life policy, but the payments are limited to ten or twenty years, or they are complete at age sixty-five.

After all premiums are paid, there are no more monthly bills, but the insurance death benefit remains in effect. It feels like term insurance, but it costs like permanent insurance.

Accidental death. Also known as accidental death and dismemberment policies. These are generally added to life insurance policies and can increase the benefit in the cast of an accidental death or serious accident. They often do not cover death during dangerous activities, such as flying an airplane.

Annuities. Beware! Annuities are the most complicated of all life insurance plans. To annuitize means that a company promises to pay you a certain amount until the day you die. That's an unknowable date, of course, but insurance companies are great at guessing when people will die, and that's why they are in this business. Of course, by making good bets (i.e., that people will die sooner rather than later) they make good money. When fixed-annuity holders die, all their money is gone—none left to heirs.

One way to think about annuities is as the reverse of life insurance. Whole life protects a surviving spouse against the premature death of a loved one; an annuity is designed to protect against the poverty that might come from outliving your money.

There are a long list of types of annuities. Some begin payouts immediately, some delay until a certain "accumulation" period has passed. Some actually confine payouts to a time period (say, ten years), rather than until death.

The problem with annuities is that they offer very high commissions to salespeople, charge high upfront and annual investment fees, and offer real benefits to few consumers. Consumers should fully exhaust all 401(k) and IRA options before even considering an annuity, for example. That cuts out anyone who contributed less than $16,500 to their retirement last year. Even though sales folks will tout the tax benefits of annuities for high-net-worth individuals, it's not hard to make a case that index funds are cheaper and more tax efficient. Here's one case: Annuity payments are taxed as income (up to 35 percent), while index-fund withdrawals are generally taxed as capital gains (currently 15 percent).

If you are tempted by the offer of an annuity, you should really keep asking yourself, "Why am I taking investment advice from a life insurance salesman?"

I'll tell you why: They are trained to deceive you in diabolical ways. Several years ago, a *Wall Street Journal* reporter sat in on a training class for annuity sales agents called Annuity University. The teacher began the session like this:

"Treat [senior citizens] like they're blind twelve-year-olds."

Things went downhill from there.

"There's the technical answer," the teacher said. "Then there's the senior answer. Tell them it's like a CD—it's safe, it's guaranteed.

"Toss hand grenades into the advice to disturb the seniors. You're there to solve their problems, but you have to create those problems first. No problem, no sale. So at the seminars, you're creating problems, and you tease them with the solutions. . . . They thrive on fear, anger, and greed. Show them their finances are all screwed up so that they think, 'Oh, no, I've done it all wrong.' "

But now, you know better. You know exactly how to get a good deal. Usually, that means avoiding advice from salesmen.

Don't Get Screwed by Insurance Companies

- Pay as little as you can to ward off personal ruin, but no more. Insurance is for catastrophes, not convenience.
- Most folks never switch insurance and overpay. Take advantage of competition! Pick a month every year and get fresh quotes on your policies.
- Insurance isn't an investment vehicle either. Leave retirement savings to your retirement account, and use life insurance as . . . life insurance.
- You often get a significant discount by buying multiple kinds of insurance from the same firm, but not always. Don't fall for the "25 percent discount" pitch (discount from what?). Insurers

make up those discount numbers out of thin air. Always get a second quote from a competitor to make sure the multipolicy discount is real.

- You'll never know how much your credit score might be raising your insurance-policy price. That's why you need to compare overall prices from several firms.
- Get your credit report, your CLUE report, and your Medical Information Bureau report once each year, for free, to make sure you aren't paying extra because of a reporting error.

9

Get a Twenty-First-Century Raise
The real way to make money: Make something!

CHARLIE, a programmer: I think I deserve a raise, John.
I've worked here seven years and always done everything
you've asked. And I have a sense that the people around
me are making a lot more than I am.
JOHN, his manager: Charlie, I love your work, but there's
just no way I can give you a raise in midyear, you know
that. We'll review your salary when we do every year, in
June.
CHARLIE: But I really think you should reconsider.
JOHN: Thanks, Charlie. I'll make a note in your file. Now,
what's the status of that project you were working on?

To this point, we've been talking exclusively about the
places you get screwed when someone takes your money,
the places and people that take your money while you trust them
with it, and the places to keep your money safe. But of all the places
you get screwed in life, no one does it better than the organization
that gives you money. I want that to change, and I want you to begin
the only journey that will really make you comfortable in old age.

You've spent your entire working life using your annual salary as a
proxy for your value to the world, and as the source of much of
your self-esteem. This old-world thinking will leave you in the dust

and perhaps put your family at risk as the twenty-first century progresses.

It's good to put a dollar value on your time. But when you do that, I'll bet you are selling yourself short. Very, very short. And I want you to make it big.

A $75,000 annual salary would sound pretty good to most of you. After all, the median U.S. household income is around $50,000.

But if I told you that a $75,000 salary is the same as making $37.50 an hour—roughly $25–$30 after taxes—would you still feel quite so smarmy about that paycheck? When you think about how easy it is to spend $30 on a lunch that takes a half an hour to eat, you might consider this disturbing proposition: On many average days, you engage in deficit spending. In other words, you can easily spend more in an hour than you earn in an hour. It's a good thing we sleep so much. Now let me darken the picture a shade more. My calculations assume a forty-hour workweek during fifty weeks of the year. Let's say you are like most Americans and now routinely eat at your desk and work late. Say you put in fifty hours a week. Your hourly salary is $30, and you're taking home $22–$25 an hour. Is that the pinnacle you dreamed about when you went to graduate school and put in ten years climbing the ladder and counting paper clips at your cubicle desk? Yes, you would be better off waiting tables. You'd almost be better off working at a mall. After all, minimum wage in California is $8 an hour, and overtime work (i.e., more than eight hours in any day) is worth $12 an hour.

It's good to put a value on time, however brutal the calculations can be. Money is a great tool for clarifying thought and focusing energy. A price tag on a thing we buy conveys a tremendous amount of information about the item—what it costs to make, to market, and to transport, for example. A salary is a price tag on you. It says how much you value your time.

Knowing your hourly rate will help you make intelligent decisions about what tasks to take on yourself, and what tasks to outsource, for example. If you pay someone else $35 to change your automobile oil—a task that might take you three hours, once you factor in time to buy the new oil and time to dispose of the old—that's probably a rational economic choice. But if you make $12 an hour and you're pretty handy, changing your own oil makes more sense.

These, however, are small-time calculations.

Don't get me wrong. It's good to keep these kinds of numbers close at hand when you make life decisions about spending. Keeping a rough idea of your earning power in mind while you shop will help you make better choices when you buy things, leading to healthy private thoughts like these: "This television will cost one week's work" or "This expensive dinner will wipe out all the money I made today."

But not enough people spend their energy and creative juices working on the other side of the equation, finding an easier way to make the numbers work. Not enough people focus on making more money.

I'm not saying people don't complain about the money they make. I'm saying people don't focus on ways to make more money. Sure, driven by an occasional fit of pride or anger, people occasionally storm into their boss's office and demand more "respect." Some even walk out smugly, having secured 2.5 percent annual increases. These efforts are misguided. They show a basic misunderstanding of the nature of markets and pricing and, in the end, do little good. Using our calculations from above, our friend with the 2.5 percent increase has just made himself about $5 extra per day. If he marches out of the meeting and congratulates himself with a celebratory latte, he's just spent the entire raise.

That's small-time thinking.

The twenty-first century, however, is the big time. Labor markets have forever changed. Employee-employer relationships have forever changed. I want your aspirations to change. I don't want you to shoot for $40 an hour, or even $100 an hour. I want you to create a fertile environment where you can have truly remarkable moments, a day here or there that earns you a month's worth of extra cash.

This is something personal-development author Steve Pavlina calls the "$10,000 hour." That should be your goal.

So far, we've talked about efficiently fighting for refunds on hidden fees and surcharges. I hope I've convinced you that a lunch hour spent getting a $15 monthly surcharge removed from your monthly cable bill is as good as a $180-an-hour job, when you consider the annual savings. An hour's worth of comparison shopping for auto insurance could save you maybe $300 a year. Even though these might be the classic "most dreaded tasks," when they are placed in context, it should be easy to find the motivation to make those calls.

I'll bet near the top of your list of most dreaded tasks is perhaps the most valuable hour you could spend: an hour with your boss asking for a raise. It's obvious, but it bears repeating: The quickest way to save money is to make more. However, as you'll see, "getting a raise" is not what it used to be. What I call a "twenty-first-century raise" is a much different proposition. Getting a raise is much easier when you don't ask your boss for any additional money. Time and freedom are really what you need anyway; and they are precisely what you'll need to find that $10,000 hour.

A FUNNY THING happened during the economic collapse at the end of 2008. Companies began experimenting with new ways of conducting "layoffs." Armed with much more sophisticated management software tools, firms began cutting wage expenses rather than personnel. They introduced four-day workweeks, unpaid vacations, and shorter work schedules. As Matt Richtel of *The New York Times* described it, instead of slashing workforces, they started "nipping and tucking." We're not talking about mom-and-pop delis. Tech giant Dell gave employees up to five unpaid vacation days in January 2009. *The New York Times* forced employees to trade 5 percent of their salaries for ten vacation days. Companies all over Silicon Valley began mulling plans for a shorter workweek. Honda offered workers voluntary unpaid vacation time.

Naturally, many employees at these companies were unnerved, suffering small wage loses and a big dose of uncertainty.

But you should see this as an opportunity. An opportunity to found You Inc.

WHEN IS A RAISE NOT A RAISE? WHEN IT'S TIME TO FREELANCE

It's important to understand what future CEOs are being taught in today's business schools—that you are completely disposable. Thanks to the brutality of accounting principles, it's much easier for companies to spend money on buildings (acquiring an asset) than on employees (an expense). The "flexible" workforce is a euphemism for saying that you can lose your job at any time for any reason. Gone—long gone—are the days of loyal companies and loyal employees. Just think about the shift away from pensions and defined benefit plans! Companies don't care about you! Karl Marx would say such loyalty was always a myth anyway. Regardless, every worker in the twenty-first century needs to understand this harsh reality: You really could lose your job tomorrow.

There's only one way to fight back: You need to open your own firm. Call it You Inc. You must be just as flexible as your company. You must be willing to let go of your employer at any time for any reason. You must always be looking for your next customer. Whether you like it or not, you are in the sales business. We all are.

It's incumbent on any rational employee today to understand why their job makes someone money, because being a profit center is the only way to create job security. If you are making money for your boss, and you could make money for another boss, then someone will always hire you. If you can't explain why you make money for someone, your job is at risk.

Many people, once they find themselves in the comfortable arms of a large organization, ignore this simple truth. They go to work, often work hard, write emails, make presentations, type up meeting agendas, laugh at the CEO's jokes. But they have no idea how their everyday tasks improve someone's bottom line. There's a reason *The Office* is so funny. It's because much of corporate America really does spend sixty hours per week fighting over the size of manila folders and the font that's used at the top of the weekly meeting agenda memo.

Such naïveté will likely end in personal disaster. If you don't know why you make your company money, then one day, someone above you will fail to find a reason, too. And you'll be gone. There is a simple solution to this problem, however.

MOONLIGHTING

Moonlighting is the great equalizer of our time. For starters, a small part-time job outside your company can easily provide that 10 per-cent raise your boss wouldn't give. Thanks to Craigslist and network-ing at industry functions, finding a couple of outside projects each year isn't difficult.

Don't do anything that's salable to outside firms? Then return to principle number one. If you don't have an obviously salable skill, you are at grave risk. Go find one.

On the other hand, with a few outside gigs, your stock will rise inside the company, too. When you see the world of employment as You Inc., then your day job will simply become your most important customer. But it won't be your only customer. The more you can diversify your income, the less you are subject to the whims of your company's bottom line. As a side benefit, your relationship with your boss will inevitably improve as well, because the slings and arrows of your crazy office politics just won't hurt as much, thanks to the added perspective you get from having multiple bosses (or, as I like to say, multiple customers). It's easier to laugh off a bad day at work when things are going well at your "other" job.

Don't think your company will let you moonlight? Now, we're on to the twenty-first-century raise. Many bosses truly have no salary flexibility. When you ask for that 10 percent raise, you'll get the familiar helpless shrug. You might even be asked to take a furlough and a forced vacation instead. Good.

The next time you have that uncomfortable conversation and the helpless shrug, you are ready. You bring a novel idea. "Okay then, I won't ask for a raise. I just want permission to do a few things outside the company," you say.

The proposal can run the full gamut from a formal, written understanding to a wink, a nod, and a "don't ask, don't tell" policy. But all of those things are much easier for most companies to grant than a salary increase.

I know many of you think you couldn't possibly take on more work because you are already overworked. While that's true, something magical happens when you are working for yourself, when every hour you spend directly translates into dollars in your pocket. I would never recommend stealing company time or supplies for outside projects. Doing so, a slimy practice that's acquired the icky name *daylighting*, would rightly get you fired. But you will discover surprising efficiencies once you make the leap to You Inc. Your primary employer will benefit, too. You'll learn things in your outside work that you can bring back to the office, and you'll be more efficient there, too.

In his bestseller *The 4-Hour Workweek*, author Timothy Ferriss explains the importance of negotiating a remote-work agreement for getting out from under your bosses' prying eyes, and why that gives workers a chance to be more creative. While his idea of a four-hour-per-week job is a bit farcical, applying his methods to create a four-hour-per-week side job is realistic for anyone. Using remote-work agreements to extract yourself from long commutes, company meetings, and from impulsive orders to do menial tasks given by your boss, you'll easily recover the four hours you need to start a new adventure, and to start your road to independence.

Many workers are uncomfortable selling themselves. But it's not easy to be buried under credit card debt, and it's not easy to be in a dead-end job either. Moonlighting is a great alternative to office hopelessness. It's also the only way you can find your $10,000-an-hour job.

Predictably, when you begin working a little for yourself, you'll stumble. You'll struggle with generating bills, with collecting payment, and probably with annoying customers. But you'll quickly be gripped by the entrepreneurial spirit. You will develop a hunter's taste for a home-run project. Your good work for a client will land you a big side job; or you'll hit on an idea that you can easily resell over and over. Or you'll move to a new and more profitable advertising engine for your side-venture website. In one single hour of decision making and creativity, you'll see an opportunity to earn $10,000.

Most critical of all, you will be available to take it on.

Here's how Steve Pavlina, the personal-development blogger, puts it in his essay "All Hours Are Not Created Equal":

> My income isn't based on how much time I spend working. It's a function of the value I create. I can work a whole month and produce less monetary value than I do in one breakthrough hour. Every hour is unique.
>
> I stopped thinking in terms of a fixed hourly rate many years ago. In practical terms an hour of my time could be worth $0, or it could be worth $10,000 or more, depending on what I do with that particular hour. Much of the time I pursue activities that don't generate any income at all, even though I still consider it to be productive work. Answering email doesn't seem to pay too well, and I don't get paid an hourly rate for writing blog entries and articles. But sometimes I'll get an idea which I can implement in just 30–60 minutes that will earn me an extra $10,000 over the course of a year, often continuing for many years thereafter. So the concept of an hourly rate, even an average hourly rate, is meaningless to me.
>
> A recent specific example was adding those . . . ads to this site. As I previously reported, this took very little time to implement (less than an hour), but it should ultimately generate thousands of dollars a year in extra revenue. And it takes me virtually no work at all to maintain this income aside from depositing checks.

HAVING THE CONVERSATION

I've already suggested that asking for a raise—even a twenty-first-century raise—is probably among your most dreaded tasks. In a down economy, asking for anything might even seem crazy. The only thing crazier is keeping your head in the sand and hoping your company will take care of you.

The dread comes, I suspect, from a presumption that the conversation has to be confrontational. It doesn't. In fact, when cast in the right light, it could be a relief for all parties. Let's start with our main premise: The easiest raise in the world to get is the raise that doesn't require more money. You might even consider asking for less money, in exchange for a little time. If you negotiate a four-day workweek and take 85 percent of your salary, for example, you've come out ahead.

But let's take this concept a step further. Most men don't pop the question to their girlfriend unless they are pretty darn sure they know what the answer will be. How? They've done a lot of research beforehand (kissing seems to go all right; her parents don't hate him; she seems to like visiting jewelry stores; they've picked out children's names; etc.). Before having the raise conversation with your boss, you should have done similar market research (sans the kissing part). The more information about your salary and benefits you get, the more compelling a business case you can make to get what you want.

1. Doing the Research

Many salary seekers are far too naïve about the realities of the labor market, just as many home sellers were far too naïve about the reality of the housing market in the early part of this century. In many cases, workers take a good long look at their monthly bills, their credit card statements, and their growing children, and they realize they need more money. Then they march into the boss's office and demand a raise. This might work occasionally, but it's fundamentally flawed.

Here's a simple truth: A company will pay you the going rate that other companies would pay you if you worked there instead. The labor market is not perfect, of course, and so some distortions occur. But you will be paid the least a company can pay you to keep you; that's the company's job. Your company doesn't care about your kid's braces.

This means you must find out what you are worth in the labor market, which is a very, very different amount from what you think you should be earning, or what you hear your cousin Elmo is making at that company on the other side of the country. Or what you think you need to survive financially.

Fortunately, the Internet has made discovering your true market value much easier. Dozens of websites—some free, some paid—offer glimpses of salaries at other corporations. For example, the salary wizard at Salary.com will give you at least a rough idea of your real value. Think of these price points as "comparables" or "comps" in the housing market. Naturally, not every job has an exact parallel. But you can still easily get a ballpark figure and see if your compensation is comparable to others in your field. If you are underpaid, great. You have a fantastic opportunity. If you find yourself on the high side of the spectrum, then you'll have to make some realistic choices about how to enhance your income (new skills, new schooling, etc.). And you should probably be aware that your company's HR department knows you are overpaid, too. When times get tough, and budget cuts come, you'll have a target on your back. That makes having a plan B even more important.

An even better comp is a job offer from another firm. Looking for a job while employed can be risky, and if you have no intention of taking the job, some might consider it unethical. If you can, it's always best to be up-front about what you're doing when you poke around at other firms, largely with the goal of making sure you are being paid enough at your current shop. Needless to say, you'll always entertain a knock-your-socks-off offer, so you'll never be lying if you say you are simply "testing the waters."

Only workers who are deliriously happy at their current job should fail to test the waters at least once every three years.

2. Timing the Discussion

Emotional intelligence was the buzzword of business five years ago, but when it comes to selling yourself to your boss, it couldn't be more relevant. Here's where having a tin ear can ruin the best-made plans in the time it takes to say "Can we get coffee?" Once again, don't be self-absorbed when the time comes to plead your case. Do not grab your boss on payday. Do not grab your boss after he/she has just left a tough budget meeting with management. Don't grab your boss on Monday at 9:15 a.m.

Instead, find the best, least stressful time in your boss's week and schedule a meeting that's entirely about you—don't let the meeting be hijacked by some other project or blended into some other meeting. How do you know when the best time is? Ask! "Hey, do you have a bad week next week?" You can even go one step further and say, "Hey, what kind of a quarter are we having?"

You can even open the door to the most critical element of research: Ask your boss, "Are you happy with the work I'm doing?"

The easiest way to curry favor with a boss is to make him or her look good to his or her superiors. Perhaps you don't like your boss and you don't want to do that. Too bad. If you want a raise, you have to make your boss look good.

That's why a great time to set up such a meeting about you is immediately after you've finished a successful project and received some praise. "Great work, Christine!" "Thanks, Carol . . . that reminds me, I'd like to talk about my career a little bit. How about next week?"

When the time comes, remember, the only case a company understands is a business case. Do not take the conversation personally. Do not imagine that rejection would be a personal disaster. And most important, just like our young lover with the engagement ring, only have the conversation when you know you'll get a yes.

Huh?

I'm not saying you should expect a yes to everything. I'm saying you should always have a plan B, if not a plan C, and make sure you get a yes to something. Be ready, of course, for a yes to this question: "Should I take this other job offer I have then?"

If you haven't figured out how to make an offer your company can't refuse, you should probably reconsider your proposals. Remember, your proposals should be much more sophisticated than a simple "I want more money." You can ask for four hours per week of time.

You can ask simply for the right to moonlight. But only ask when you know you can get a yes.

Now, let's revisit our programmer's dilemma:

CHARLIE, a programmer: I think I deserve a raise, John. I've worked here seven years and always done everything you've asked. And I have a sense that the people around me are making a lot more than I am.

JOHN, his manager: Charlie, I love your work, but there's just no way I can give you a raise in midyear, you know that. We'll review your salary when we do every year, in June.

CHARLIE: I hear you—that you have no authority to give me more money right now. But with Julie pregnant, we need it. So instead I'm going to take on a little side project for a hardware store in my town that wants some custom billing software.

JOHN: You know we have rules about moonlighting.

CHARLIE: Okay, but I think we have to figure out how to say yes to something I'm proposing here. I will limit the work to five hours per week. I'll always do the work on nights and weekends. And I won't keep asking for a raise.

JOHN: I don't know, Charlie.

CHARLIE: I want to make this work, John. It's the best option for both of us. The truth is, if I can't supplement my income, I'll have to find another place to work. I've gotten a lot of offers for outside work, and I could probably make a go of it on my own if I had to. But I'd much rather stay here. How about this: Let's try it for one month and then meet again and see if it's working for everyone.

JOHN: All right. We'll talk in one month.

This conversation went farcically easy, of course. It might take two, three, or four conversations to beat back a company's no-moonlighting strategy. But just because your boss says no doesn't mean you have to hear no. Charlie went into this meeting with a plan B, in case his offer was rejected.

Some elements of these conversations are implied, of course. For example, a no answer from a boss to a raise question is a clear yes to shop around for other jobs. Whatever guilt you might feel about look-ing around should completely be alleviated by such a rejection. One response to a no about moonlighting would be to moonlight anyway, though that choice should be made with great care—you've obvi-ously raised a red flag saying you're willing to cheat on the company, and it might find out and fire you.

If your job is so fragile and your boss so close-minded that you can't find any flexibility or room for creativity, your plan B should be shopping around, anyway. You'll never be in a position there to find your $10,000 hours, and you're certain to be left behind in the twenty-first century.

3. The Tricks to Diversifying Your Revenue Stream

Moonlighting, of course, is nothing new. The U.S. Department of Labor says about 4 million Americans have a full-time job and a part-time job—a number that steadily rose as the economy faltered at the end of the last decade. Without moonlighting, many restaurants would have no waitstaff. But what's new here is the idea that you can do it on your terms, rather than someone else's. If you secretly har-bor a love of classical music, doing ten hours per week of public rela-tions work for the local orchestra is far better than slinging hamburgers. So is writing a blog that you augment with advertising. You will give yourself at least a glimpse of a dream you've always had, and you will give yourself a shot at something much more lucrative. Maybe you can sign up community orchestras all around the country and make good money promoting Mozart from home. You can do a ten-hour-a-week part-time job during sixty minutes each morning and sixty minutes at night. From home.

Getting an idea is easy. I'll bet you have one right now. Just com-plete the simple sentence "I've always wished I could . . ." Thanks to the twenty-first-century raise, you have the chance to dabble in that dream without risking everything.

Like everything else, the trick is getting started.

First, you must figure out what your real company policy is. It's best to find out quietly, without asking your boss directly, because you will have more options later. I'm not saying you should hide things from your boss. But you don't need anyone to know prematurely about your ideas.

Strike up conversations with coworkers. Note that your company's written, formal policy may be one thing, but in practice another set of rules may govern. If anyone at your company has already blazed the moonlighting trail, you're in business.

Approach the topic delicately. Don't ruin opportunities for everyone by flaunting your work despite a company policy and embarrassing someone into enforcing the policy.

Finding customers shouldn't be hard if you love what you're doing. Just call the orchestra or pester the conductor after a concert. If you will moonlight in a similar field, such as programming, you will have delicate ethical waters to swim. Don't take revenue away from your day job, that'll get you fired. But of course that job will provide you with endless networking opportunities, and you should take full advantage of them.

You should also take full advantage of Craigslist, which is incredibly effective at linking people with skill and people with money. And it's free. Write, rewrite, and rewrite your Craigslist ads, trying different key terms all the time. You never know what someone will type into a search engine. You could even consider a small keyword campaign at Google or another search engine. Depending on your field, these can be fairly reasonably priced. Small campaigns can cost $500 to $1,000 a month.

One nice thing about moonlighting is the amount of control you'll have over the work you do. You do not have to accept every job that comes along; in fact, doing so is a bad idea. It's easy to recommend taking only the most lucrative jobs, but I'm not a fan of that either. It's most important to do jobs where you are assured of quick payment. The number one hassle for freelance workers is billing and payment. Freelance writers are well acquainted with waiting months for checks to arrive in the mail. That's typical in all freelance fields. That's why it's better to work for reliable customers than lucrative ones. If you only have ten hours per week to work on your side gig, you don't want to spend half of it chasing down payments. That's way beyond your field of expertise.

To make things easier, you might consider an electronic payment system such as PayPal. Of course, these cut into revenue. But PayPal essentially allows you to accept credit cards, which makes getting quicker payment much easier.

Naturally, earning side income has tax implications. Most over-the-counter tax-prep software handles moonlighting income easily. But you could end up with a hefty tax bill, so tread carefully here.

When you file your taxes, you'll have to fill out a "Profit or Loss from Business" form, also called Schedule C—assuming you've made more than $400 in side income. In this form, you'll include your income and your deductible expenses. These can include driving to or from work sites, buying special equipment, and so on. It's important to keep careful records of all your business expenses because taking all the deductions you are entitled to is important to not overpaying in taxes on moonlighting income. Using a separate credit card for expenses related to your side business can help you keep track of them.

Companies that paid you may send you a 1099-MISC form at the end of the year, which means the IRS will know directly about your extra income. But even if you don't get a 1099-MISC form, fess up to the income anyway. No one likes taxes, but cheating is cheating. And you could land in a lot of trouble, with a very big tax bill, and facing very large fines, if you lie.

At your day jobs, you split the cost of Social Security and Medicare taxes, also called FICA. When you work on your own, you pay both halves of that tax, which works out to a profit-strangling 15.3 percent. That's over and above the federal tax rate you'll pay on the income itself. It sounds almost depressing enough to discourage you from moonlighting. Don't let it. When you add up the real business expenses you've had connected to your venture and deduct them from the income, you'll probably get that tax bill under control. And if you are successful enough—when your total income rises above $90,000 for singles, for example—your Social Security tax obligation is capped, so the self-employment tax penalty is eliminated beyond that.

Finally, balance is the ultimate challenge. There's a reason it's called moonlighting. You don't want to get in the habit of working through the night. Many traditional moonlighters say their social lives suffer as they run out of time for family and friends. That's why I'm advocating twenty-first-century moonlighting as part of a comprehensive lifestyle strategy that includes negotiating fewer work hours from your primary employer. The best way to do this, however, is to leave big blocks of time that you will preserve for family and friends—all weekend nights, every other evening, whatever it might be. Time management is the key to successful moonlighting, just as it's the key to getting away from those $30 an hour days and finding the $10,000 hours.

PART III

HOW TO PITFALL-PROOF YOUR FINANCES, PAST, PRESENT, AND FUTURE

Introduction

How do you expect to win this race when you are walking
along at your slow, slow pace?

—The Rabbit

Now, it's time to put all your Gotcha-stopping knowledge
into practice. As you know by now, this is not a book
about getting rich quickly. It's a book designed to prevent others from
getting rich quickly at your expense. Right now, this is almost certainly happening to you. If your financial situation is so fragile that
you must live paycheck to paycheck, you are a prime target for banks
and their relentless attacks of overdraft "protection" and overlimit
credit card fees. But even if you have a fairly solid financial foundation and you are dutifully saving for the future (a home, education
expenses, or retirement), you are probably getting ripped off, too.
The more you have, the more sophisticated the Gotcha scams that
target you. Even if you are well on your way to funding a hearty
retirement, it's almost certain Wall Street is slowly sucking the life
out of that money, one 2 percent expense ratio at a time. You will
probably have to work an extra four or five years—postpone your
retirement—to compensate for this theft of your money. I don't want
that to happen. I want you to catch Wall Street in the act, and to tell
those brokers to get their grubby hands out of your cookie jar. In the
following section, I will introduce you to the Pitfall-Proof Pyramid—a

way to get, keep, and grow your money, no matter what stage of life you're at. After reading the introduction, feel free to skip ahead to the life stage that best describes your personal situation. But you will probably benefit from reading through the entire pyramid and making sure, as you pass through each stage, you never get ripped off.

It's your money, and I want you to keep it. Let's get started.

Stage 1

The Solid Foundation—Plan B Basics

When Mike Templeton looked at the credit card application his college-aged son had received in the mail, his blood started to boil. The card promised an attractive 9.9 percent interest rate. But there was a catch. Buried in the fine print was a list of fees that seemed almost comical.

- Account setup fee: $29
- Program fee: $95
- Annual fee: $48
- Monthly servicing fee: $84 annually
- Additional-card fee: $20 annually

Then, at the bottom, was a sentence that's hard to imagine someone could write with a straight face:

"If you are assigned the minimum credit limit of $250, your initial available credit will be $71 ($51 if you select the additional-card option)."

This is the world of low-credit-score credit cards. Millions of consumers who, for whatever reason, have their backs up against the financial wall are forced to sign up for credit cards under these hard-to-believe conditions.

Most consumers take credit cards for granted as a necessary tool for living in twenty-first-century America. It's difficult to rent a car, book a hotel room, buy anything online, or even rent a movie without a credit card. With billions of preapproved credit card applications sent out each year, it's easy for many Americans to get plastic—perhaps too easy. But another segment of the population—those who've got low credit, or no credit—find themselves in an alternate universe, where credit card plastic can literally cost its weight in gold. The card Templeton was studying, issued by South Dakota–based First Premier bank, essentially has a $250 sign-up fee disguised in a series of smaller fees.

First Premier is hardly the only bank charging high fees. In 2007, the National Consumer Law Center issued a report about what it called "fee-harvesting" cards aimed at the low end of the credit card market. With some of these cards, after fees are counted against the credit limit, consumers have virtually no credit left to spend when they receive the card.

Consumers who have trouble getting credit cards are faced with two bad choices. They can either opt for what's called a "secured" card, which requires a hefty upfront deposit; or they can sign up for a card with hefty upfront fees.

With a secured card, consumers send a bank $200–$500, then get back a credit card with an identical credit limit. The bank holds the deposit in case the consumer defaults on the card. With secured cards, the consumer is essentially borrowing his or her own money, and paying interest, for the right to carry plastic. After a user demonstrates a good payment history, some banks extend the credit limit and eventually offer the consumer a chance at a traditional unsecured card. But secured cards are no picnic. Unlike with regular cards, consumers who buy things with some secured cards get no grace period. They must pay interest immediately on every purchase. They are literally paying interest to a bank on their own money!

Those with bad credit might have trouble coming up with deposit money for a secured card, however. Fee-harvester cards fill this gap because they require no upfront payment before the card arrives. Some also don't require immediate payment of the fees; the $200 or so in extra charges can be financed by the consumers. That can lead to even more credit trouble down the line.

The trouble begins, of course, when the consumer ends up with a low credit score and few options. Corporate America smells consumers who are backed into financial corners the way sharks smell blood. The single best way to avoid these sharks is not to bleed in the water. In this section, we will be talking about how to avoid hidden fees by taking a fundamental approach—by putting your financial house in order, from the ground up, with a strong foundation and well-timed forays into the investing world. I will not tell you how to get rich quick. But I will tell you that if all you ever do is manage to avoid getting screwed, to avoid secured credit cards, subprime loans, and charlatan financial planners, you'll be in pretty good shape.

THERE ARE TWO things that virtually no one likes to talk about: death and old age. In fact, I'll bet you are probably perfectly happy to outsource these things to other people. From the moment you get your first real job, and someone puts that 401(k) form on the table in front of you, you know you should be planning for the future. But you'd rather not. Talking about investing is akin to talking about old age, and you want no part of that. So you'll do just about anything to avoid the topic, and that includes outsourcing the task to someone else. Plus, you figure that someone else must know more about it than you.

You're wrong.

And in so doing, you have made *rookie money mistake number one*—assuming that everyone knows more about money than you do. In fact, very few people know more about money than you. The telemarketer who is pitching you a loser stock certainly doesn't know more about money than you. Neither does that nice man in the white shirt at the bank, or Joel, the guy down the block who mows his lawn impeccably. Nobody knows your needs better than you, and figuring out where to put your money for today and tomorrow just isn't that complicated.

But wait, isn't this a book about hidden fees? How did it suddenly turn into a book about investing? It didn't. We're just taking a broad view. Today's money is the grandparent of tomorrow's money; today's debt, the father of tomorrow's outrageous fee. People tend to look at their financial picture in silos, as if their 401(k) has nothing to do with credit card interest rates, or their insurance policy has nothing to do with their credit card balances. *That's rookie money mistake number two*—looking at your financial picture without looking at your entire financial picture. So now, we're going to step back and take a wide view.

But before we start, I'm going to warn you about *rookie mistake number three*—automatically trusting Joel the lawn mower, Uncle Leo, Cousin Lenny, or anyone whom you happen to know with your money. Lots of people give advice. Very few people give good advice. Never trust anyone else—not Uncle Leo, not that guy from church, not even me—to give you perfect advice. When I interview people who were scammed out of money, it's amazing how often the trouble began with a family member or friend.

Most people don't understand where their money is, so they certainly can't keep track of how it's doing. Okay, here's a quick Gotcha quiz: Name the mutual funds you hold in your 401(k). If you passed that quiz, can you describe your mutual funds? Do you know the fund's top holdings? Know how much you are losing in fees every year? Why not?

Knowing is important, because you and your financial adviser will almost certainly disagree on the definition of critical terms such as *conservative, aggressive,* and *low-risk.* If you have carefully saved some money to buy a new car, and you tell your broker you might need the money in two or three years, that broker may put your money in a fund with a name like Capital Appreciation or Value Institutional or Dividend and Growth. Tell your moneyman to shove it. If you really need your money in two years, your money should stay as money. Put it in a high-interest account that's backed by the guarantee of the U.S. government, and forget about it.

But let's say you followed a broker's advice and put money you need for a new car within two years into his idea of a conservative investment—say in a "dividend and growth" fund, or a bond fund. Let's say you bought the fund in mid-2008. It might be ten years before you see it all again. You would have made *rookie mistake number four*—tying up money in a risky investment when that investment has a looming expiration date, such as a broken-down Ford Mustang that needs replacing.

For many people, it all comes down to a gross misunderstanding of a concept that is central to money, yet quite elusive. Risk.

Risk may sound like a simple word. Drive at fifty-five on the highway, you're conservative. Drive at eighty-five, you're risky. But risk, in the world of money, seems to befuddle most people. I think that's because risk is often misunderstood as a black-and-white assessment. It's risky to arrive at the airport thirty minutes before a flight. It's safe to arrive three hours early. It's risky to start a business. It's safe to put money in a savings account. It's risky to travel to foreign countries without updating your vaccinations. It's safe to take aspirin. As I'm sure you can see, none of these statements are completely true. They all have gradations and subtleties. To get a bit closer to the truth, you would need data— what foreign country? How crowded is the airport? But even with that, there's no sure thing. There's always at least some risk.

It's certainly possible to make better-informed decisions. But in the end, people must roll the dice. They must make a bet. Perhaps you've never entered a casino, but you are making thousands of bets every day, even if you are simply betting on safety. You bet someone driving down the highway won't plow into you; you bet the water in the faucet will work. You bet the boss won't fire you. Safe bets, perhaps, but not 100 percent safe.

On the other hand, risky bets make people money. The only way to turn money into more money without producing something of value is to put money at risk.

Here is a rule of thumb I want you to keep in mind as we walk through the five stages to financial screw-proofing your life: If someone is giving you money for nothing, that means the money is at risk. The more money for nothing you might get, the more at risk that money is. There is no way around this rule.

Investors earn premium returns for putting their money into risky investments, such as mutual funds. The greater the risk, the greater the potential reward. A mutual fund will almost certainly never grow

500 percent in a year, but an individual stock certainly could. On the other hand, it's very unlikely you'll lose everything you put into a mutual fund, but you could certainly lose it all if you invest it in a stock.

Not all risks are created equal. It's easier to lose money in some ways than others. I encourage the devoted among you to begin the arduous task of evaluating what companies or what investments might be a little less risky and earn a little better return. But you should know that a multibillion-dollar industry has sprung up around the complex topic of risk. Credit scores define risk for banks; life insurers make gigantic bets based on fine-tuned actuarial tables, guessing what month you will die; car insurance companies work incessantly to quantify risk and calculate what year you'll have an accident. Firms that make billion-dollar bets on the stock market use huge computer programs to inform their bets. And still, they get it wrong. Often.

When you assess risk, all you have is a few hunches. Really, you don't stand a chance.

Remember, we learned in the introduction that the vast majority of people overestimate their abilities and their knowledge of subjects. Combine that with all these computer programs working against you, and that's why Warren Buffett has concluded that the average investor simply cannot "beat the market" anymore. The vast majority of Americans just shouldn't play the market game.

So let me give you a basic rule of thumb for investing. The small amount of money you can earn through interest payments on a savings account is not magic. And neither is the money you can make investing in stocks. These are directly related. This is not a game you can "beat." But the game *can* beat you.

I want you, as a financially sophisticated person, to have one number in your head at all times. It's not hard to find. You can ask your friends. You can look in the newspaper. You can even notice signs in banks. It's the going interest rate on a mortgage—preferably a thirty-year, fixed-rate primary-home mortgage. But at least keep some mortgage-rate number in mind. That number will set the tone for the chart I'm about to share. Here's the essence: The best interest rate you can get on a savings account—one of those Internet savings accounts, for example—is a bit less than half the rate of a mortgage. That makes sense, doesn't it? Remember, loosely speaking, the bank is taking your money and lending it to other people. For the bank to make money, it has to "mark up" the rate. That means if mortgage rates are around 6 percent, your top saving rate would be perhaps 2.5 percent. A long-term CD might earn you a little bit more than that. But no-risk financial accounts will always return considerably less than mortgage rates.

(As always, the truth is a bit more complex—the going rate for ten-year U.S. treasury notes is a better guidepost than mortgage rates for the top high-yield passbook savings-account rates, but we're going for simple rules of thumb here. If you are the kind of person who's familiar with treasury-note rates, feel free to skip ahead.)

Down the chain are bad savings accounts, low-interest checking accounts, and low-yielding money-market funds, which pay less interest. Up the chain are bonds, mutual funds that hold bonds, other kinds of mutual funds, stocks, real estate, and private investments. These things form a sort of triangle.

In good times, you might expect an exceptional stock fund to earn you a 50 percent better return than the mortgage rate. If mortgage rates are 6 percent, a good fund might earn you 8 or 9 percent. Stocks offer a much wider range of returns, but if you take out the outlier IPOs and penny stocks, you are doing fantastic if you earn double the rate you would get on a good mutual fund. In this same year we are discussing, a 15 percent rise in stock price would be a great return, and a 10 percent return would be solid indeed. The winnings from starting a successful business or investing in one can be astronomical (ask Bill Gates or Michael Dell). But the triangle, and the font, get pretty tiny up there near the top. There are very few winners at the top.

Obviously, the percentages fluctuate. But the relationship between these things *has* to stay the same. No one would ever invest in high-risk stocks if they could get the same return in a safe bank account. No one would start a company if mutual funds offered the same kind of return.

The problem with my triangle, as I'm sure you are all screaming by now, is that it's a farce. In 2008, you could have cut the head right off my triangle and it would have looked like this.

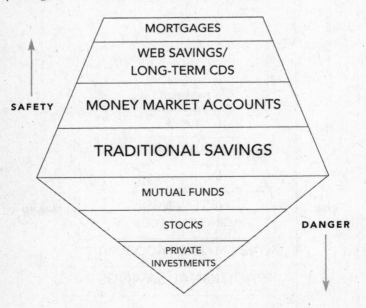

What's the lesson here? Risk actually does mean risk. You can actually lose money when you invest. People don't hand out something for nothing, and you should act accordingly.

Another reason I think consumers have an underdeveloped ability to assess risk is that it seemed to disappear from view during 1993 to 2008. Sure, there was a brief lesson during the dot-com bust in 2000, but that wasn't, strictly speaking, a scary event. Most people were playing with house money at the time. All the losses were on paper, and the event seemed to feel more like narrowly missing a Powerball lottery win ("Damn! Off by one number!") than losing a lifetime of savings.

Risk, however, reemerged with a vengeance in 2008 when the housing-market collapse spilled over to the wider market and people started losing real money. I suspect an entire generation of investors was forever scarred by the experience. If the dot-com bubble and the housing bubble filled Generation X with the idea that it was possible for everyone to get wealthy without doing anything, the collapse taught Generation Y they better live for today, before the money disappears.

But aren't you tired of living like that? Things can really be less volatile—when you build a house on a strong foundation. That's why I want to draw a very different kind of triangle for you. We're going to call it the Pitfall-Proof Pyramid.

STAGE 1: SIX WEEKS

Get comfortable
- The 21st-century raise
- Wealth investing

Set for the future
- Dabble in wealth building
- Firm retirement plan
- Set-asides for home, cars, college

6 months
- Ready for any surprise
- Mutual funds/risk in 401(k)
- Serious debt reduction

3 months
- Strong plan B • Conservative 401(k) retirement
- Debt map • Down-payment savings

6 weeks
- Emergency kitty
- Maybe a Roth IRA or Roth 401(k)

PITFALL-PROOF PYRAMID

COULD YOU LIVE OFF YOUR SAVINGS FOR SIX MONTHS?

Want real peace of mind? Get a rainy-day fund, now. It's the foundation of financial security. Without one, you'll always have a nagging sense that you are one bad illness or one disagreement with the boss away from disaster. You should feel that way. Because you are.

The foundation for any strong future is to have a plan B sitting securely in a virtual box with glass on it that says, "Break in case of emergency." That's true in every area of life—but in the world of finance it means having old-fashioned cash on hand. There's no point in saving for the long term if you don't have any savings for the short term. Without the confidence that comes with having a shelter against any financial storm, the Gotcha Capitalists can have their way with you. High credit card fees, outrageous interest rates on car loans. Out-of-sight insurance costs. Fee-harvesting credit cards. But you'll have to pay, because you have no negotiating leverage. They will be your last resort.

Conveniently, sound financial advice neatly dovetails with Gotcha prevention advice. Being prepared for emergencies also means you will be prepared to say no someday when you have to—as in, "No, I don't have to take that rotten car loan, I have other options." The key to not getting screwed is the simple ability to say no. You must always be in a position to walk away from a deal. By building a strong financial pyramid, you will give yourself the gift of the strong no, and that's the key to avoiding every financial trapdoor you'll ever find. As a bonus, your emergency kitty will act as a buffer against bank overdrafts or credit card late fees. See, it all fits neatly together: Mastery of checking accounts and credit cards is achieved, in part, by preparing for the future.

Most financial gurus will tell you to have three to six months' worth of emergency savings, that the first step to financial security is preparation for long-term emergencies such as job loss or health problems. That's a grand idea, but for many it's out of reach. Completely unrealistic. If that's you, don't worry, you have lots of company.

A survey commissioned by the Federal Reserve and the Consumer Federation of America revealed that only 40 percent of consumers have a separate emergency account, and only half of those savers said they have more than $2,000 saved up. A similar study by the Consumer Federation of America revealed that 42 percent of women don't even have $500 saved. And HSBC found that 40 percent of Americans don't even have one month's savings in the bank.

Living so precariously obviously has serious financial consequences. If you're faced with an unexpected money emergency—say, your car breaks down and you need to borrow money fast—you'll almost certainly get screwed on an interest rate.

But the life impact of living on the edge goes beyond the bank account. The added stress can have serious health implications, too. A study by Stephen Brobeck, director of the Consumer Federation of America, found that those with less than $500 in savings were 50 percent more likely to say they'd lost sleep over money, and twice as likely to say financial anxiety contributed to a decline in health and loss of productivity at work. Brobeck's work champions an incredibly modest, but important, goal for all Americans: Start with a $500 emergency kitty.

That's an important benchmark, and a great starting point. But it's certainly not good enough. So I've drawn a slightly more pragmatic picture. As you are considering the grand topic of where your money goes, who gives it to you, who takes it from you, and who screws you, I want you to keep your entire financial picture in mind. To seize control of your money, and your life, your first task is to put all your financial energy into stockpiling six weeks' worth of living expenses.

How much is that? You must be realistic about your real cost of living. When we talk about a month's costs, for most people we're talking about three times your monthly rent or mortgage payment. That means six weeks of expenses is a little more than four times rent. So if your rent is $1,000 a month, you should have $4,500 socked away somewhere close by. This is Stage 1 of our Pitfall-Proof Pyramid, and until you have six weeks' emergency savings, you aren't allowed into Stage 2.

Please note that I said "close by." I want you to place the funds in a completely liquid, immediately accessible account. Emergency funds that aren't in cash are just as good as a fire extinguisher that's at a friend's house while you're trying to put out a kitchen fire. Close by means a modest savings, checking, or money market account. Not stocks, not even bonds, not even certificates of deposit.

Why is this plan B kitty so important—important enough to consider forgoing free matching retirement funds from your company? One of the foundations for financial independence and personal happiness is the ability to quit your job if the need arises. I'm not saying you should quit your job. I'm saying it should always feel like a real alternative to you. Many Americans get to the "I hate my boss, I hate my coworkers, I hate my prospects" place but do little to improve their lot in life because they believe they have no alternatives. The presence of a plan B kitty is imperative to mental health. Again, ideally this is a weapon you'll never have to use. But it should be in your holster, just in case, providing you with sanity on the day that layoffs are rumored at your company, or the day your boss asks you to sharpen all the pencils in the mailroom and line them up by length.

At this point, perhaps you are thinking that—while you don't have emergency money per se—you do have a 401(k) account. Can't that serve as a backup plan? Or you might have a related question: Should you contribute to your 401(k) even though you don't have an emergency fund?

There's no cookie-cutter answer to either question. For many people, the automated deduction of a 401(k) is the only way to realistically begin a disciplined savings program. Company matching funds and tax benefits also make this an attractive option. But can your 401(k) double as your plan B? As you'll see in the next section, I think that's a fine idea when you're talking about the second tier of your financial foundation, your kitty of three months. But at this basic level, many factors would tilt the scale in favor of funding an emergency savings account over a 401(k). Here are a few:

- If your company match isn't generous. Much of the value in a 401(k) comes from the "free money" that arrives in the form of a company match. If you're not getting at least 50 cents on the dollar, it's not a great deal.

- If you don't vest immediately. Some companies require that you work for a period of time before you get to keep their matching contributions. If that's true, it's not a suitable emergency fund.
- If there's no cashlike investment choice, such as a money market fund, in your plan. If you only have a few mutual funds to pick from, and there's no ultrasafe option, then keep your emergency money elsewhere.

Also, let's keep the company match in perspective. I know, everyone is in love with the concept of free money, but here's the truth. Let's say our renter—we'll call her Katherine—is paying $1,000 a month in rent and earning $50,000 per year. Using the standard 6 percent salary contribution, even with a generous 50-cents-on-the-dollar match, Katherine will get an extra $62 twice each month for the 401(k). Not bad. But remember, if the money is ever needed as part of an emergency kitty, there will be a 10 percent early-payment penalty. That makes the emergency value of the 401(k) company-match dollars more like $56 twice a month, and after a roughly 25 percent income tax hit, more like $42. Still a nice amount, but not worth putting your entire financial picture at risk. For most people at the six-weeks stage, simply putting aside money into a traditional, completely safe, completely accessible savings account is the best bet.

If you really, really feel a need to begin automatic retirement savings today, and you're worried about having an emergency fund, consider a Roth IRA instead of your 401(k). The money you place into a Roth can be withdrawn penalty-free. That makes it a suitable emergency-fund placeholder, *as long as it is invested very conservatively*, perhaps in a money market fund. Sure, you'll surrender the company match, and the short-term tax benefits, of a 401(k). But you'll have far more investing options, and you won't risk early-withdrawal penalties on the money you've invested (you will be liable for tax on your investment gains, if you have any).

After you've built up a little Roth IRA buffer, then you can start piling money into your 401(k) as you arrive in Stage 2. This won't take long, by the way. Our $50,000 earner, Katherine, could have $4,500 in a Roth IRA by putting 9 percent of her paycheck into the account for one year. After that, she has a rock-solid foundation for climbing the ladder of financial security.

Finally, if your company offers a Roth 401(k), you are in luck, and when you are building your primary emergency fund, you should definitely take the Roth 401(k) option. Should an emergency hit, money that both you and your employer have put into a Roth 401(k) can be withdrawn penalty-free—only your investment earnings are subject to income tax and penalty. That makes a Roth 401(k) an acceptable emergency-fund vehicle, as long as your company plan offers conservative options and you invest in them. With just 6 percent of salary and 3 percent of company match for one year, Katherine's Roth 401(k) would hit that magic $4,500 amount in a year.

Why pick a Roth account instead of a traditional savings account at this point? Well, the tax-free benefit is nice. More important, however, is beginning the good habit of investing for the future. Simply opening a Roth account is a good step for some folks. But as I've already mentioned, most savers at this level should leave the retirement toys alone until they get their six-week kitty in order. Here's a word of caution about both Roths, however. Just because you've opened a Roth account doesn't mean your money is safe; and if you've been talked into placing the money in a mutual fund you don't really understand, the money is definitely not safe enough to double as an emergency fund. Move it to cash, or a money market fund, for now.

HERE ARE A few other notes about Stage 1. Some will advise you to take your $4,500 kitty and pay off credit card balances. I disagree. You always need flexibility, which means you always need liquidity— cash on hand. Do what you can to minimize finance charges on credit cards, of course. Shift the money to your lowest-interest card, if you can do so without incurring high fees. But keep the kitty.

Emergencies do happen.

But as part of a realistic plan B, be sure to peg the size of your kitty to include keeping your credit card payments current—i.e., increase the amount to include at least minimum payments on all cards. If Katherine owed $5,000 on credit cards and had a minimum payment of $200 per month, her six-week kitty would have to be about $4,800 to make sure she's financially secure. Your emergency savings won't do you any good if they don't cover compulsory credit card payments, students loans, etc.

Finally, if you aren't even in a position to put aside that $4,500— or while you are taking the year or so required to build up that amount—at least plan for where you could get your hands on that kind of money if something happened to your health or your job. Combine $2,500 in savings with a $2,000-limit credit card and save it for a rainy day. Open a "line of credit" with a family member. But always have in mind a plan for how you'd stay afloat for at least six weeks if disaster struck. Not having one is perhaps the biggest rookie mistake you could make.

Until you have your six-week emergency kitty in place, you shouldn't spend a single moment considering other investment options. All your energy should be focused on squirreling away this safety net.

I want to offer one exception to this plan B rule. If I had my way, every college graduate would take the $500 they receive in graduation gifts from family and open up an account at a discount broker such as Ameritrade or Charles Schwab. Then, that twenty-two-year-old would immediately begin investing. Why? The single best way to avoid getting scammed is to have experience. Or, put another way, the single biggest predictor of scam victimhood is inexperience. Even if the $500 disappears entirely through bad stock picks, that's a good lesson. Age twenty-two is the best time to lose that kind of money, when the emergency kitty is still the childhood bedroom. Nothing teaches someone about the stock market, investing, hidden fees, and money quicker than real-life experience. Investing is boring until you can watch your own money go up and down every day on the Internet. It has an amazing impact on young people's knowledge of the market. Parents, aunts, and uncles—give your kids a little house money to play with soon after graduation. It'll truly be the gift that keeps on giving.

KATHERINE'S PROGRESS

	Time Required	Savings	Money In
Stage 1	One year	$4,500	Savings account

Stage 2

Three Months—401(k) Basics

Get comfortable
- The 21st-century raise
- Wealth investing

Set for the future
- Dabble in wealth building
- Firm retirement plan
- Set-asides for home, cars, college

6 months
- Ready for any surprise
- Mutual funds/risk in 401(k)
- Serious debt reduction

3 months
- Strong plan B • Conservative 401(k) retirement
- Debt map • Down-payment savings

6 weeks
- Emergency kitty
- Maybe a Roth IRA or Roth 401(k)

PITFALL-PROOF PYRAMID

Once you have six weeks of living expenses in a safe place, you can begin to spread your financial wings just a little bit. You're still not in the clear to take big financial risks—if disaster strikes, six weeks will go by very quickly. Just ask the victims of Hurricane Katrina. So at this stage, you must still concentrate on building up your emergency fund, clear up to three months of living expenses. It won't take long—our $1,000-a-month renter, Katherine, only needed a year before she got on solid ground. Another year of disciplined savings will send her through Stage 2 clear up to Stage 3.

Because of the way investment accounts work, you can now feel free to park some of your kitty in retirement vehicles, or to apply what you already have there to your emergency fund. The vast majority of people in Stage 2 should join their 401(k) or similar plan. But don't take on risk yet. You can't graduate to the next level until you have completed the debt inventory that follows.

To have three months of emergency savings in place—which is really the minimum amount for financial sanity—a person who pays $1,000 per month in rent should have about $10,000, but that's unrealistic for the vast majority of savers. At this stage, someone like Katherine will almost certainly be dreaming of buying a house or a condo and be tempted to hoard cash for a down payment. That's understandable, and we can blend that into this model.

Here's the good news. Some of these funds in Stage 2 can overlap. Money you are saving for retirement can overlap as a backup rainy-day fund, and in some limited cases, a down payment on a home. You must keep that first six-weeks fund a virtual lockbox, sacrosanct, unavailable for all but the most serious emergencies. But Stage 2 money can be applied toward both long-term needs and emergencies.

But all the while, the money must still be invested conservatively because you might need it should an emergency hit. Our $1,000 renter, Katherine, would aim for $4,500 in cash and $4,500 in a retirement account with low-risk investments to fill out her pyramid. If she dreams of buying a condo, she should keep that second $4,500 out of a retirement fund and in cash—preferably a high-yielding savings account or money market account—so it's available for a down payment at some point.

Here I will repeat rookie mistake number four, which is tying up money in an investment that might be needed in the next three to five years. Say Katherine talks to Uncle Leo, who hooks her up with an investment account and convinces her to put that $4,500 down-payment money into a seemingly safe mutual fund. Markets are fickle, and prices go up and down over the short and medium term. It would be common for Katherine's fund to rise as high as $6,000 or drop as low as $3,000 during the next few years. Such oscillations are fine, if she has time to ride them out. But let's say exactly eighteen months after the investment, Katherine finds the condo of her dreams. But Katherine's fund is on a downswing, thanks to a drop in exports to China (or a hurricane in Florida; or a drop in the value of the dollar versus the euro; you get the idea). Now Katherine has only $3,121. She's young enough to wait out the market volatility, but she probably won't be able to buy the condo.

That's why medium-term money must always be kept in a safe, safe place.

Of course, even if Katherine did do well and used the mutual-fund money as a down payment, she's taken a step back on the pyramid. She now has only the absolute minimum in her emergency fund. She's reverted to Stage 1. If the condo's hot-water heater busts a month after she moves in, she won't have any money to pay for new floors. If she loses her job, she might have to stop paying the mortgage in as little as six weeks. So there is serious risk dipping into Stage 2 money for a major purchase, and it should be done with great care. Restoring the emergency fund should take precedence over all else after the purchase—before the new carpeting, the kitchen renovation, even the new couch.

That's why, ideally, Stage 2 is all about kick-starting a retirement fund.

401(k) Basics

Before we move on, I'm going to take a short detour and explain a few 401(k) essentials. In my experience, 401(k) plans are like the weather—everyone talks about them but no one does anything about them. Many people don't think about them for more than the ten minutes it takes to fill out the forms on the first day of work. But there's a lot to know, and not all of it good.

The name 401(k) refers to a section in the federal tax code that allows companies to defer compensation to employees without tax implications—in short, your company can give you bonus money that you don't have to pay taxes on. These 401(k) plans were almost unheard of until the 1980s, when companies quickly realized the plans were far cheaper to provide than traditional pension plans.

Having a 401(k) means you are putting aside money, tax-free, with every paycheck. In most cases, your company kicks in some matching funds, too—maybe 50 cents on the dollar, maybe 25 cents. There's usually a cap—the firm will match 50 cents of every dollar up to 6 percent of the employee's salary, for example. It is generally accepted that all employees should take their company up on this offer and contribute at least enough to their 401(k) get the maximum company match, lest the worker miss out on the free money. Thanks to the tax savings and cash matching, skimming 6 percent of your salary into your 401(k) will really only feel as if you were losing 4.5 percent of your take-home pay, but it will put nearly 9 percent into your retirement account. Unquestionably, a good deal.

Just because money is put into your 401(k) does not mean it's "invested," however. It could just be sitting in the retirement account doing nothing (the same is true of IRAs). Or in some cases, it could be swept into a nearly worthless money market account earning 0.1 percent interest. So once you begin contributing to your retirement, the critical question becomes, where is the money that's *in* your 401(k)?

When you set your contribution levels (3 percent? 6 percent? 9 percent?), you will usually be asked to set your investments, too. In

401(k) plans, these are usually an incredibly limited set of mutual funds—often ten, or fewer—that have been handpicked by your company and its 401(k) administrator. You should know that your administrator, often a third-party company, makes a lot of money because it chooses to offer one set of funds over another. The firm that manages the mutual fund also earns fees, called expense ratios. These are explained below.

It's important to know that 401(k) plans are not portable. If you change companies, your 401(k) will not move with you. You'll probably get a new one, adding to the confusion. When you leave your company, you should transfer your money from that 401(k) into an IRA account. The process is called a rollover, and it's incredibly important that you do it correctly. Doing it wrong—say, withdrawing the money first and then later opening an IRA—would cost you a hefty early-withdrawal penalty.

One critical thing to understand about 401(k) investments is that it's challenging to determine exactly how well (or poorly) you are doing. Generally, because you are adding money every month, your 401(k) account will increase in value. That might make you feel good. But you could be gaining money and losing money at the same time. Let's say you put $100 into the account every month; the funds you buy, however, are losers, dropping 1 percent every month. After ten months, you'd have $946 in your retirement fund. You might feel pretty good about your self-discipline. But you'd be losing money, and you should consider a new investment.

This is a very, very simple example, of course. Most people purchase multiple mutual fund shares several times each month, at multiple prices. It's easy to lose track of the most important things: how much money you (and your company) have put in, and how much it's growing. In some cases, this is called your personal rate of return. Don't be satisfied that your bottom-line figure is simply growing. Always know what you've put in, and what your investments have really done for you. Use this brutal assessment, which I call the mattress assessment, to keep you grounded. Always keep in mind your investment return if you simply put your money under your

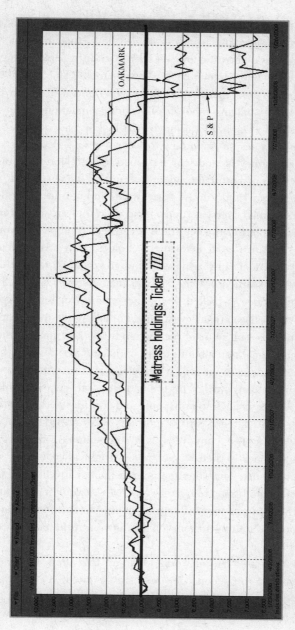

MSN Money

mattress, and use that as a baseline to determine if your 401(k) is doing anything for you. In our example above, the "mattress fund" outperformed our investor by $44. For a sobering look at this possibility, I compared two popular baskets of stocks (The S&P 500 and the conservative Oakmark Equity & Income Fund) with my mythical mattress fund—ticker symbol ZZZZ—during a recent five-year span. (See page 245.) Ouch! Flatlining doesn't look so bad, does it?

This is why it's so important to always have a decent grasp of where your money is, and why it's a bad idea to store a future car down payment in a mutual fund, or to count on money there to serve as an emergency fund. Always know what kind of mutual funds you hold (bond funds? overseas funds?) and what they are doing for you.

It's also important to keep track because as time passes, you will have to "rebalance" your investment choices. Why? Say your international fund does rip-roaring well and grows much faster than all your other investments. One day you may discover that half your retirement money is locked up in the fortunes of foreign governments. Maybe that's okay with you, but it's wiser to spread that money around—sell some of the foreign funds, buy some domestic.

One additional note about 401(k) options. If you work for a publicly traded company, it will likely give you the option to invest directly in company stock. This is a bad idea, particularly at this critical investment stage. Later on, you could consider putting a small—such as 5–10 percent small—portion of your 401(k) funds in company stock. But employees as a rule shouldn't bind up their retirement money in their own company. It already pays your salary! You never want to have so much of your financial well-being bound up with a single firm. Things may look rosy at your shop right now, but anything can happen. If your company starts underperforming, you wouldn't want to lose your job and all your retirement savings at the same time.

Don't have a 401(k) at work? Open an IRA then. But in either case, money in this second tier must still be invested conservatively once it's deposited in the 401(k)/IRA because it's doubling as part of your emergency fund. Yes, if the world came crumbling down and you found yourself out of work and out of unemployment benefits for more than two months, and you had to tap into your retirement account, you'd have to pay those early-withdrawal penalties. But then, you'd be in the middle of a life disaster, and that's what we're preparing you for. You don't want this Stage 2 money invested in risky mutual funds because you could end up with a picture that looks like the one above.

What does conservative look like? It's simple: It says FDIC INSURED on the label. It's a savings account, or perhaps a money market deposit account, that returns slow, steady returns and promises to preserve your principal.

I know you have heard the trite advice that young people should invest aggressively and older people conservatively. There's truth to that statement, but it's far too vague and general. Of course Wall Street wants the maximum number of new consumers investing in the riskiest ways! That's how it makes money. But now, you know better. You know how to really plan for the future. Build a solid foundation first. Take risks only after you've built a solid foundation. Rather than the straight line that most investment advisers give consumers—high risk when young, low risk when old—I believe the right graph should look a lot more like a camel's back. Low risk when initially starting out, gradually rising risk as your footing becomes solid, and gradually falling risk when retirement creeps within ten years.

NONE OF THESE pretty formulas work, however, if you aren't dealing with your debt. At this stage of the pyramid, while funding your retirement and/or saving for a home, you must simultaneously make a careful inventory of all your debts—your student loans, your credit cards, your car loans, everything. Before you leave Stage 2, you must come up with a single, crucial number that crystallizes your debt—your Debt-Free Day. Add up all you owe. Then look at how much you're contributing to pay down this debt every month. Then, do some division. Say you owe $10,000, and you can afford $400 per month. Divide one by the other, and you get 25. Now, go to a five-year calendar you have in the house, flip ahead twenty-five months, and circle a date. Now you have a Debt-Free Day.

The exercise is imprecise, of course. Interest rates, new debts, bonus payments, and many other items will impact your eventual date. But the exercise is necessary before graduating to Stage 3. You cannot begin saving for the future when you've already spent it. And you can't leave Stage 2 without paying down debt at a steady rate and knowing what kind of uphill battle you are in for.

But the good news is, you can pay down debt and save money at this stage without spending additional funds. So at this level, it makes sense to split your money between paying off debt and beginning a retirement fund. By keeping with the same savings level of 9 percent as at the last stage, Katherine would easily reach level two in an additional year, with no change in savings amount! Sticking with our example, she would finish tier two in a year by putting 6 percent of her salary into a 401(k) and receiving the 3 percent company match. In reality, because she is now accepting the company match, she could be saving less while staying within the model. If she chooses a traditional 401(k), the investment will feel like only 4.5 percent off her paycheck, thanks to the tax savings. If she maintains her 9 percent contribution, she could take the remaining 4.5 percent and pay down $2,250 in debt during the year.

If Katherine receives even a modest 4.5 percent raise, the debt savings can be even bigger. Applying the raise to pay off more debt, she'd rid herself of $4,500 and save $4,500 that same year.

Which debt should she pay? Plenty of good strategies exist for attacking mountains of bills. There's the confidence-building "snowball plan," popularized by Dave Ramsey, which starts with the smallest debt, polishes it off, then moves on to the next largest, and so on. There's the more fiscally sensible "high interest" approach, which devotes the most money to the most expensive debt. For example, pay down the 22 percent store credit card first, then the 18 percent Visa, then the 13 percent MasterCard, then the 6.25 percent student loans. That obviously saves more money in the long run.

At this stage, I don't much care which plan you use. I want you to commit to the plan and stick to it.

In just two years, with a modest savings plan in effect, our young woman now has a rock-solid foundation that includes provisions for three full months of emergency funds, a great start at retirement, and a substantial contribution toward reducing debt. She's headed in the right direction and now sailing with the wind.

KATHERINE'S PROGRESS

	Time Required	Savings	Money In	Debt Payments
Stage 2	Two years	$9,000	½ savings account, ½ conservative retirement account	$4,500

Stage 3

Six Months—Mutual Fund Basics

Get comfortable
- The 21st-century raise
- Wealth investing

Set for the future
- Dabble in wealth building
- Firm retirement plan
- Set-asides for home, cars, college

6 months
- Ready for any surprise
- Mutual funds/risk in 401(k)
- Serious debt reduction

3 months
- Strong plan B • Conservative 401(k) retirement
- Debt map • Down-payment savings

6 weeks
- Emergency kitty
- Maybe a Roth IRA or Roth 401(k)

PITFALL-PROOF PYRAMID

Now that you have a nice, comfortable kitty, and you know you can withstand even a three-month interruption of income with nary a care, your financial confidence should begin to grow. Remember, in only two years' time, with modest tools and a small investment, we've put Katherine's financial house in order. She's got a great emergency savings account, a solid start on retirement, and she's paying almost $400 a month toward reducing her debt. Two years isn't overnight, but it is a quick turnaround. Start today and you'll be on solid ground quicker than you could earn a master's degree!

Now, after achieving this level, as you start to shoot past three months' living expenses—and only now—should you begin to play the market. Now is the time to begin experimenting with more risky mutual funds in your 401(k) or IRA.

Since it's simple and at hand, your first experiment should be researching other options within your 401(k). There won't be many. Most plans have around ten funds to pick from, in addition to company stock. That's a serious limitation. But the good news is you can trade for free in many plans, with liberal limitations on the number of trades you can make. So 401(k) experimentation is a low-pressure way to learn about the market. Read up on your options, familiarize yourself with the types of funds (bond funds, blended funds, overseas funds, oh my). To get you started, take 10 percent of your retirement money and drop it into one or two of these funds. Then, look every week and follow your performance. The best way to learn is to do, and now you're doing. Later, you can increase the at-risk amount to 20 or 25 percent while in Stage 3.

Now is the time to visit your company's 401(k) website. Study the names of all your mutual fund options, visit an investment site such as MSN Money or Yahoo! Finance to discover their five-letter ticker symbol, compare them to the benchmark S&P 500, and examine their hidden fees. At this point, we're climbing up the camel's back, but still only dabbling in the market. Never invest in a mutual fund before you have reached this solid level, as you'll know the whims of up-and-down investing cannot topple your financial house—which is built on stone, not straw! But even now, you'll want to put only some of your retirement money at risk. Only later, in Stage 4, when you have a full six months' worth of emergency funds socked away, will we move into the world of wealth investing. Once there, you can think about putting money away for a sunny day in twenty-five years instead of a rainy day next year.

But for now, we're still taking small steps. In this section, we'll show you a little bit more about how to evaluate mutual funds. Then, we'll make sure you are well on your way to a debt-free life before you move up to the next level.

Many workers automatically dump 6 percent of their salary into their 401(k) accounts, or whatever amount gains them the maximum company match. But you don't have to stop at 6 percent of your income when electing to put money into your 401(k) just because your company has stopped matching your contribution. You can put in more and reduce today's tax burden. In 2009, the maximum was $16,500, and you should consider putting extra money into your 401(k) if you can. That'll give you even more to work with at this stage. Remember, every 1.5 percent of your salary you contribute to your retirement only feels like a 1 percent deduction of your paycheck, thanks to the tax savings.

How do you pick what investments to try? You do a little reading. Here's an example of how to research a mutual fund. Back to the Oakmark Equity & Income Fund we mentioned in the prior section. Let's presume this fund is offered by your 401(k), or a friend has recommended it for your IRA. Find the ticker symbol on a site such as Yahoo! Finance.

Note the ticker symbol is OAKBX (see page 253). Use the symbol to get a full quote on the fund. A ton of information is packaged neatly for you when you look up the ticker symbol.

Pay close attention (see page 254) to the expense ratio, under "More information." In this case, it's 0.81 percent, not bad. Let me translate *expense ratio* for you. That's the amount of money a fund manager takes from you every year as his/her fee. You never notice it's missing because it's automatically taken out of your investment. Most investors should never buy into a fund with an expense ratio higher than 1 percent. If you think about it, 1 percent is a lot of money—after twenty-five years, the manager will have taken 1 percent twenty-five times, which works out to roughly one-quarter of your money. You'd better be getting a lot for that! (Don't believe me? That's the tyranny of compounding costs at work. Read the footnotes and I'll prove it to you!)

High expense ratios are epidemic in U.S. 401(k) accounts. The average American investor is losing about one-third of his or her retirement money due to the compounding effects of these annual fees. The longer the time horizon, the worse the impact. In one example that's been described by Vanguard founder John Bogle, a twenty-year-old who invests in a mutual fund with a 2.5 percent annual fee will see fully 80 percent of that money disappear in fees by the time the precocious investor turns eighty-five. Four for Wall Street, one for him. That's no way to plan for retirement. Make sure you keep more of your money by watching expense ratios like a hawk. As Bogle is fond of saying, "You get what you don't pay for."

Also, notice the top holdings of the fund in the chart above. You should always have a grasp of where your money is invested within each mutual fund you pick. Don't rely on terms such as *aggressive growth* or *wealth preservation*. In this case, the fund is top-heavy in a U.S. power utility company and U.S. treasuries, which are generally safe.

One reason for paying attention to top holdings is that many rookie investors simply split their money up between three or four mutual funds and think they're "diversified," because someone once told them to be diversified. However, investments in behemoths such as Microsoft, General Electric, and Cisco are so popular among fund managers that they are top holdings in thousands of funds. Many investors who think they are diversified are not—they just hold funds with different names that are invested in basically the same companies. If that's you, be sure to find other places for some of your money, lest you be enslaved by the fortunes of a single industry.

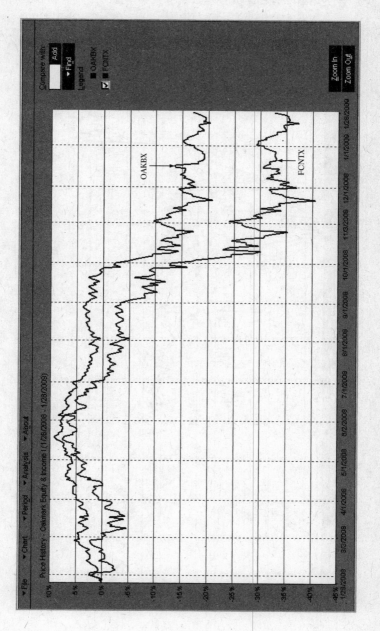

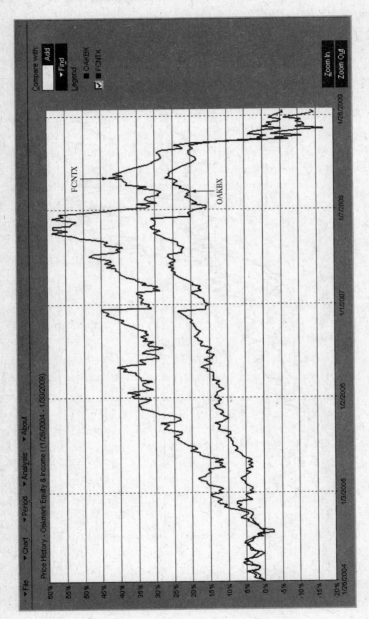

Now, I want you to put your five-letter ticker symbol to the test. Comparing mutual funds can be difficult, but it doesn't have to be. Charts of past performance, while no predictor of future performance, do make comparisons easier. So take a chart of that Oakmark fund and compare it with another. How about Fidelity's Contrafund, which is described as a collection of companies that the fund's manager believes are undervalued. Its symbol is FCNTX. Notice how neatly the charting software switches from price to percent gain/loss, so it's easier to compare the two funds (see page 255).

Okay, we all know 2008 was a brutal year, but it was obviously more brutal for the Fidelity fund. So that makes it an easy choice, right? Oakmark is better? Not necessarily. Here are the same two funds (see page 256), this time compared during a five-year stretch. Note that the Fidelity fund is ahead for almost the entire time span, until that devastating end to 2008.

But the Oakmark fund is still a winner. So let's compare it to the true benchmark: an S&P 500 index fund. I want you to remember that name, because that's the kind of fund I want you to invest all your money in when you are in this stage of the pyramid. (So, by the way, does Warren Buffett.) Index funds are not like other mutual funds. They are not managed by a person who is actively buying and selling stock. Instead, a computer simply works to match the stocks that are in a large, popular index, such as the S&P 500 you always hear about in the news. In other words, owning an S&P 500 fund is like owning a little bit of stock in all five hundred stocks that compose the S&P 500. Fundamentally, it's like investing in the entire stock market, or even the entire U.S. economy. You won't get filthy rich doing this. But you will nicely follow the gains made by the U.S. economy as a whole.

And here's the best part. Because the fund isn't actively managed by a person, it's nearly free to invest in. There are many S&P 500 index funds. Here's one: Fidelity's Spartan 500 (ticker FSMKX). Notice the low, low expense ratio (see page 258):

Fidelity Spartan 500 Index Investor (FSMKX) [Trade Now]

FSMKX quote

68.42 ▲ **+0.05 +0.07%**

Previous Close	68.37	Category	**Large Blend**
Net Assets	5.65 Bil	Dividend Yield	2.81%
Morningstar ratings:		Minimum Initial Purchase	10,000
Risk	Average	1 Year Return	-19.95%
Rating	★★★☆☆	3 Year Return	-6.20%
Return	Average	5 Year Return	-0.19%

Cumu
2004
$14,000.00
$12,000.00
$10,000.00
$8,000.00
$6,000.00

	2004
Growth	10.73%
Value	$11,073

Last NAV

Your latest quotes: OAKBX, FSMKX, $INX, HEMMX, VFINX, EEM

MSN Money fund commentary

How Whole Foods profits in lean times 7/31/2009

Financial planner as therapist? 7/30/2009

Overview

The investment seeks results corresponding with the total return of common stocks represented by the S&P 500 index while keeping transaction costs and other expenses low. The fund normally invests at least 80% of assets in common stocks included in the S&P 500. It may lend securities to earn income for the fund.

More information for FSMKX

Fees and expenses	
Front load	0.00%
Deferred load	0.00%
Expense Ratio	0.10%

Top holdings for FSMKX	
Company Name	% Net Assets
ExxonMobil Corporation	3.96%
S&P 500 Index (Fut)	3.68%
Fidelity Cash Central Fund	2.93%
Microsoft Corporation	1.85%
Johnson & Johnson	1.76%

Now, let's compare the S&P fund to our current champion, the Oakmark Equity & Income Fund (see page 259). To avoid the crazy fluctuations churned out by that nutty 2008 collapse, here are the two funds compared between 2003 and 2008.

The two funds peak and valley at similar times. But notice the S&P fund is nearly always slightly higher. Why? Partly it's because the S&P fund starts every year with a nearly 1 percent head start over the Oakmark fund, because its expenses are so much lower.

In real dollar terms, here's the difference for $10,000 invested in both funds:

	January 28, 2003	January 28, 2008
Oakmark	$10,000	$16,114
S&P	$10,000	$17,762

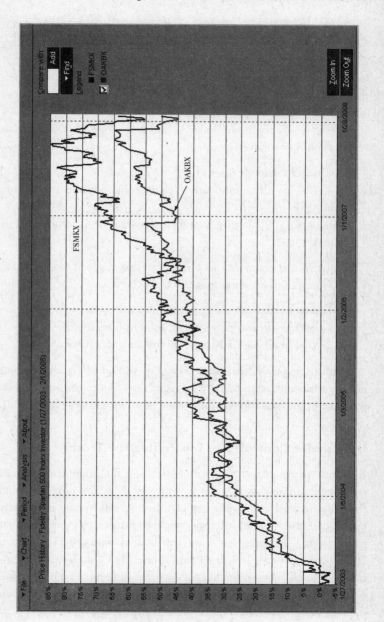

That's a serious difference! I hope it's enough to convince you that S&P 500 funds are the best place for you to start putting money when you don't know where to start. Most 401(k) plans now offer at least one index choice. If you instead have an IRA (Roth or traditional), you're in luck: You can pick any S&P fund you want. They are all virtually identical.

To review: To complete Stage 3, Katherine, our $1,000-a-month renter should now have:

- $4,500 in cash (six weeks tier)
- $4,500 in ultraconservative retirement investments (three months)
- About $10,000 (and growing) in low-risk S&P 500 fund (six months)

Adjust your investments accordingly. For example, if you're paying $2,750 per month for a mortgage, you should have:

- $12,500 in cash
- $12,500 in ultraconservative retirement investments
- $25,000 in an S&P 500 fund or similar index fund

In either example, that Stage 3 money should be in savings, and not in retirement, accounts if it's pegged toward a car or home down payment in the next three to four years. Ditto for a college tuition bill.

Debt under Control? Are You Telling the Truth?

But now we reach the moment of truth. So far, along the pyramid we've made some casual references to your debt. But now, we reach the crossroads. If you want out of Stage 3, you must have a fully drawn debt map—what you owe, what the finance charges are, what you're paying, and precisely when it will all be paid off. This is not a circle on a calendar. This is a commitment. For couples, it's a commitment to each other. I'm not saying every debt must be paid in full before moving into beginner's aggressive investing, where you will take on some risk in the hope of higher returns. You wouldn't hold off on investments until your primary mortgage is paid off, for example. I'm saying the plan must be in place and well under way.

If you don't have your debt under control, then you shouldn't read on. (Okay, go ahead.) What does "debt under control" mean? You'll find a lot of opinions on this, and a lot of data, too. Most frequently, you will hear banks and financial advisers talk a lot about the "debt-to-income ratio" or DTI. That's a calculation of all your debt payments—mortgage, car loan, student loan, credit cards—divided by your income. For example, take a consumer who earns $72,000 per year, or $6,000 per month. If he owes $1,300 monthly on a mortgage, $300 on a car loan, $200 on a student loan, and pays $200 on a credit card each month, his DTI is $2,000/$6,000 or 0.33. It's often said that if you are spending more than one-third of your income on debt—if your DTI is over .33—you're in trouble.

I think this is a terrible calculation, however. The mingling of good debt (a mortgage at 5.07 percent) with bad debt (a credit card at 21.99 percent) is stupid. Further, not all credit card debt is equal. People with $200 balances that are paid off every month aren't really paying debt, they're just paying monthly expenses. On the other hand, someone who owes $8,000 on a credit card and pays the minimum payment of $200 each month would take five years to pay off the card—presuming not a single additional item is purchased on the card. Why would you equate someone who pays a $200 minimum payment with someone who pays their bill in full at $200? The normal debt-to-income-ratio calculation fails to account for these variations.

Instead, I want to focus on an entirely different, and much more tangible, number. I want you to think like the big boys, the way corporations and governments do. I want you to focus on opportunity cost—the cost of servicing your debt. Every dollar spent on interest is a dollar you don't have to invest, or to buy food or to go on vacation. Interest payments strike right at the heart of your income and rip it away from you. Over the long term, they'll kill your investing future. You'll be surprised at how the math works.

It costs more to service an $8,000 credit card debt than a $45,000 student loan, for example. Carrying $8,000 in credit card debt for a year on a card with a 25 percent interest rate means you'll pay about $2,000 in interest charges that year. If your take-home pay is $50,000, and you work twenty days per month, that means you work an entire day every month just to pay interest to the credit card company. A whole day's work, up in smoke. This is why I don't care what your minimum monthly credit card payment is, or even how much you pay regularly. I care about the cost of the borrowing, and that's all you should think about, too.

By the way, servicing $45,000 in student loans only costs you $1,850 per year (averaged over twenty years). In our example, you'd be finished paying for the student loan just before the closing bell rings on day one—and before a credit card debt that's almost six times smaller is paid off.

If you have significant credit card debt—if the outstanding balance after next month's payment is more than 10 percent of your annual income, or if you can't pay down that debt within the next twelve months—you have no business investing in the stock market. Ideally, your amount of credit card revolving debt would be zero, but if you are aggressively paying down your credit card debt and can see the end in sight, within twelve months—and you have a little money left over at the end of the month, and you now have three months of emergency funds identified—it's okay to begin dabbling in aggressive investing.

But even if you don't have any credit card debt, you might still have too much debt, or just plain too many bills, to dive into the deeper end of the investing pool. Calculations of appropriate debt levels involving "good debt"—mortgages, low-interest car loans, and student loans—are a bit more complex. Generally, consumers who have already spent more than one-third of their salary making long-term-debt payments before they even cash their payroll checks are living on the edge. If your mortgage is $2,000 a month, your car loan is $250 a month, and your student loan is $350, that's an annual hit of more than $30,000. If you don't earn at least $90,000 per year, you're probably struggling. Ridding yourself of that $350-a-month student loan (and its annual $1,850 interest charge) should take precedence over risky investments.

At this level, I'm not as concerned about good debt ratios. Making aggressive contributions to an investment account—what you do with the other two-thirds of your income—is merely a matter of budgeting. If you can afford it, based on your other monthly expenses such as food and entertainment, have at it.

A quick note to renters: You're not off the hook in this debt math. Just because you aren't paying a "debt" for a place to live, you don't get to screw with this good-debt-ratio calculation. Rent, obviously, is a monthly obligation. Insert your rent amount in the calculation where homeowners would place a mortgage payment. If your car loan, student loan, and rent add up to more than one-third of your income, you should tread carefully.

KATHERINE'S PROGRESS

	Time Required	Savings	Money In	Debt Payments
Stage 3	3–4 years	$18,000	¼ savings account, ¼ conservative retirement account, ½ S&P 500 fund	$4,500/year

Stage 4

Get Set for the Future— Basic Risk Investing

Get comfortable
- The 21st-century raise
- Wealth investing

Set for the future
- Dabble in wealth building
- Firm retirement plan
- Set-asides for home, cars, college

6 months
- Ready for any surprise
- Mutual funds/risk in 401(k)
- Serious debt reduction

3 months
- Strong plan B • Conservative 401(k) retirement
- Debt map • Down-payment savings

6 weeks
- Emergency kitty
- Maybe a Roth IRA or Roth 401(k)

PITFALL-PROOF PYRAMID

For many, "real investing" begins with a free lunch. Maybe a friend invites you to be part of a group of ten or so lucky pals who "won" a free meal at a swanky downtown restaurant. Maybe you slipped your card into a fishbowl four months earlier.

Meals like this always begin the same way. One participant is supremely overdressed and overcologned. Golf and football are discussed. There's wine. And then, right around the time dessert arrives, an innocent question is floated:

"What do you guys think about retirement?"

If you've ever been to one of these free lunches, perhaps you felt you were suddenly thrust into the middle of a bad speed-dating experience. You watched as business cards were exchanged and phone numbers were scribbled on napkins. Maybe you even forked over your card. Then came a months-long string of phone calls from that friendly guy with the white shirt who bought lunch. The result, of course, is the opening of some modest investment accounts.

Sometimes, something much worse happens.

In 2007, the Securities and Exchange Commission investigated investment free lunches. Here's what the agency found:

Half of the meetings contained exaggerated or misleading claims. About one-quarter included unsuitable investment recommendations. One in eight were outright scams that the agency referred to other regulators for disciplinary or enforcement actions.

And—surprise!—100 percent weren't free lunches. They were sales pitches.

I know most of you are clever enough to realize there is no such thing as a free lunch. That's not why I relay this story. I tell you because you probably don't know that almost all the investment advice you've ever heard comes from a sales guy (or gal). It's not always a free-lunch invitation. Sometimes, it's just a cold call at the office. Often it's a call from a friend of a friend, or your third cousin's husband, or a new neighbor.

I have a friend with an important job at the Securities and Exchange Commission who tells me whenever we talk that almost every single con artist she has ever prosecuted got started by scamming friends, cousins, uncles, nephews, and so on. Blind faith is at the heart of every investment scam, and what better place to get it than from friends and family? That's how Bernie Madoff, the scammer who stole nearly $50 billion from the rich and famous of New York, built his classic pyramid.

THINK ABOUT THE wonderful Will Smith movie *In Pursuit of Happyness,* if you've seen it. The movie retells the trials of a man named Chris Gardner as he tries to learn the ways of Wall Street. His struggle—which includes sleeping with his young son in a homeless shelter while working as a trainee in a brokerage house—is unfathomable for most of us. But if you watch the movie with a careful eye, you'll notice the real lesson Gardner learns about being a broker throughout the film: It's all about the sales pitch. He spends virtually all of his time in the movie making cold calls, and getting hung up on. He's selling investment advice, but he could just as easily be selling vacuum cleaners or Caribbean vacations.

The next time you work with a financial adviser, I want you to keep that image of Chris Gardner in your mind. You should realize that sales staff at brokerages are not very different from sales staff at car dealerships. And in some ways, they have more in common with telemarketers.

I don't say this to insult the entire financial industry. Being a salesman is no dishonor, and most professions are, at their core, sales jobs. But you should understand that the person talking to you is engaged in a well-orchestrated dance to steer you toward doing things that are very profitable for *them*. Most of you are good at simply hanging up on telemarketers. You are, at least, wary of car salesmen. When you're told about crash-test results and cupholders, you probably realize you're not getting the whole truth and nothing but the truth about that car, so help their God.

Yet many people trust their stockbrokers and financial advisers as they would their family doctor. Doctors, at least, have to go through six years of school. Stockbrokers often get the training that Gardner did—in sales pitches. Some have a little additional finance training. Some really do have your best interests in mind. Many do not. Many brokers do not understand the products they are pitching and are simply reading scripts given to them by superiors. They have little or no financial expertise. Remember rookie mistake number one— assuming others know more about money than you? As you enter Stage 4 of the Pitfall-Proof Pyramid, it's critical you remember this lesson. You've made it this far, why not continue to trust yourself? Doing otherwise can be a costly mistake.

NOW THAT YOU'VE got six months' money, developed a little expertise, dipped your toe in the water of risk, and generally taken care of the basics, you can indulge in a little short-term thinking. Katherine, our protégé, now has nearly $20,000 in mostly ultrasafe investments, which she's accumulated in three to four years. And she's well on her way to being free of all bad debt. And at least some of that money is at hand, ready to help her raise a down payment on a car or a house.

At this stage of the financial journey, Katherine—and you—can start to invest for the present instead of the future. You're not going to get rich by investing in your 401(k). But you'll get solid. Now that you have taken care of the security part of the pyramid, you can start thinking about building up wealth. Now you should consider dabbling in an effort to sock away money that might grow and make you even more comfortable at an even earlier stage in life. Don't plan on it; just open the door to the possibility. At this stage, I'm talking about taking 10 or 20 percent of the money you are saving and setting it aside to make dreams come true—money that in ten years you might be able to use for a boat, or for that two-month vacation around Asia, or to take a one-year leave of absence from work.

One thing I don't want you to do at this stage, however, is lunch. There are far easier ways for you to plan for the future than to give a salesman your money.

Wealth investing—what might be called medium-term investing—

means opening up an investment account just for this purpose. It probably means opening a brokerage account so you can invest in the stock market outside your retirement savings. It might mean hiring a professional financial adviser.

Just don't take a free lunch. Those can be expensive.

This is a book about gotchas and fees; not a book about investing trends. So why have I spent so much time discussing the finer details of the Pitfall-Proof Pyramid? Because I want you to always be operating from solid ground. The best way to avoid getting scammed is to avoid being desperate, and to always invest from a position of strength.

What's fair game at this stage? Notice the dreams I listed earlier—the boat, the sabbatical. None of these are a must-have. When I'm talking about wealth investing, I am talking about playing with house money. I'm talking about money that could shrink by half and you wouldn't lose sleep.

This is important for two reasons. One, it's fiscally sound. The stock market is like the girl you kept asking out on a date in high school: She may eventually say yes to you, but you have little control over the timing. She'll say yes when she's ready. The biggest-money mistake investors make is putting cash that's saddled with a deadline into the market. When the car breaks down, and you need the money right away, you might also find out you had a lemon of a mutual fund. It's true that over the long term, the stock market generally goes up. You may have heard something like this when discussing the market with friends: "There's never been a ten-year period when the stock market hasn't gone up." If you look at the history of the Dow, that might *seem* true (see page 269):

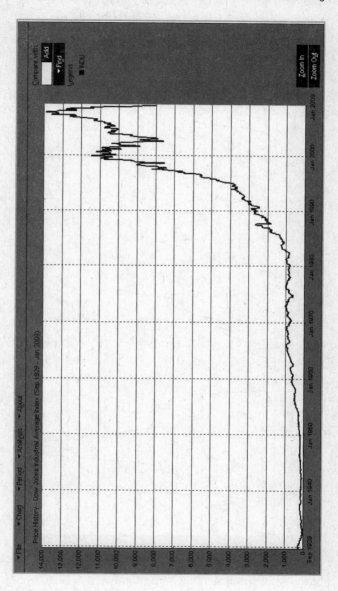

But remember, numbers, and even charts, can lie. The idea that the stock market will always make money in the long run—or even over ten-year periods—is a dangerous myth. Lookie here:

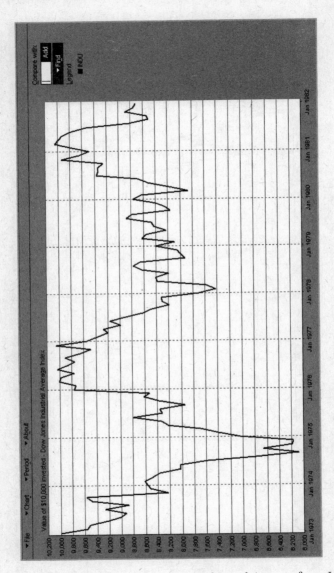

Above is a chart of the Dow Jones Industrial Average from January 1973 to January 1982. If you invested $10,000 on the first day of 1973, you'd have $8,719 in 1982—and that's not considering the commission costs of buying and selling the investment. Notice, this

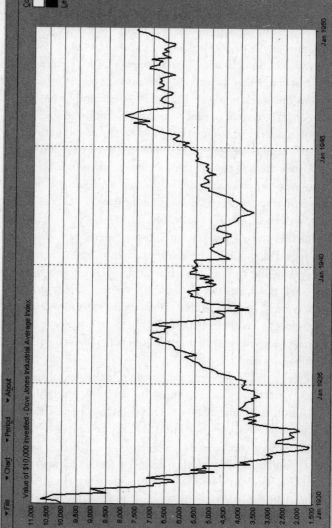
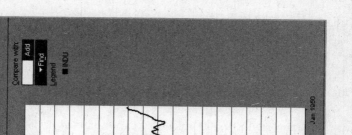

chart is not a fluke. It's not the product of a bad quarter, or even a bad year. It was a ten-year malaise.

Perhaps, you are now hoping, that was a once-in-a-lifetime event. Perhaps, you are thinking (wisely), that ten years isn't a long enough time horizon to guarantee positive returns. How about twenty years? Nope, not good enough.

If you invested $10,000 in Dow stocks on January 1, 1930, you'd have . . . $7,492 on January 1, 1950 (see page 271). Twenty years, 25 percent loss. No, there is no time horizon long enough to guarantee a return in the stock market, although it is currently true that there hasn't been a thirty-year period when stocks haven't risen.

Careful readers might note that I picked the absolute worst times to enter the market in both charts, and that's true. It's not quite fair to cherry-pick the bad times in this analysis. But no one really knows when the next ten-year-long doldrums might begin, and before you start investing for anything with a time horizon that's less than two decades, you need to know the real risk.

And at this stage I really want you to remember rookie mistake number four. Don't put any money into a wealth investment that you might need in the next four to five years. Planning to buy a new house? You'll need a down payment. Keep the money out of your wealth accounts. Kid headed for college in the next few years? Ditto. Have an old car that might need replacement in two years? Don't count on an "aggressive growth fund," or even a "capital preservation fund," to bail you out.

If the house or car purchase might come in the next three, four, or five years, that money must simply be kept off the table here in Stage 4. Put it in a safe place, such as a high-yielding Internet savings account or money market fund. That's the only way to be sure it'll be there when you need it.

A deep understanding of this financial truth will also help you weed out the charlatans who will take your money, take their cut no matter how your stocks perform, and place your money at unnecessary risk. Anyone who gives you the idea that you can easily make money in the stock market is lying to you. Anyone who promises you that medium-term money is safe in a fund is lying. If your feet are planted firmly on the ground, you are less likely to get suckered by the nice man in the white shirt who promises a can't-miss, low-risk investment such as auction-rate securities or municipal bond funds.

Auction-rate securities swept through the private investment world after 2005, at the height of the stock market boom, as the "can't miss" wealth builder with medium-wealthy clients. In most cases, the minimum investment was $25,000. At their core, auction-rate securities were a newfangled way for large institutions such as student-loan lenders or municipalities to raise short-term cash without going to banks. Small investors could get in on the lending, which promised better returns than high-yielding money market accounts. Advisers whispered about them to clients, promised 8–10 percent returns, and regularly said there was no risk, often comparing auction-rate securities to supersafe money market accounts. By 2007, about $330 billion was invested in these mysterious instruments, about half by private investors. By 2008, the market for auction-rate securities had literally disappeared. Many holders couldn't access any of their money. Lawsuits and a government investigation eventually got much of the principal returned to investors, but only after many spent months with their supposedly "safe" money in limbo, looking at statements that said merely "null" where the balance was supposed to be listed.

Municipal bond funds, meanwhile, probably sound like a supersafe investment to you. Buying bonds means paying for the construction of schools and roads, with a promise from stable local governments to pay investors back with interest. What could be safer? If your town can't pay its bills, you'll have bigger problems than a loss of investment income (you'll have no police, for example). A collection of such bonds into a fund should be incredibly safe, right?

Wrong. Bonds aren't just for schools and roads anymore. Nearly anything can be "securitized," as they say on Wall Street. States can borrow off future lottery revenues, for example, or toll-road receipts or even future income-tax collections. Sure, that means trading $10 billion during the next ten years for $4 billion today, but what governor running for reelection wouldn't make that trade? By the time the bill comes due, he'll be long gone.

That kind of short-term thinking led to the ruin of a large segment of the bond fund market in the late 1990s. This requires a bit of explanation. In 1998, to settle a massive lawsuit filed by forty-six states, the tobacco industry promised to make $200 billion in payments to states during the following thirty years. Many states couldn't wait for the money and "securitized" it. That meant they sold bonds against future payments and spent all the money immediately. These so-called tobacco bonds made their way into the bond fund market, right along all those promissory notes that were tied to schools and roads.

The bonds inside bond funds, I should remind you, rise and fall like stocks—and specifically with the market's perception of the issuer's ability to repay those bonds. Even a small event, such as a poorly constructed state budget, can spook bond investors into paying less for bonds. You can probably imagine what happens to the value of tobacco bonds every time a new state passes a law banning smoking in public places. In fact, investing in tobacco bonds, and in funds that hold tobacco bonds, is little different from investing directly in tobacco companies.

Let's review: Perhaps millions of inventors who picked what they thought were supersafe investments in local governments found their financial futures tied directly into the health of the tobacco industry. When I asked Morningstar to review the holdings of all 660 bond funds it researches, the firm told me that 260 held tobacco bonds. And, yes, that money eventually went up in smoke.

Oppenheimer Rochester National Municipals, a fund heavily invested in tobacco bonds, was the single worst performing fund of 2008—and that's saying something. Investors in this allegedly safe haven lost 48.9 percent of their money, a disastrous drop even in a year known as one of the worst ever for the stock market.

So much for safe investments. Remember our original pyramid, the risk/reward pyramid? I'm telling you these horror stories to convince you that no one can revoke the financial rules of gravity. In a normal market, where mortgage rates are around 5 or 6 percent, no one can promise 10 percent returns with no risk. If you make a choice that turns $50,000 into $30,000, no one is going to give you that money back. So I want you to search around for moderately solid returns and moderate risks. Even if you are trying to create medium-term wealth, I want you to be the tortoise, not the hare. Putting $50,000 into a vehicle that averages a tidy 5 percent return for twenty years—even if you never add to the original amount—will leave you with $126,000. After thirty years, you'd have $205,000. That's a pretty tidy sum. You really shouldn't hope to do much better than that.

I'm also telling you all this because at Stage 4 you need to carefully separate your retirement savings from your wealth savings. Your retirement needs to take priority. Experiment with 10 to 20 percent of the leftovers. Leave the serious risks for Stage 5.

But how much risk do you really have to take? Here are some tortoiselike ideas that will be surprisingly satisfying in the end.

Let's take an even more conservative investment than the example above—a high-yielding savings account earning 3 percent each year. Internet-based savings accounts can give you that kind of return. Let's say you water and feed a Web savings account every year, adding $2,500 (a little more than $200 a month) to your original $50,000. After twenty years, the $50,000 will be $150,000. After thirty years, $230,000.

There's one solid way to build wealth. Remember the trite but true Wall Street saying: Bulls make money, bears make money, but pigs get slaughtered. Don't be a pig, and don't give your money to one, either.

I tell you this because financial managers would have you believe the only way to build wealth is by giving them your money and having them put it in some kind of complicated fund. Now you know better. If you fall for a broker's get-rich-quick speech, I will still blame the broker, who should know better. But you should probably look in the mirror, too.

I know if you discuss this simple savings-based approach with investment advisers, they will begin to yammer on about keeping up with inflation, and about the inflation-busting returns they could earn for you. Perhaps. In a moment, we'll discuss your best hedge against inflation. But for now, let me assure you that chasing after speculative stock market returns isn't exactly a brilliant strategy. Financial advisers cannot defy financial gravity. The buying power you'll lose to inflation using a simple savings plan is nothing compared to the money you'll lose through nickel-and-dime investment fees. Here's one example.

Let's say you put that $50,000 into a managed mutual fund instead of a savings account. To keep the numbers simple, let's say the mutual fund earns 5 percent each year, and the manager keeps 1.3 percent in fees (remember the expense ratio?). We'll ignore the issue of disbursements and taxes (these wouldn't impact your tax-free 401(k), but they would impact both your unsheltered, wealth-building brokerage account and the savings account). After twenty years, your return would be $99,716. After thirty years, $134,401.

Let's compare:

	Savings at 3%	Fund at 5%–1.3%
Today	$50,000	$50,000
20 years	$87,675	$99,716
30 years	$117,828	$134,401

The mutual fund wins . . . barely. But remember, the mutual fund can, and will, fluctuate. The year you need it, it is as likely to be down as up. Yes, a savings account can keep up with a mutual fund. Annual fees are deadly to your investment.

Venerated investment titan John Bogle, the father of the index fund, talks often about "the tyranny of compounding costs," and there you see it. Wealth investing gets killed by annual fees. The pain caused by the fees above shows you would get just about the same results by putting your money into an FDIC-insured, can-never-lose-value Internet savings account as in a mutual fund. So why would you take the risk? Why are you paying someone to manage your money? Invest in a low-fee S&P 500 fund, even in this wealth account, and the returns using the example above (assuming a 0.10% fee) are $124,000 after twenty years and $200,197 after thirty. Now you're cooking.

	Savings at 3%	Fund at 5%, 1.3%	Index fund at, 5%–0.10%
Today	$50,000	$50,000	$50,000
20 years	$87,675	$99,716	$124,000
30 years	$117,828	$134,401	$200,197

Mark Kritzman, president of Windham Capital Management of Boston and an adjunct professor at MIT's Sloan School of Management, ran an elaborate study in 2008 that took into consideration far more detail than I have, including annual tax payments. He showed that an actively managed fund with moderate expenses would have to beat an index fund's return by an average of 4.3 points every year just to keep up with the index fund. A much more expensive hedge fund would have to beat the index fund by 10 points every year. Since only a tiny fraction of managed funds beat index funds in even one year, the chance of picking investments that outperform the S&P over twenty years is virtually zero, Kritzman said. During the twenty years he studied, only 13 out of the 452 mutual funds that Morningstar had records on beat the index funds when expenses were considered.

In other words, making money doesn't require a guy in a white shirt with an Italian suit and greasy hair. Making money takes time, discipline, and careful protection from nickel-and-diming fees.

When inflation comes, it does, of course, destroy purchasing power. That's true whether your money is in a savings account or an investment account. But trying to stay an inch ahead of inflation by taking on big stock market risk is a fool's game. It's likely that interest savings rates will rise along with inflation—not enough to eliminate the risk entirely, but enough to balance the risk of taking on stock purchases. The only real hedge against inflation is to own hard assets, such as real estate. Once upon a time, real estate didn't seem so risky, either. But if you are at the life stage of wealth investing, true diversification of your assets can certainly include a well-considered second home or investment property. Just don't expect to get rich overnight.

KATHERINE'S PROGRESS

	Time Required	Savings	Money In	Debt Payments
Stage 3	3–4 years	$50,000	$10,000 savings account, $10,000 conservative retirement account, $20,000 S&P 500 fund, $10,000 risky stocks/funds	$4,500/year

Stage 5

Get Comfy—Advanced Risk

Get comfortable
- The 21st-century raise
- Wealth investing

Set for the future
- Dabble in wealth building
- Firm retirement plan
- Set-asides for home, cars, college

6 months
- Ready for any surprise
- Mutual funds/risk in 401(k)
- Serious debt reduction

3 months
- Strong plan B • Conservative 401(k) retirement
- Debt map • Down-payment savings

6 weeks
- Emergency kitty
- Maybe a Roth IRA or Roth 401(k)

PITFALL-PROOF PYRAMID

I told you that you wouldn't get rich quickly by reading my book. But getting rich slowly is the next best thing. Katherine is now four to six years into the pyramid and about to embark on serious wealth investing. Four to six years doesn't seem like all that long a wait, does it?

As usual, I'd like to start by telling you how not to go about Stage 5; and how to avoid backing yourself into a corner and getting screwed, which can happen if, like the Greek mythical character Icarus, you try to fly too close to the sun.

When should you move from beginning wealth investing to aggressive wealth investing? Here's my benchmark: after you have six months' living expenses stored up in cash and retirement funds, you are fully funding your retirement accounts, and you have a solid foundation of medium-term wealth savings in safe places like index funds.

One size does not fit all however. Practically speaking, for most folks, the point hits when you are contributing the maximum amount to the tax-sheltered 401(k) account (currently $16,500 per year for an individual). But the most specific answer is this: You become aggressive with medium-term investing when your retirement plan is accounted for. Many Americans have wildly unrealistic ideas about the money they'll need to retire. At the beginning of 2009, the average balance for an American who had a 401(k) (and half of Americans don't) was $50,000. For most people, that's barely enough to make it from sixty-five years old to sixty-seven years old. But what happens after that?

Thirty years ago, an employee who spent twenty-five years at a company could retire with the promise of a pension—a guaranteed monthly check for life. Even a paltry pension for a lower-wage job might offer $1,500 per month and discounted health insurance.

Today, pensions are dead, replaced by these spiffy 401(k) accounts. The result has been the creation of a ticking time bomb. Obviously, our retiree in the above example will not want to draw on the $50,000 balance at age sixty-five. Instead, she'll want to put it into some kind of income-generating investment. Would you like to know what kind of monthly checks a $50,000 401(k) account can generate?

I'll tell you—$200 per month.

And remember, I'm talking about the average 401(k) account balance. Roughly half of America has less than that, less than $200 a month coming to them from their retirement account.

I don't know how much money you'll need to retire, only you know that. One popular formula suggests you'll need to generate two-thirds of your annual income after retirement. Whatever the amount, it's a lot more than $200 a month. So when I say you shouldn't try aggressive wealth investing until your retirement plan (and the kids' college, and the new car, and the new home) is in order, I mean *really* in order. I don't mean strictly speaking that you'll have the $1 million saved today, but if you think you need $1 million to retire, you need to have a plan for how you are going to get that $1 million ($1,000 every month into a special account? A big promotion?), and to have implemented that plan, before you begin aggressive wealth investing.

Here's a rough guideline: For every $100,000 in your retirement account, you'll be able to generate about $400 a month in income. So if you think you'll need $2,000 a month, in addition to Social Security, to live comfortably, you'll need $500,000.

Notice, by the way, how incredibly valuable those old-fashioned pensions were. A $1,500-a-month pension is the equivalent of roughly $375,000 in a 401(k) account.

Whenever discussion of regular retirement income comes up, annuities are not far behind. These insurance-like products do promise perpetual income, but they come at a hefty price. We can dispense with this subject rather quickly. Annuities, which are explained in detail in the insurance chapter earlier, are only suitable for high-net-worth individuals who are looking for elaborate tax shelters. For more than 95 percent of consumers, annuities are a bad deal. They are a great deal, however, for the annuity salesman. Agents often get commissions of 4 percent to 7 percent of the principal invested for selling variable annuities, and 5 percent to 12 percent for equity-indexed products. An agent who convinces a retiree to roll over a $200,000 IRA into an annuity can earn as much as $24,000.

Suffice to say you should avoid annuities. You don't want to help some agent's retirement plans, you want to help your own. Stick to the simple math. Realistically, anyone under forty probably needs something closer to $4,000 per month to sustain a familiar lifestyle. Generating that kind of income requires a retirement account stocked with $1 million!

I don't want you to see this as an impossible goal. Behavioral economists Richard Thaler and Shlomo Benartzi have come up with an incredibly simple, effective way to get started. I've been holding out on you until this stage of the pyramid, but really, you could use this technique to begin saving money at any stage.

Each time you get a raise, a bonus, or moonlighting income, pretend you didn't. Just take that 4 percent raise or that $1,000 payment and automatically shift the new money into your wealth account. You'll never notice it's gone if you don't get used to spending it. Or, to give yourself a little reward, split the raise or income fifty-fifty. Take that raise and give 2 percent to yourself now and send the rest off to your buy-a-big-boat-someday account. Thaler and Benartzi have done extensive research on which consumers meet investment goals, and which give up, and found "raise-skimming" to be one of the best predictors of success. They call their plan Save More Tomorrow. During one experiment, the researchers found that consumers who used raise-skimming increased their savings rate from 3.5 percent to 13.6 percent.

Here's why: Let's go back to our ultraconservative $50,000 investment placed in a savings account earning 3 percent interest. Leave it alone, and after thirty years, it would be worth $117,000. Now, let's say you earn $75,000 a year and average a 6 percent raise every year. You take half of that, 3 percent, and blindly drop it into this savings account. You'll never notice it's gone.

The importance of incremental increases in savings, just like incremental fees, cannot be overstated. That's why I have an entire chapter devoted to the twenty-first-century raise in this book. It sounds obvious, but it's easily forgotten—the easiest, most effective ʼɔ grow your savings is to consistently grow your contributions.

Socking away all these little increases into savings is a bit like a tulip bulb planted in the fall. It might seem as if nothing is happening all winter, but underground, that bulb is working very hard for you. By spring, it's something beautiful.

Back to your raise-skimmed $50,000 investment. The bad news is that after thirty years, your account will no longer be FDIC-insured. It's grown too much.

But there's very good news. Our little savings account, augmented simply by 3 percent investment returns and 3 percent raises, is worth $449,622 after thirty years. Now, that's wealth building, all with no risk. (Too good to believe? Check the endnotes.) The truth is, what you want is those 3 percents working for you, not against you.

Now that you've accumulated a half million dollars with no risk, you'll want to split the savings up at different banks so you are FDIC-insured (accounts are only insured to $250,000). And perhaps you should think about getting professional money management help.

Throughout this book I've been very hard on financial planners. I've overstated that case just a bit, largely because I am convinced that in the majority of cases consumers can handle their finances as well as, if not better than, so-called financial professionals. But for all the reasons I outlined before, most are afraid. Afraid of screwing up, afraid of missing out, and in general afraid of money. That sets them up to be victims. And I want you to know the truth: The vast amount of financial professionals you meet have very little training in money managing or markets; they are trained in sales. You should believe that you are as smart as they are. The vast majority of investors could simplify their financial lives and severely reduce their exposure to unnecessary risk by following the simple tactics I've outlined here.

But of course, there is plenty of room for even more creativity, and more moneymaking, and every rule has exceptions. Some financial advisers are great. Some really do have their clients' best interests in mind, despite the strong economic pressures that surround them. You probably think you know someone like that. Maybe you do. But remember what we've said about confirmation bias—once you've given your money to someone, something deep inside you pressures you to find evidence that you made the right choice, and to ignore evidence to the contrary. You want to think you've made a good choice. If there's a problem, you will almost certainly be slow to recognize it. But I promise you, you will never know how honest your adviser is until you become interested in money and understand exactly what he or she is doing.

This brings me nearly all the way back to the beginning, to *rookie mistake 1*, when dealing with advisers: Never, ever, ever invest in something you don't understand. This is related to the rule I've been implying all chapter, namely, never invest in something that defies the rules of the pyramid. Here's a good test: Before you invest in anything, try to explain what you are about to do to a friend. If his or her eyes glaze over at terms like *auction-rate securities* and you can't convincingly unglaze them, you shouldn't put any cash into it.

I hate fees, of course. But one fee you should gladly play an adviser is a flat fee. In the world of business, everything is about incentives. You need to understand the incentives behind every person you talk money with. An adviser may well believe he or she has your intentions at heart. But the principle of economic bias is impossible to ignore, and just about impossible to eliminate. If someone stands to benefit by selling you something, that person will see the merits of your buying that something and be blinded to any downside. How else can we explain the annuities market? You should always know—go ahead and ask—the economic bias of the person you are talking with. Always ask advisers to put in writing what their sources of compensation are. Then, whenever their advice and their compensation converge, take the advice with a huge grain of salt.

That's the good thing about fee-based advisers. They aren't working on commission; they make money whether you buy this or sell that. They make money strictly on their time and advice. Their bias is to keep you as a client. That's a far superior economic relationship to that of the "free" advisers who make money only when you buy or sell things they recommend, or when they buy you lunch. If you find yourself believing that you simply must have a financial adviser, go ahead and pay for one.

The real value in the world of financial advice is in tax advice. The U.S. tax code is awful, and blatantly unfair to middle-range earners and investors. Tax planners bring a decided trade skill to this area. I've so far left taxes out of this discussion, but they obviously impact every part of the pyramid. Federal income tax will suck up a lot of those wonderful savings-account interest earnings I've been telling you about. That lovely $449,000 I told you about gets knocked down to $323,000 if you factor in Uncle Sam sucking 25 percent of those interest earnings every year (this is why your 401(k) is so valuable: tax-free growth). The issues become much more complex as the wealth grows, and even more as you approach retirement and death issues. When you enter the world of wealth investing—that is, beyond your tax-free 401(k)—you should consider hiring a CPA to optimize your tax situation and handle estate planning. If you're paying for tax help, you're getting more than a sales job. In some cases, a financial adviser will double as a CPA. As long as you're paying a flat fee for the stock tips, and not taking advice laced with economic bias, that's fine.

When you begin interviewing financial advisers (you are interviewing at least three, aren't you? You're not going with Uncle Earnie, are you?), one indispensable tool is the BrokerCheck at the Financial Industry Regulatory Authority, or FINRA. The agency's database covers more than six hundred thousand registered securities brokers and five thousand brokerage firms. If an agent has any violations on his or her record, they'll turn up in this database. Even better, the page lists the agent's employment history. Beware agents who jump around a lot. It also lists the agent's certifications, examinations, and even other associations. Obviously, it won't tell you if the agent gives good advice. But it's a good start.

You can learn a lot more about the financial-planner industry by visiting that association's website at CFP.net.

One place not to look for an investment adviser—your local bank. Let your bank handle your mortgage. Any advice that lands in your lap from a drop-in at a bank is sure to be sales-oriented and inferior.

Here's another reason to carefully research your choice of broker.

Breaking up is hard to do. Brokers typically charge hefty fees to move your money somewhere else—often at least $500.

If you already have a broker and you get that sinking feeling that something has gone wrong—that your money for a new car next year was placed in a too-risky mutual fund—put your concerns in writing ("I thought we agreed to keep this in cash"). And get the responses you receive in writing. If you discuss anything verbally, write a letter or email afterward that summarizes your understanding of the discussion and send it. Creating a paper trail is incredibly important, and it will definitely get the attention of your broker. As we've said before, the SEC has a broad definition of misbehavior. A paper trail will be important should your complaint escalate to the next level.

I want you to think much more broadly about the notion of "investment scams." The SEC does. Any financial professional who recommends an inappropriate investment vehicle for a consumer is subject to disciplinary action. That's a pretty broad definition. If we took that literally, our jails would be full of most brokers who ever sold annuities.

But by the time you're in Stage 5, you know money. You know better than to take bad advice. And you're about to find out how to avoid losing money on the things you buy, too.

KATHERINE'S PROGRESS

	Time Required	Savings	Money In	Debt Payments
Stage 3	7 years and beyond	$1 million	$10,000 savings account, $10,000 conservative retirement account, $20,000 S&P fund, vacation home, boat, college fund, happily ever after	None

LeeAnn Gaunt, head of investigations for the SEC's Boston office, offers these succinct tips on how to avoid getting screwed while investing.

Five hallmarks of false promises:

1. **"Guaranteed returns with no risk!"** There are no guaranteed returns in financial investments. Anyone who says you're going to get a guaranteed return, *even a very modest one,* is flat-out lying to you. The same goes for "risk-free" investments. There aren't any. Period.

2. **"You're special."** If the financial professional claims that an opportunity is secret, highly confidential, and/or available to just a select few, be suspicious. You're really not that special. The same goes for anyone who pressures you to "hurry up" and invest or you might miss your chance. There will always be people who are willing to let you invest your money with them. You should take all the time you need to fully understand what you're investing in.

3. **"It's complex."** If the investment sounds like mumbo jumbo, it probably is. If the investment professional explaining the investment sounds as if he is speaking a foreign language and/or you are made to feel ignorant because you don't understand the investment strategy, either he is trying to pull a fast one on you, or he is an ineffective communicator. Either way, you deserve better. Move on.

4. **"Trust me, we've known each other since grade school."** Don't trust your friends or your family (when it comes to investments). Never, ever invest money just because someone you know from high school, your church, or the Elks Club told you that they are getting a really great return. It could be a particular kind of fraud called an affinity fraud, which targets social groups, churches, neighborhoods, etc., and which preys on people's inherent willingness to trust people they know personally. Often, the "recruiters" are people you have known and trusted your entire life, people who would give you the shirt off their back and who honestly believe that they have made a great investment and want you to as well. Too often we find that those people have been misled, are also victims of the scam, and are devastated to learn they have unwittingly participated in the

victimization of their friends and families. It's like a chain letter, only it involves your life savings and leaves you bankrupt.

5. "Just write the check out to me." Never, ever write a check out to the investment adviser or to the broker personally. Doing so puts you at risk of having your money intercepted by the bad guy before it ever reaches a legitimate investment. Your account should be held with an independent third-party custodian (a registered entity that holds the actual securities), typically a brokerage firm. Whether you're dealing with an investment adviser or a broker, your check should be written out to the *brokerage firm* and mailed to the *brokerage firm*. This is important: You should get periodic account statements showing your holdings from the *brokerage firm*, not just from the adviser or the broker himself. Dishonest brokers or advisers can easily gin up false brokerage statements that make it look as if you have a lot of money invested with them. If you don't get the statements *directly from the brokerage firm*, you don't know what your account really holds. If there is anything about your statement that looks suspicious (typos, "clerical errors," for example), call the firm's compliance officer for an explanation.

And Gaunt offers two things to do if you feel your broker has been misleading you:

1. Call the SEC at the very first sign of trouble (the adviser failing to honor redemption requests promptly, inexplicable delays in returning calls, just not answering the phone, sudden requests for more money, including requests that you withdraw *retirement* funds to invest). I'd much rather catch one of these scams before it completely implodes and all the money is gone.

2. Save documents (checks, statements, offering materials) and make contemporaneous notes of discussions. That allows us to identify misrepresentations quickly and makes it easier for us to seek an emergency court order to freeze whatever money might be left.

Conclusion

> The depressing truth is that financial literacy is impossible, at least for many of the big financial decisions all of us have to make.
>
> —RICHARD THALER

Richard Thaler, one of the founders of modern behavioral economics, has a rather discouraging outlook on the subject of consumers and money. People are poked and prodded and tricked with all manner of advertising and rogue mathematics. We are lied to with "fixed interest rates for life" that change. And most important, we often don't care or don't notice because we are too busy trying to raise children, trying to get promoted, or taking care of elderly parents. The average consumer, Thaler believes, cannot be expected to negotiate a fair rate on a complex mortgage product and keep track of expense ratios in their 401(k) plan mutual funds.

"If these things are perplexing to people with Ph.D.s in economics, financial literacy is not the right road to go down," he says.

He's right, of course. We have turned all of these basic life decisions into complex games with arcane and whimsical rules. Only those with inside knowledge can get a good deal. The vast majority suffer. This is a terrible way to organize a society.

But it's not going to change anytime soon. That's why I wrote this book. I want it to be your insider's guide to life in our unfair times. Every time you make a sound, informed financial choice, you help keep your fiscal ship in order. Every time you fight over an unfair fee, you are taking care of your family's bottom line. But I believe you are also doing something much more important than that: You are joining a volunteer army that aims to restore fairness and honor to America's marketplace. Each time you raise your voice to fight a hidden fee, you are doing your part to restore our system.

For now, these are the things you must do to stop getting screwed. I think it is your patriotic duty to take up this fight. This is no time to surrender.

But of course, much more must be done. Thaler supports simplification of most financial choices. For example, he wants most American workers to be automatically enrolled in retirement savings plans. Workers not wanting to be involved would have to opt out; today, they must opt in. By making the default option the "right" option, consumers could be saved strife in many financial arenas.

It's easy to forecast some trouble with this idea. Who would decide which choices were right, for example? In hindsight, the most sensible thing to do from 2004 to 2008 was to avoid investing in the stock market. Those who procrastinated in joining 401(k) plans during that time are happy they did so. Pushing an additional segment into stock market investment seems a little dubious since the 2008 crash.

But in general, this is a good idea. The default option is to buy a car with working brakes and a house that's up to code. We should make the default option safe mortgages and credit cards. It shouldn't be legal to give someone a loan that any reasonable person would know can't be repaid. The default option should also be cell phone plans that don't have outrageous fees with punishments that don't fit the crimes. We can't protect people from every financial hazard. But we should protect people from obvious and avoidable financial disasters.

In other words, we should be willing to regulate more and be much more willing to enforce the law. How many times have you walked into a store and bought a shirt from a table that said "two for the price of one," only to be told at the cash register that the shirt you picked is not included in the deal. That's false advertising. So are fixed-rate credit cards with rates that change. So are dealership ads that promise $200 new cars that don't exist. Some of these ads are outright fraud; others are designed to walk gingerly along the edge of the law ("Well, we had one two-hundred-dollar car"). But much of the time, they still run afoul of the basic Federal Trade Commission Act, and state consumer-protection laws, which require "clear and conspicuous" notice of all terms and conditions. Where are the government regulators? It would take only one or two prosecutions a year per industry to keep businesses in line. Fully funded state consumer-protection offices and federal regulators would be the single best way to restore credibility and strength to the American marketplace—and to make sure we never build another house of cards.

Setting such rules is not as hard as people like to make it sound. It's not fair to take money from people when they never intended to give it to you, or to sell them a product they don't fully understand. "Regret laws" or "free-look" laws offer a neat solution to this problem. In many states, consumers who buy certain products have five to ten days to change their minds—or to have their friends talk some sense into them. Currently, these laws are limited to such products as gym memberships, auto warranties, and life insurance. Additional regret laws should be considered. In the long run, no one wins when someone buys something or spends money by accident. The existence of additional regret laws would force companies to be more clear at the point of sale.

Fixing our problems will take much more than new laws, however. One quietly anonymous group of guilty parties in America's meltdown are the employees themselves. Here's a secret problem with our country: the rampant lack of conscience from some people who work at car dealerships, cell phone sales kiosks, and banks. Consumer advocates like to criticize faceless corporations and distant characters such as CEOs. But behind every bad transaction is a bad choice by an employee. Tens of thousands of mortgage brokers and loan officers made a killing by selling toxic products from 2001 to 2007. They are guilty, too.

So I call on all fair-minded Americans to stop doing what profit-driven, heartless companies tell them to do. And to tell fellow employees when they're crossing the line. In short, to speak up. If no one sold pay-option ARM mortgages, there wouldn't have been any market for them. Fair-minded employees everywhere should be willing to raise their hand and say, "No, I won't do this. I won't cheat my fellow man or fellow woman anymore."

In particular, I call on all mathematicians and business-school graduates to take some kind of an oath—akin to the physicians' Hippocratic oath—that they will use their superior numbers skills with honor. It might be a fun mental challenge to predict the percentage of customers who will send in late payments to credit card companies if the payment-due date is moved by one day. But you don't have to use your skills for evil. Doctors promise to do no harm. Mathematicians should promise the same thing.

Also, there needs to be serious and sustained investment in financial education. Why graduate students who can read if they can't add? Only three states mandate financial-math classes; only another dozen or so require personal-finance study as part of another class. That's starkly inadequate and should immediately change. Mandatory financial education is a public health issue and should be treated with that same urgency.

Nonprofit groups such as Jump$tart and Junior Achievement offer helpful course outlines to schools and some independent programs. But these efforts are tiny compared to the size of the problem. Remember, the world was sent into a deep financial freeze because millions of individuals made terrible financial choices. Changes must be made to prevent such an avoidable calamity from happening again. But of all the changes that could be made, I can say with certainty that only one single change would have prevented all of it:

Smarter consumers.

To restate the opening of this book, I'll remind you that Jefferson said a functioning democracy requires an informed electorate, and I say a functioning economy requires informed consumers. The housing collapse and the subsequent halving of everyone's retirement savings should make clear that I am not simply a raving consumer advocate with an ax to grind. Financial literacy is the civil rights issue of the twenty-first century, as John Bryant, founder of the financial-literacy organization Operation HOPE is fond of saying. People like Staff Sergeant Rolon should not have to travel to Iraq to save their home from foreclosure, nor should they believe that a desert war zone is safer than an ocean full of financial sharks. This should be our new cause.

SO WHAT SHOULD you do now? I'll give you a five-step plan:

1. **Complain.** Every time you are mistreated by a company, complain. Complete the Kabuki dance, even if it seems pointless. Fill out the form, send the letter to the CEO, write a critical note on the company blog. Tell the appropriate federal-government regulator, the Better Business Bureau, and your state attorney general. Even if you don't get your money back, speak the truth out loud. It's just as important as voting in a presidential election.

2. **Change.** Vote with your wallet, too. Never patronize a bank or company that cheats you. Hold your grudge. The best way to rid the world of thieving corporations is to cut them off at the knees. Pay a little extra to work with fair companies, so they succeed.

3. **Organize.** It's hard to make a difference with one lonely voice. Large groups get more attention, both from regulators and from company PR departments. The best way to get satisfaction, and change, is to find another five hundred or so people who've suffered the same indignity as you and organize a protest. You've seen a family picket outside a car dealership or mattress retailer at least once in your life. Be that family. Thanks to the Internet, it's easy to find other people who've been harmed like you. One place to do that is through my blog, the Red Tape Chronicles, or my volunteer advocacy group, the Red Tape Raiders. But the Web offers numerous similar outlets, such as Consumerist.com, ConsumerAffairs.com, Complaints .com, Yelp.com, TheSqueakyWheel.com. Sign up, find each other, and make a lot of noise.

4. Sue. Nothing says you mean business like a nasty letter on a law firm's letterhead. Once you've found some other victimized consumers, consider taking your case to a class-action lawyer. Often, the only way for consumers to exact retribution after a wrong is to take the legal route. No consumer who's eyeing a $30 refund will ever interest a lawyer. But one hundred thousand consumers eyeing $30 refunds sure will. Jeffrey Carton, one of the nation's top class-action lawyers, offers this advice: Create a massive paper trail. The more paper the better. Write down every phone call, every registered letter, every disputed payment. Nothing turns on a class-action lawyer more than a compelling plaintiff with excellent records. Not long ago, a woman emailed Carton asking for help, and when he returned her note, she sent him an Adobe Acrobat file that was one hundred pages long. She got his attention.

5. Demand change. Finally, I hope I've impressed on you the dire need for systematic change. I'm always astonished at the level of mistreatment American consumers will tolerate. I'm hopeful that we've reached the end of our rope, however. I've said it before in this tome, but it bears repeating: Today, our system requires all consumers to fight for their economic survival every day. It's barbaric. For now, I want you to fight for yourselves. But in the long run, this is a terrible way to run a society. We need a government that is for the people, of the people, and by the people, rather than what we have now: a government of, for, and by the corporations. Elect officials who are willing to give agencies such as the Federal Trade Commission real teeth. Don't see them? Run for office yourself. Write letters to your local news organizations. Start blogs when you are wronged. We are spending far too much time generating a nation of cynics, and we would be much better off making the world safe for dreamers, optimists, and risk takers. Work for that world and we will give our children a decent place to live in the second half of the twenty-first century. Without that, all bets are off.

ACKNOWLEDGMENTS

My prior book, *Gotcha Capitalism,* succeeded beyond my wildest dreams, hitting *The New York Times* bestseller list in the crowded advice category. I believe I was lucky; the timing was perfect. Americans angry about the economy were looking to assign blame. In scheming, conniving, dishonest corporations, they had a great target.

It is a bad and annoying habit to stand over rubble and say, "I told you so." But it's downright nauseating when journalists do it. Like any typical reporter, I am sometimes guilty. I point out what's wrong from the sidelines, declare myself thoughtful by calling it ahead of time as a trend, and move on.

Jill Schwartzman, my editor at Random House, would have none of that. Don't just point out what's wrong, she urged me, repeatedly. Tell people what they should do. People who are paying $15 for a book don't just want problems, they want solutions. Don't you really want to be helpful?

In part to answer her challenge, I've written *Stop Getting Ripped Off.* If you like it, you should thank Jill, as I am now, for continually urging me to hone my problem-solving skills.

There are a host of other people at Random House to thank—not just for helping me publish a book, but for believing in an idea. Jane von Mehren, who runs Random House's fine trade paperback division, has invested in me twice now, and I hope to show she was wise for doing so. No one works harder than my publicist Lisa Barnes, helped by Caitlin Kuhfeldt and Alison Masciovecchio. Thanks also to editor Lea Beresford and production editor Penelope Haynes.

Helping tie all those folks together with me was my agent Daniel Lazar of Writers House. Every time there is anything to discuss, I find myself quite relieved that he is on my side.

My chief research assistant, Lauren Serpe, also deserves a huge helping of gratitude. By day her task is even more impressive—she works to keep the world safe for democracy—but she spent many evenings researching ways to keep your money safe. I also thank Colleen Sanvido for supplying me with additional research help.

I could not be of any help at all without the continued support of the great folks at msnbc.com. My day job, writing "The Red Tape Chronicles" for msnbc.com, has provided me with the best platform a twenty-first-century journalist could hope for. Editor Michael Brunker has continued to be a good ear and an unflinching advocate for my ideas and stories. Technology editor, Michael Wann, has also offered steadfast support. Editor in chief, Jennifer Sizemore, has managed to preserve a newsroom that allows serious, important journalism to thrive during what has been perhaps journalism's darkest hour. And CEO, Charlie Tillinghast, continues to show good news can be good business.

Producers at NBC News have also given me ample face time and opportunity to share my ideas to its television audience—including Kim Grabina-Como, Andrew Gross, Jay Blackman, Albert Oetgen, and Patricia Luchsinger. And I thank NBC News president, Steve Capus, for his commitment to consumer news, and for believing that websites and TV networks have a lot to offer each other.

But most important, I want to thank you, dear reader, for caring and making a stand. To everyone who's ever stood up to a hidden fee, waited on hold for an hour to obtain a $4 refund, who demanded better customer service and quit a company when they weren't satisfied: I salute all of you. You are the most important engine in a market economy, and you are the only fool-proof tool for fixing what ills our economy now.

My grandfather, who died before I was born, was a train engineer. On August 17, 1941, he was driving for the Delaware, Lackawanna, and

Western Railroad headed to Hoboken, New Jersey, when there was a deadly derailment. The ugly crash, which saw the engine skid on its side for a quarter-mile, was the news of the day, the equivalent of a major airline crash today. My own father got the news that his dad had died from a premature radio announcement.

There were four casualties and one death that day, but my badly injured grandfather had luckily survived. While he was recovering from his injuries in the hospital, a government inquest publicly declared him responsible for the accident.

Recently, I used my reporting skills to track down the accident investigation report completed by the Interstate Commerce Commission, that day's equivalent to our National Transportation Safety Board. I learned that the revolving door between industries and their regulators was even more egregious in the early 1940s than it is today. A bunch of former railroad company officials had found my grandfather guilty of speeding: "Accident was caused by excessive speed on a curve," the report declared on its cover page.

But anyone who bothered to read the entire report could see it was contradictory. It said that the speed of the train by itself could not have caused the crash. There was a laundry list of other causes: poor signage, misaligned tracks, and inadequate banking on the curve. My grandfather was railroaded.

Fortunately, after many months, he got healthy, got out of the hospital bed, took on the industry, and got his job back.

My grandfather's saga influences my family and I to this day. We are all fighters. I hope Grandpa Sullivan can influence you, too. Look for revolving doors between corporations and the regulators who are supposed to keep them in line. Complain about the shuttle flights between Wall Street and Washington D.C. In the meantime, fight for what is yours, and don't accept the first ruling against you—even if you have to fight City Hall.

But don't forget to smile. As Grandma McFadden would say: "You get more bees with honey than vinegar." She had the ability to argue while maintaining dignity and grace, a winning combination sorely lacking in our world today.

NOTES

PART I: WHY CONSUMERS GET SCREWED

3 **Staff Sergeant Sandra Rolon** Sergeant Rolon's story initially appeared in "Helping to Keep Homelessness at Bay as Foreclosures Hit More Families," by Manny Fernandez. *The New York Times,* February 4, 2008. With additional reporting by Colleen Sanvido.

5 **Look at the menu below** This question and all subsequent questions are taken from the National Assessment of Adult Literacy, a massive study performed occasionally by the U.S. Department of Education's National Center for Education Statistics. Basic information can be found at the organization's website http://nces.ed.gov/naal/index.asp.

Sample questions can be found and downloaded from http://nces.ed.gov/NAAL/sample_items.asp.

13 **The problem of adult illiteracy** Robert Roy Britt, "14 Percent of U.S. Adults Can't Read," LiveScience.com, January 10, 2009, http://www.livescience.com/culture/090110-illiterate-adults.html.

13 **John Allen Paulos tried** John Allen Paulos, *Innumeracy: Mathematical Illiteracy and Its Consequences* (New York: Vintage, 1990).

14 **The same people who cringe** Ibid., 4.

14 **For example, he'll be** Scott LaFee, "Odds and ends: Eventually, everybody's number comes up," *The San Diego Union Tribune,* February 22, 2004.

15 **In another great tome** Joseph Ganem, *The Two-Headed Quarter: How to See Through Deceptive Numbers and Save Money on Everything You Buy* (Baltimore: Chartley Publishing, 2007).

17 **As for that bar bet** For more on the birthday problem, there is a great explainer (and a little bit of math) in an article titled "Understanding the Birthday Paradox" at BetterExplained.com, written by Kalid Azad. He blames self-centeredness. It can be viewed at http://betterexplained.com/articles/understanding-the-birthday-paradox/.

18 **In a wonderful children's book** Demi, *One Grain of Rice: A Mathematical Folktale* (New York: Scholastic Press, 1997).

18 **50 million Americans** Mark Roth, "Tax reform plan would shift tax return preparation to the IRS". *Pittsburgh Post-Gazette,* March 23, 2008.

19 **In one classic example** Matthew Rabin and Richard Thaler, "Anomalies: Risk Aversion," *Journal of Economic Perspectives* 15 (2001).

20 **Here's another behavioral puzzler** There is a growing body of research and literature which combines neuroscience and economics, a field that's been given the name "Neuroeconomics." When used by a sales team, the term "Neuromarketing" has been used. For an excellent introduction to the subject, see *The Mind of the Market: Compassionate Apes, Competitive Humans, and Other Tales from Evolutionary Economics*, by Michael Shermer. Times Books (December 26, 2007) p. 131–138.

20 **Here's one study** G. Northcraft and M. Neale, "Experts, amateurs, and real estate: An anchoring-and-adjustment perspective on property pricing decisions," *Organizational Behavior and Human Decision Processes* 39 (1987): 84–97.

20 **Here's one you can** For more, see Daniel Kahneman, Jack Knetsch, and Richard Thaler, "Anomalies: The Endowment Effect, Loss Aversion, and Status Quo Bias," *Journal of Economic Perspectives* 5 (1991): 193–206.

21 **One more: *confirmation bias*** Confirmation bias is a long-observed trait. Leo Tolstoy made the point in his book *The Kingdom of God Is within You*. He wrote, "The most difficult subjects can be explained to the most slow-witted man if he has not formed any idea of them already; but the simplest thing cannot be made clear to the most intelligent man if he is firmly persuaded that he knows already, without a shadow of doubt, what is laid before him."

21 **72 percent of online daters** Steven D. Levitt and Stephen J. Dubner, *Freakonomics: A Rogue Economist Explores the Hidden Side of Everything* (New York: William Morrow, 2005), 60.

It's also noteworthy that 94 percent of college professors rate their performance as above average. See P. Cross, "Not can but will college teaching be improved?" *New Directions for Higher Education* 17 (1977): 1–15.

21 **42 percent of workers** T. R. Zenger, "Why do employers only reward extreme performance? Examining the relationships among performance, pay, and turnover," *Administrative Science Quarterly* 37 (1992): 198–219.

21 **93 percent of drivers** Ola Svenson, "Are we all less risky and more skillful than our fellow drivers?" *Acta Psychologica* 47.2 (February 1981): 143–48.

Also worthy of note: Overconfident drivers are dangerous drivers, according to researchers. Driver Safety Services of Australia has developed a training manual for ambulance drivers, for example, that expressly forbids teachers from complimenting students' skills, lest they drive more dangerously. "People who have an exaggerated sense of control—who are unrealistically optimistic—tend to be less cautious than those who have more realistic views," the manual, called "Guard Against Promoting Optimism," says. That clearly applies to financial decisions as well. See http://www.ambulancedriving.com/changedriving/optimism.html.

21 **nearly everyone believes** In the book *Nudge*, author Richard H. Thaler describes an experiment he runs on his college students. He asks how they compare against each other. Less than 5 percent say they expect to be below the fiftieth percentile.

The definitive work in this area is a paper titled "Unskilled and Unaware of It: How Difficulties in Recognizing One's Own Incompetence Lead to Inflated Self-Assessments," by Justin Kruger and David Dunning of Cornell University, *Journal of Personality and Social Psychology* 77, no. 6 (1999): 1121–34. Their research was a bit more subtle, and the results more nuanced, than I have described. Essentially, the smarter you are, the more likely you are to underestimate your intelligence; and the reverse is also true. This probably isn't hard to observe in everyday life. People who don't get it are often the last to know they don't get it.

21 **Perhaps more on point** Vanessa Gail Perry et al., "Is Ignorance Bliss? Consumer Accuracy in Judgments about Credit Ratings," *Journal of Consumer Affairs* 42.2 (2008): 189.

22 **During the 1990s** Amy Kamenick, "Small PR agencies snap up accounts: Shifting strategies in tough climate," *Minneapolis / St. Paul Business Journal* December 28, 2001.

22 **In his book *The Undercover Economist*** Tim Harford, *The Undercover Economist* (New York: Random House Trade Paperbacks, 2007).

23 **Every three years** The OECD study referenced in the following pages is "Learning for Tomorrow's World," published by the OECD's Programme for International Student Assessment. Studies were published in 2003 and 2006. Details and copies of the reports are available at www.pisa.oecd.org.

24 **"The gap between the best"** Floyd Norris, "U.S. Students Fare Badly in International Survey of Math Skills," *The New York Times,* December 7, 2004.

24 **Its complaints run the gamut** The National Mathematics Advisory Panel presented its results in a paper titled "Foundations for Success: The Final Report of the National Mathematics Advisory Panel," published on March 13, 2008. It can be downloaded from www.ed.gov/about/bdscomm/list/mathpanel/.

24 **"Close to half"** Ibid., 31.

24 **"The sharp falloff"** Ibid., xiii.

25 **The National Council on Teacher Quality** The National Council on Teacher Quality, "No Common Denominator: The Preparation of Elementary Teachers in Mathematics by America's Education Schools," June 2008.

25 **"Almost anyone can get in"** Ibid., 11.

26 **"Elementary teachers are phobic about math"** Maria Sacchetti, "Teachers' math skills are targeted," *Boston Globe,* Jan. 2, 2007.

28 **I'll leave it to the footnotes** Sorry to be difficult there. You would need eighteen Mini Moo's for nine cups of coffee, or eighteen three-eighths-ounce containers, or 18×3 divided by 8, which is $6\frac{3}{4}$ ounces—considerably less than three-quarters of a sixteen-ounce, pint container of creamer.

30 **Welcome to the world of Bobos** David Brooks, *Bobos in Paradise: The New Upper Class and How They Got There* (New York: Simon & Schuster, 2001).

31 **Before the decade was out** Eric Abrahamson and David H. Freedman, *A Perfect Mess: The Hidden Benefits of Disorder—How Crammed Closets, Cluttered Offices, and on-the-Fly Planning Make the World a Better Place* (New York: Little, Brown, 2007).

31 **square footage of a new home** John W. Schoen, "By Some Measures,

Houses Are Still Cheap," MSNBC.com, July 13, 2005, http://www.msnbc
.msn.com/id/8544466/.

31 The price difference between George Will, "Stimulating Times: Cows
should die in Wisconsin so that mothers in Watts will pay more—a price
government deems 'reasonable'—for their children's milk?" *Newsweek*, February 9, 2009.

34 Generational Shift The chart and the figures concerning income and price
first appeared in "Life Is Harder Now, Some Experts Say," by the author,
on MSNBC.com, published October 16, 2007, at http://www.msnbc
.msn.com/id/21309318/.

35 Where the Money Goes The Bureau of Labor Statistics annual consumer-
expenditure report, available online at http://www.bls.gov/cex/.

35 "Yes, people are spending" Sullivan, "Life Is Harder Now."

36 The U.S. Census Bureau Stephen Ohlemacher, "Americans Spend More
of Incomes on Homes," Associated Press, October 3, 2006.

36 And a full 15 percent Adrian Sainz and Alan Zibel, "Millions spend half of
income on housing," Associated Press, September 24, 2008.

36 Compare that to 1975 Elizabeth Warren and Amelia Warren Tyagi, *The
Two-Income Trap* (New York: Basic Books, 2003).

37 "Madoff Securities" This Markopolos memo was sent to the SEC on November 7, 2005. It can be accessed courtesy of the Reuters news service at http://
static.reuters.com/resources/media/editorial/20090127/Markopolos_
Memo_SEC.pdf.

38 The Consumer Product Safety Commission Stephen Labaton, "Bigger
Budget? No, Responds Safety Agency," *The New York Times*, October 30,
2007.

38 The Federal Trade Commission issued "FTC Warns Mortgage Advertisers
and Media That Ads May Be Deceptive," press release issued by the Federal Trade Commission, September 11, 2007.

39 By 2006, the staff The actual number shrank from 1,746 in 1979 to 1,007
in 2006. It hit its low point in 1989, with 894 employees. From "FTC Full-
Time Equivalent History" on the agency's website http://www.ftc.gov/ftc/
oed/fmo/fte2.shtm.

39 During the throes David Corn, "Foreclosure Phil," *Mother Jones*, July/August
2008, http://www.motherjones.com/politics/2008/05/foreclosure-phil.

42 "If there is a radio" "Secrets of the Psychics," *Nova*, 1993.

43 The video of the episode Ibid.

44 "Hello, Peetie" Ibid.

44 Randi has collected James Randi and Arthur C. Clarke, *The Encyclopedia
of Claims, Frauds, and Hoaxes of the Occult and Supernatural* (New York: St.
Martin's Griffin, 1997).

45 "In the end" Interview with the author, July 2008.

46 The people who are uploading From Uri Geller's home page, http://site
.urigeller.com/to_all_skeptics_-_a_big_thank_you.

48 Math nerds play A set of classic Fermi problems (and their answers) can
be found at http://mathforum.org/workshops/sum96/interdisc/classicfermi
.html.

51 **At this point** A number of good auto-loan calculators are online. My favorite is at bankrate.com, http://www.bankrate.com/brm/calc/rebatecalc.asp.

53 **Researchers at Johns Hopkins University** Natalie Angier, "Gut Instinct's Surprising Role in Math," *The New York Times,* September 15, 2008.

54 **Such raw math instinct** info Tk

55 **In her groundbreaking book** Martha Stout, *The Sociopath Next Door* (New York: Broadway, 2005).

59 **In a recent study** "Getting it right on the money," *The Economist,* April 3, 2008.

59 **Robert Manning** Robert D. Manning, *Credit Card Nation: The Consequences of America's Addiction to Credit* (New York: Basic Books, 2001).

59 **Study after study** Amy Finkelstein, "E-ZTax: Tax Salience and Tax Rates," MIT and NBER Working Paper Series, February 2007.

60 **In his groundbreaking relationship research** John Gottman, *The Seven Principles for Making Marriage Work: A Practical Guide from the Country's Foremost Relationship Expert* (New York: Three Rivers Press, 2000).

PART II: STOP GETTING RIPPED OFF—ONE DEAL AT A TIME

CHAPTER 1: THE TWENTY-FIRST-CENTURY
CHECKING ACCOUNT

70 **In 2007, Americans spent $17.5 billion** Center for Responsible Lending, "Out of Balance: Consumers Pay $17.5 Billion per Year," report, July 11, 2007.

70 **In 2007, 20 percent of banks** Government Accountability Office, "Bank Fees: Federal Banking Regulators Could Better Ensure That Consumers Have Required Disclosure Documents prior to Opening Checking or Savings Accounts," report, March 3, 2008.

70 **In total, Americans donate** Ibid.

CHAPTER 2: CREDIT CARD MATH

84 **I thank personal-finance writer** Liz Weston, "The Truth About Credit Card Debt," MSN Money, undated, http://moneycentral.msn.com/content/Banking/creditcardsmarts/P74808.asp. With updated data at http://articles.money central.msn.com/Banking/CreditCardSmarts/TheBigLieAboutCreditCard Debt.aspx.

86 **Average Daily Balance Calculator** The average daily balance charts were calculated with a spreadsheet provided by the "No Credit Needed" blog at NCNBlog.com.

86 **After thirty-one days** See chart. Here's the math: Add 27 days of $3,000 plus four days of 0 and you get $81,000. Divide that by 31 and you get an average daily balance of $2,612.90. Multiply by the daily interest rate of about 8 cents per day per $100 and you arrive at $64.36.

88 **percent interest penalty** For many reasons your monthly statement might not precisely match these examples. Here's one. Beginning in the late

nineties, banks found an even seedier way to enhance their revenue at your expense. It began with the addition of this tiny phrase into your credit card agreement:

"To get the daily balance we take the beginning balance for every day, add any new transactions, fees, and any finance charge on the previous day's balance."

It means that every day, day after day, your interest charges are added to your balance. That means interest is charged on interest. By switching from monthly compounding to daily compounding, banks have changed the real interest rate on your card without having to advertise higher rates. For example, according to a Philadelphia Fed report, a card with an advertised rate of 18.99 percent interest has a real rate of 20.73 percent when interest is compounded monthly, but a 20.91 percent rate when compounded daily. That's an 18 basis-point increase you never noticed—and another number you're unlikely to see on credit card offers. It's also another reason to pay early and charge late.

93 **In 1990, the average late fee** Mark Furletti, "Credit Card Pricing Developments and Their Disclosure," Payment Cards Center, Federal Reserve Bank of Philadelphia, January 2003, 15; "Credit Cards: Increased Complexity in Rates and Fees Heightens Need for More Effective Disclosures to Consumers," GAO report 06-029, September 2006.

97 **Sometimes, you can just ask** Bob Sullivan, "Want a better credit card rate? Just ask," msnbc.com, February 26, 2008, http://redtape.msnbc.com/2008/02/if-interest-rat.html.

97 **Kevin McPhail of Austin** Bob Sullivan, "Want a better card rate? Just ask," MSNBC.com. February 26, 2008. http://redtape.msnbc.com/2008/02/if-interest-rat.html.

CHAPTER 3: BUYING A CAR

100 **When you negotiate** Chandler Phillips, "Confessions of a Car Salesman," Edmunds.com, undated, http://www.edmunds.com/advice/buying/articles/42962/article.html.

105 **In some cases** "Dealer holdback" is just one way dealers make money from selling a car outside the money you pay. Manufacturers also offer dealer incentives, sometimes called dealer cash or dealer rebate. These numbers are held fairly close to the vest, but it does mean that the dealer makes money even if they sell you a car at invoice price. Because you don't know the number, it's hard to negotiate, but you can certainly use it during your negotiation. When the dealer tries to say they're not making any money in an invoice-price sale, you can call the bluff.

105 **You probably know** Loan prices from John Nay-Eve's story calculated with the help of the Edmunds.com auto-loan calculator at http://www.edmunds.com/calculators/auto_loan_calculator_index.html.

111 **If you are a visual person** Rob Gruhl, "How to Buy a New Car," speech given at Ignite Seattle conference, August 2008, http://www.youtube.com/watch?v=pPor5b7JLLE.

111 **remember the assertion in** Martha Stout, *The Sociopath Next Door* (New York: Broadway, 2005).

112 **You can tell a salesman** Phillips, "Confessions of a Car Salesman."

113 **writer Tom Evslin** The neat and clean rebate calculator is available at Tom Evslin's Fractals of Change blog, http://blog.tomevslin.com/zero-cost-calculator .html.

CHAPTER 4: BUYING A HOME

116 **In early 2009** Mara Der Hovanesian, "Report: 1 in 5 Mortgages Are Underwater," *BusinessWeek*, March 3, 2009. More than 8.3 million out of 45 million mortgaged homes were under water.

116 **But in most of the country** Federal Housing Finance Agency, "Record Home Price Declines in Fourth Quarter; Isolated Pockets of Strength," report, February 24, 2009.

One grand error nearly everyone makes when discussing the U.S. housing market is to describe it as a single entity. It's not. Housing markets are virtually isolated small markets. Nearly all the real drama of the housing collapse—the stories of home prices falling 50 percent—occurred in California, Florida, Nevada, and Arizona. In December 2008, at the absolute worst point of the U.S. housing collapse, six U.S. states showed price increases during the previous year. In another thirty-five states, price drops averaged about 5 percent in 2008. Finally, and most compelling, is that 87 of 292 metro areas in the report actually gained in market value during 2008, and 200 of the 292 areas fell by less than 5 percent.

117 **The median commission** U.S. Department of Justice, "Home Prices and Commissions over Time," 2008, http://www.usdoj.gov/atr/public/real_estate/ save.htm. See also Stephen Gandel, "Closing Cost Scams," CNNMoney.com, October 10, 2006, http://money.cnn.com/2006/02/13/real_estate/closingcosts _money_0603/index.htm.

120 **Because people buy homes** Determining average home stay is a bit of a vexing problem for statisticians because of the extremes at either end of the spectrum. First-time home-buyers stay only an average of four years, but retirees tend to stay for decades. Data from the U.S. Census Bureau's American Housing Survey indicate an overall average of fifteen years for single-family dwellings, and six years for condo owners. For more, see Paul Emrath, "How Long Housing Buyers Remain in Their Homes," for the National Association of Home Builders, February 11, 2009, http://www.nahb.org/generic .aspx?sectionID=734&genericContentID=110770.

121 **The lender will tell you** A comment left on the author's blog.

135 **The moment you agree** You can get a Settlement Statement (HUD-1) in lots of places, but it's best to get it from the horse's mouth at http://www.hud .gov/offices/adm/hudclips/forms/files/1.pdf.

139 **"Standard of Practice 12-2"** "NAR: Real Estate Resources: 2009 Code of Ethics and Standards of Practice," Realtor.org, http://www.realtor.org/Mem PolWeb.nsf/pages/COde.

141 **But note that** Blank Good Faith Estimate forms can be seen at HUD.gov, http://www.hud.gov/offices/hsg/sfh/res/resappc.cfm.

CHAPTER 5: CELL PHONES

148 **I have an 18-year-old** Bob Sullivan, "Price for 'Premium' Text Messages? $10,000," MSNBC.com, October 30, 2007, http://redtape.msnbc.com/2007/10/sean-clark-pays.html.

154 **nothing compared to** Susannah Cahalan, "This Kid's a Text Maniac," *New York Post,* January 11, 2009.

157 **Richard Branson** Richard Branson, *Business Stripped Bare: Adventures of a Global Entrepreneur* (London: Virgin Books, 2008).

CHAPTER 6: PAY TV

163 **Today, about four in five** Nick Wingfield, "Turn On, Tune Out, Click Here," *The Wall Street Journal,* October 3, 2008.

164 **I'll bet you don't know** Melina Fulmer, "Kill the cable box: Get free TV," MSN Money, undated.

164 **The price is up 77 percent** Matt Richtel, "Cable Prices Keep Rising, and Customers Keep Paying," *The New York Times,* May 24, 2008.

166 **I don't know why people** Jeffrey Strain, "50% Off Cable TV Bill," PFAdvice.com, June 15, 2006, http://www.pfadvice.com/2006/06/15/50-off-cable-tv-bill/.

169 **In 2009, complete episodes** Wingfield, "Turn On, Tune Out."

169 **CancelCable.com** "Like Buying a New 50-Inch TV Each Year and Tossing It in the Dumpster," http://www.cancelcable.com/why-keeping-cable-tv-is-like-buying-a-new-plasma-tv-each-year-and-tossing-it-in-the-dumpster/14/.

CHAPTER 7: STUDENT LOANS

172 **Stacey dreamed of teaching children** Stacey and Natalie's stories, along with analysis from hundreds of similar stories, were supplied by Student LoanJustice.org and supplemented with the author's own interviews.

174 **One in ten college students** "Student Loans," FinAid.org, http://www.finaid.org/loans/.

174 **The cost of college** Tamar Lewin, "College May Become Unaffordable for Most in U.S.," *The New York Times,* December 3, 2008.

177 **"Live like a student"** The quote seems to have originally appeared on the FinAid.org website, attributed to Mark Kantrowitz.

CHAPTER 8: INSURANCE

181 **The average American consumer spends** Determining an average consumer cost for all insurance is tricky because individual circumstances vary widely. Most challenging: the real cost of health insurance, which for a

majority of Americans is provided as an employment benefit and should rightly be considered an expense as a subtraction from annual salary. The best available estimates that contribute to the $4,000 figure are home-owner's insurance, $729 per year; auto insurance, $829 per year; health insurance, $1,800 per year for an adult individually, and $4,800 per year for a family; life insurance, $500 per year. Estimates are from the National Association of Insurance Commissioners, Insurance Information Institute, and Compuquotes, http://www.compuquotes.com/average-costs-of-insurance .html, accessed March 23, 2009.

The annual premium for an employer health plan covering a family of four averaged nearly $12,100. The annual premium for single coverage averaged over $4,400. Workers contributed nearly $3,300, according to the Henry J. Kaiser Family Foundation, "Employee Health Benefits: 2007 Annual Survey," September 11, 2007, http://www.kff.org/insurance/7672/index.cfm 3.

Because most consumers have few choices about their health care costs, and because of the complexity of the subject, discussion of health insurance will be left to another forum.

182 **only about one in fourteen drivers** Insurance Information Institute, November 2008 report, http://www.iii.org/media/facts/statsbyissue/auto/?table_sort_746260=5. From 2005 to 2007, claim frequency for all passenger vehicles averaged 7.2 percent.

182 **The average comprehensive-claim payment** Ibid.

186 **Raising a deductible from $200 to $1,000** Insurance Information Institute, "Auto Insurance Checklist," undated, http://www.iii.org/individuals/auto/checklists/auto/.

187 **a calculation based on complaints** To find this number, check your state insurance commissioner's website. You can find yours at the Insurance Consumer Advocate Network home page at http://www.ican2000.com/index .shtml. Or just google your state name, *insurance commissioner,* and *complaint ratio.*

187 **Prices have remained relatively flat** Insurance Information Institute, "Average Expenditures for Auto Insurance, United States, 1997–2006," http://www.iii.org/media/facts/statsbyissue/auto/.

188 **Essentially every state requires drivers** Wisconsin and New Hampshire do not require liability insurance; instead the states have a financial-responsibility law, which requires that consumers without insurance have the ability to pay for damages they cause.

190 **77 percent of drivers bought comprehensive** Insurance Information Institute, http://www.iii.org/media/facts/statsbyissue/auto/.

193 **90 percent of all natural disasters** "National Flood Insurance Program: Oversight of Policy Issuance and Claims," Government Accountability Office report GAO05-532T, April 14, 2005.

195 **A more common rule of thumb** Chart adapted from "How Much Insurance Should You Own," LifeInsuranceHub.net, http://www.lifeinsurancehub .net/HowMuchLifeInsurance.html.

197 **Other Kinds of Life Insurance** List adapted from LifeInsure.com.

CHAPTER 9: GET A TWENTY-FIRST-CENTURY RAISE

205 **instead of slashing workforces** Matt Richtel, "More Companies Are Cutting Labor Costs without Layoffs," *The New York Times*, December 21, 2008, http://www.nytimes.com/2008/12/22/business/22layoffs.html?hp.

208 **the importance of negotiating** Timothy Ferriss, *The 4-Hour Workweek: Escape 9–5, Live Anywhere, and Join the New Rich* (New York: Crown, 2007).

209 **Here's how Steve Pavlina** Steve Pavlina; Personal Development for Smart People; http://www.stevepavlina.com.

209 **My income isn't based on how much** Steve Pavlina, "How to Earn $10,000 in One Hour," Personal Development for Smart People blog, November 9, 2005.

214 **about 4 million Americans** Eve Tahmincioglu, "More Workers Forced to Try Moonlighting," MSNBC.com, April 14, 2008, http://www.msnbc.msn.com/id/24070585/.

PART III: HOW TO PITFALL-PROOF YOUR FINANCES, PAST, PRESENT, AND FUTURE

221 **How do you expect** A retelling of Aesop's fable "The Tortoise and the Hare," adapted from StoryArts.org, http://www.storyarts.org/library/aesops/stories/tortoise.html.

STAGE 1: THE SOLID FOUNDATION—PLAN B BASICS

233 **A survey commissioned** "Survey Finds Few Saving for Emergencies," ConsumersAffairs.com, February 27, 2007, http://www.consumeraffairs.com/news04/2007/02/savings_rate.html.

233 **A similar study** "New Survey Finds Insufficient Savings for Emergencies Major Cause of Financial Worry among Younger Women," April 27, 2005, Consumer Federation of America.

234 **And HSBC found that** Bob Sullivan, "Study: Few Have Rainy Day Savings," MSNBC.com, February 27, 2007, based on "HSBC Survey: Most Consumers Unprepared for Life Emergencies," a press release issued by HSBC, October 17, 2005.

234 **A study by Stephen Brobeck** Liz Weston, "Want to Sleep Better? Save $500," MSN Money, undated, http://articles.moneycentral.msn.com/SavingandDebt/LearnToBudget/want-to-sleep-better-save-500-dollars.aspx.

STAGE 3: SIX MONTHS— MUTUAL FUND BASICS

253 **The average American investor** This is extensively discussed in *Gotcha Capitalism*, but here's a simple way of looking at it: If someone takes 1 percent of your money every year in fees, after thirty years they'll have about 30 percent of your money.

254 **Four for Wall Street, one for him** This hard-to-believe result of forty-five years of investing is elegantly explained in the PBS *Frontline* special "Can You Afford to Retire?" which initially aired in May 2006. The 80–20 split

claim was made by John C. Bogle, founder of Vanguard, and defended by a benefits expert who provided a year-by-year table of earnings to PBS. The table is available online at http://www.pbs.org/wgbh/pages/frontline/retirement/interviews/bogle.html#2.

260 **That's a serious difference!** Of course, things can change based on the time period you pick. Thanks to the collapse of all stocks in 2008, this chart would look very different in early 2009.

260 **Debt under Control?** Formulas for household debt and monthly costs abound. Here's another formula you can use.

When economists consider this problem, they talk about something called the financial obligations ratio, which calculates average mandatory monthly costs as a percentage of disposable income. As you might guess, this number has steadily been climbing since the go-go credit days of the 1990s. Here's a look at the numbers:

1980 Q1 = 15.90%
1990 Q1 = 17.29%
2000 Q1 = 17.62%
2007 Q1 = 19.42%

"Household Debt Service and Financial Obligations Ratios," a quarterly report issued by the Federal Reserve Board, http://www.federalreserve.gov/releases/housedebt/default.htm.

The picture for household debt is even bleaker. In the first quarter of 2008, Americans spent on average 14.34 percent of their income just on interest payments for debt. In other words, $1 out of every $7 earned is paying interest on past purchases, and not available to spend on new things. Put another way, when Americans go to work each month, the first four workdays are spent simply to pay interest to someone else. That's depressing. For renters, the picture is a bit more bleak. That group, in 2008, spent an average of 26.25 percent of their income on mandatory expenses.

261 **Carrying $8,000** Because the interest compounds daily, the interest charges are closer to $2,250.

STAGE 4: GET SET FOR THE FUTURE— BASIC RISK INVESTING

265 **In 2007, the Securities** "'Free Lunch' Investment Seminar Examinations Uncover Widespread Problems, Perils for Older Investors," Securities and Exchange Commission press release, September 10, 2007, http://www.sec.gov/news/press/2007/2007-179.htm.

273 **Auction-rate securities** Aaron Pressman, "Auction-Rate Securities: How to Get Unstuck," *BusinessWeek,* May 22, 2008.

274 **In 1998, to settle a massive lawsuit** Bob Sullivan, "Ten Years Later, Tobacco Deal Going Up in Smoke," MSNBC.com, November 21, 2008, http://redtape.msnbc.com/2008/11/ten-years-later.html.

274 **Oppenheimer Rochester National Municipals** "Oppenheimer's Fielding Falls to Worst from First Citing 'Panic,'" Bloomberg News Service, January 8, 2009.

277 **Since only a tiny fraction** Mark Hulbert, "The Index Funds Win Again," *The New York Times,* February 21, 2009.

STAGE 5: GET COMFY—ADVANCED RISK

282 **Each time you get a raise** Richard H. Thaler and Shlomo Benartzi, "Save More Tomorrow: Using Behavioral Economics to Increase Employee Saving," *Journal of Political Economy,* 2004, vol. 112.

283 **But there's very good news** It's true! Compounding raises help a lot. For example, in the thirtieth year, our investor is putting $15,786 extra into the account through raise skimming. During the whole thirty years, $252,963 in contributions come from raise skimming.

285 **BrokerCheck** See http://www.finra.org/Investors/ToolsCalculators/Broker Check/index.htm.

286 **LeeAnn Gaunt** Tips provided to author upon request.

CONCLUSION

289 **The depressing truth** "Getting it right on the money," *The Economist,* April 3, 2008.

289 **"If these things are perplexing"** Ibid.

ABOUT THE AUTHOR

BOB SULLIVAN has been a reporter for nearly two decades. For the past twelve years, he has covered computer crime and consumer affairs for MSNBC.com. Today his work appears on msnbc.com's "Red Tape Chronicles" blog. He also appears regularly on MSNBC television, NBC Nightly News, the *Today* show, and various local NBC affiliates. He is the winner of the prestigious 2002 Society of Professional Journalist Public Service Award for a series of articles on online fraud. His first book, *Your Evil Twin: Behind the Identity Theft Epidemic,* investigated the root causes of credit card fraud and other identity-related crimes. His second book, *Gotcha Capitalism,* exposed the hidden fee economy that attacks family budgets. He lives in Maltby, Washington, with his golden retriever, Lucky.